HEADMASTER

By the same author

HEADMASTER

The Life of John Percival,
Radical Autocrat

JEREMY POTTER

Constable · London

First published in Great Britain 1998
by Constable and Company Limited
3 The Lanchesters
162 Fulham Palace Road
London W6 9ER
Copyright © 1998 Jeremy Potter
ISBN 0 09 478200 8
The right of Jeremy Potter to be identified as the author
of this work has been asserted by him in accordance
with the Copyright, Designs and Patents Act 1988
Set in Linotron Sabon 11pt by
SetSystems Ltd, Saffron Walden, Essex
Printed in Great Britain by
St Edmundsbury Press Ltd
Bury St Edmunds, Suffolk

A CIP catalogue record for this book
is available from the British Library

'In the last century there are two names of
great public schoolmasters which will live in history . . .
Those names are
THOMAS ARNOLD and JOHN PERCIVAL.'
Canon J. M. Wilson

Contents

Illustrations

Percival, aged 42: portrait by G. F. Watts, R.A., 1876 *Frontispiece*

between pages 150 and 151

Percival at Oxford, aged 23: from a daguerrotype, June 1858.
Headmaster of Clifton, 1878.
Clifton's Masters, 1865.
Clifton College, c.1880.
Bust of Percival by Thomas Woolner, R.A., 1880.
Cartoon on Trinity election: Percival crowing over Woods.
Design for new quadrangle at Trinity, 1880.
Headmaster of Rugby: portrait by Sir Hubert von Herkomer, R.A.
Bishop of Hereford: portrait by H. Riviere, 1899.
At the gateway of the Bishop's Palace, Hereford.
Feeding the fantail pigeons.
Percival on his eightieth birthday with grandson Douglas.
Bishop of Hereford, aged 82.
Plaque in Hereford Cathedral.
Percival Memorial Chapel at Clifton.
Clifton College from the Close, 1997.

PART I

CREATING A SCHOOL

CHAPTER 1

Character and Upbringing

John Percival was born before Queen Victoria came to the throne and lived to witness the watershed of the First World War. He was headmaster of two leading public schools, where the budding leaders of the nation were trained. He was the reforming head of an Oxford college. He was a bishop with a seat – or, more precisely, a platform – in the House of Lords. He was one of the principal forces behind the development of education for women and the working class. All in all, he was among the most influential of the giants of the Victorian age, a prime mover in changing the face of society in England.

In his work as a pioneer of educational reform Percival stood second to none in his time. Yet a prediction that his name would live in history alongside that of Thomas Arnold has proved a sad misjudgment. Arnold's has been famous and venerated since the day of his death. Except at Clifton, the school which he created, Percival's has been consigned to near-oblivion. History has embraced the one and turned its back on the other, whose talents extended over a much wider field.

The bare facts of his life and career are these. Born in Westmorland in 1834, he became a Fellow of Queen's College, Oxford (1858–60) and an assistant master at Rugby School (1860–62) before being appointed headmaster of Clifton College. During his years at Clifton (1862–79) he became a Prebendary of Exeter Cathedral (1871–82) and was awarded an honorary LLD by St Andrews University (1876). In 1878 he was elected President of Trinity College, Oxford. While at Trinity (1878–1887) he also served as Chairman and then first President of the Council of Somerville College (1879–1887) and did duty in the Long

Vacations as a Canon Residentiary of Bristol Cathedral
(1882–1887). Headmaster of Rugby School (1887–95) was his
next appointment; Bishop of Hereford (1895–1917) his last. He
died in Oxford in 1918.

The popular image of a Victorian headmaster pictures a well-
bred gentleman in holy orders; a formidable scholar; a stern
disciplinarian conventional in outlook, Tory in politics, austere in
private life.

In scholarship, piety, sternness and austerity, few could match
Percival. His record as a student at Oxford was said to be almost
unsurpassed. As befitted a clergyman, he held a passionate belief in
Christian ideals and conduct. In the role of headmaster he countered wrong-doing and indiscipline with punishment which sometimes fell not far short of a reign of terror. In public life he deplored
materialism and all forms of self-indulgence. His private life was
ascetic. But well-bred? Hardly. Conventional in outlook? Rarely. A
Tory? Never.

If the terminology of a later age could be applied, 'far left' would
be a more apt description of his brand of politics. Yet he was
ardently patriotic, seeing the hand of God in the growth of the
British Empire. Following where God beckoned, he never doubted
which was the path of righteousness and saw no contradiction in
the roles of radical autocrat or liberal imperialist.

His greatness sprang from a well-stocked armoury of principle
and talent. Devout faith was supported by superiority of mind,
moral inflexibility and strength of purpose. These qualities were
supported in turn by practical ability, organisational skills of the
highest order and an almost superhuman capacity for sheer hard
work. While his head was in the clouds in constant communion
with the Christian God, his feet were firmly on the ground as he
laboured to put His will into effect.

God told him not only that public school boys must be brought
up to be Christian gentlemen with a mission to make the whole
world a better place, not only that undergraduates must not
squander the privilege of a university education through idleness,
but also that the rest of the population too must be educated and
poverty eradicated through social reform and the enlightenment
which education would bring.

In these and other causes he displayed a grim intransigence.
Drunkenness, gambling, illegitimacy and cruelty to animals were
among his domestic targets. Abroad, the cruelty of man to man

roused his very considerable wrath. The conscience of the nation was awakened to these evils by lengthy letters to *The Times* and Gladstonian speeches in the House of Lords.

Forthright, uncompromising, never courting popularity, Percival exercised a spiritual force and iron certainty which swept aside all obstacles and objections to what he saw as his missionary work here on earth. His long life was therefore marked as much by controversy as by achievement. In the course of it he attracted a number of faithful admirers but gave grave offence and made many enemies.

He did not, for instance, mince his words when he roundly denounced Toryism as the work of Satan. With conservative churchmen he disputed vehemently in public, and at his enthronement as bishop the 'dour looks' of the diocesan clergy were all too noticeable.[1] An inquiry about his reception in the House of Lords elicited the blunt response: 'Why, they hate him like the devil.'[2] Even to those who fell under his spell an obsession with the need to speak out, coupled with an unshakeable belief that life was a duty and on no account to be enjoyed, made him an uncomfortable man to know. As his career was to prove, Percival was your man if you were looking for results, but most definitely not someone to choose if you wanted peace, harmony and an easy life. As a colleague he could be both intolerant and intolerable.

Viewed from the end of the twentieth century, Victorians are distant figures living in an age with values very different from our own. Faith in a Christian God and the life of the spirit finds few echoes in the present period of agnosticism and materialism. God and duty were the pole stars of Percival's life, but duty too – Wordsworth's 'stern daughter of the voice of God' – is not a concept any longer in vogue. Nor is obedience to the kind of authority which Percival represented. His ideals of patriotism, imperialism, paternalism and élitism have become subjects for disparagement, the very boo-words of a later liberalism.

Yet if in those respects his is a deeply unsympathetic character when glimpsed through the eyes of post-imperial Britons, in other respects John Percival is pre-eminently a man of our times. His liberal convictions; his loudly voiced concern for the lot of the poor in Britain's industrial cities; his writings and speeches calling for action on behalf of oppressed peoples overseas; his advocacy of, and commitment to, education for women; his demands for the reform of the Church of England; even Queen Victoria's assessment of him as a dangerous subversive – all these must count in his favour in the climate of late twentieth-century opinion. The causes which he espoused were the forerunners of such modern developments as social security, the feminist movement, wider availability of higher education, and charities like Oxfam.

If these contrasted aspects of the man appear paradoxical to us, that must be attributed to the myopia of hindsight. Every one of his opinions, attitudes and actions was dictated by principle, and in the circumstances of his own life and time all his principles stemmed logically from a single source: the teachings of Christ, as he interpreted them.

Percival's appearance was as striking as his character, his voice deceptively low and gentle. More than six feet two inches tall, with a lean look, fair reddish hair, handsome features and an imposing presence, he was one of those men with a natural air of authority who cannot enter a room without attracting attention.

His daughter has described how, in 1876, George Moore, a wealthy admirer, tried to commission a portrait of him from the then fashionable G. F. Watts, whose ambition was to paint a series of portraits of great men as a historical record of the age. The artist, who had never met Percival, refused on the grounds that he always chose his own subjects and was not interested in schoolmasters. Not to be denied, Moore invited the schoolmaster to his house, where Watts was a guest. As soon as Percival appeared, Watts turned to Moore and said: 'Who is that man? I must paint his portrait.' Moore lost no time in sending him a cheque for £500, and the portrait was duly painted and hung in the next Royal Academy Exhibition.[3]

The heredity and circumstances which shaped Percival's character are no less surprising. His beginnings were both humble and inauspicious. First, he was conceived out of wedlock, born seven weeks after his parents' marriage. Common as it was in country districts among ordinary folk like his parents, extramarital conception was an unusual prelude to the making of a future public school headmaster and bishop.

Some of his colleagues in later life became aware of the circumstances of his birth, but they were never public knowledge during his lifetime. Discretion was a Victorian virtue, and it was as well that this irregularity never came to the ears of the queen herself, whose opposition to his appointment as bishop might then have prevailed. Percival's godson and biographer, William Temple,

himself Bishop of Manchester and afterwards successively Archbishop of York and Canterbury, wrapped it from view in these
carefully chosen words in his *Life of Bishop Percival*, published in
1921:

> In 1834 [his father, William Percival] was married by licence in
> St Michael's Church, Brough under Stainmore, to Jane Langmire,
> daughter of William and Ann Langmire ... It was at the house
> of his mother's parents that John Percival was born on September
> 27, 1834.[4]

The unstated date of the marriage was 9 August 1834, and the
infant John was baptised in the same twelfth-century church on 26
October. Jane was aged twenty-five, William thirty-two, and it
seems that they had had an earlier, illegitimate son, named William,
who was born outside the parish.[5]

The village of Brough under Stainmore lies in the Eden valley
eight miles from the market town of Appleby. It is overlooked by
steep, grassy fells topped with outcrops of limestone. The landscape
of this part of Westmorland has a rare, wild beauty, but in winter
it can be chilly and cheerless.

Although isolated, Brough has never been as remote as its
situation suggests. In Roman times it was a garrisoned staging post
on the cross-Pennine road built between York and Carlisle. The
Roman fort was later converted into a Norman castle, which in
turn became a medieval stronghold of the Clifford Earls of Cumberland. At the time of Percival's boyhood this had long been no
more than a picturesque ruin, but the village itself was then a busy
stage on the London/Glasgow road with a dozen coaching inns
catering to more than sixty carriages a day.

Percival's father was the son of Robert Percival and his wife
Elizabeth (née Clark). He was born at Brampton in the parish of
Long Marston near Appleby, but had come to live at Brough
Sowerby, a hamlet within the parish of Brough but outside the
village itself. He was what was known in Cumbria as a 'statesman':
a husbandman or farmer working his own land. In his case this
amounted to twenty acres. As smallholders the family were relatively well-to-do by the standards of the locality but, in the eyes of
the world at large, scarcely more than agricultural labourers.

The large Percival clan, clustered for the most part around
Appleby, included a labourer, a bricklayer, a sexton, a stonemason,

a shoemaker, a grocer and a beer-seller as well as farmers. Some were described as poor; others as 'base-born'. In 1815, for example, a son of Barbara Percival, baptised in St Michael's, Appleby, was described in the parish register as illegitimate and his father's name left blank. Jane, a daughter of Mary Percival, baptised in St Lawrence's, Appleby in 1826, was another bastard in the family.[6]

Little is known of Percival's mother. Her father came originally from Bolton, but the Longmires (or Langmires) were thick on the ground in and around Brough, where William Longmire farmed, probably on a larger acreage than William Percival. Thus, although born into a social class markedly different from the circles in which he was to move, John Percival sprang from sturdy northern yeoman stock on both sides. His father, moreover, was a cut above the ordinary. He was intelligent and well-read and excelled at the local sport of amateur wrestling, in which gentry and labourers competed together. William Percival was a champion at this, with a silver cup and belt to show his son as proofs of his prowess.

Percival was never ashamed of his family or at all concerned with distinctions of class. He was proud of his father's brain and brawn, and throughout his life made no attempt to conceal his origins. Anyone who expected a public school headmaster to speak with what became the socially acceptable southern English accent was to be disappointed in him. Regional accents among prominent men were not rare in mid-century, but the broad Cumbrian vowels which remained with Percival to the end were much remarked upon. A shortcoming which he frequently and famously deplored in school assemblies was a 'law tawn' – his version of a 'low tone'.

His mother died in the summer of 1838,[7] when he was still only three, and the sight of her face in death haunted his memory until his own eighty years later. 'The longer I live,' he once wrote to a friend, 'the more I feel how the early loss impoverished and saddened my life.'[8] This tragedy no doubt contributed to his reserved manner, the aloof air of melancholy isolation in which he cloaked himself. A protective carapace was grown to shield his inner self from the world and his emotions from public view. This resulted in some misunderstanding of his character, because a forbidding exterior concealed a kindly nature and generous spirit unsuspected by those who never broke through the crust.

Maternal deprivation may also have accentuated his shyness towards women. The societies in which he spent his working life were all predominantly male, peopled by schoolmasters and schoolboys, academics, clergy and peers. Although a devoted family man, he was ill at ease on social occasions and would seldom unbend in mixed company. Yet his first wife and his daughter were especially dear to him, and women in the abstract, women as an underprivileged class, attracted his wholehearted sympathy and support. In the movement for women's education he was among the most fervent of pioneers.

After his mother's death he suffered what must have felt like a second rejection by those he loved and on whom he was dependent, and this may have stimulated the early development of his self-reliance and independence of mind. His father took in a housekeeper, and John and his baby sister Anne, born the previous year, were sent to live with their mother's brother and sister-in-law, Richard and Elizabeth Longmire. The housekeeper was another Jane, Jane Johnston, a labourer's daughter. In 1848, after ten years' co-habitation, William Percival married her. They had three daughters: Percival's half-sisters, Elizabeth, Jane, and a second Anne born after the first had died.[9]

Percival never returned to live with his father's second family. The formative influence on his early years was his Aunt Elizabeth. Fortunately, it proved a strong influence for the good. She appears to have been a strict disciplinarian and unable to replace his mother in his affections, but he later acknowledged his debt to her in making him learn a passage from the Bible every day. Thanks to her, he had most of the Psalms by heart throughout his life. Another Christian influence was that of the Rev. Henry King, the vicar of nearby Kirkby Stephen, who made the boy welcome in his vicarage.

At the Longmires' farm young John was soon expected to earn his keep by helping in the fields. His health was not strong, but he sometimes did this work before walking or riding several miles to school. He was first sent to the village school at Winton, which was well regarded locally, and then, when his uncle and aunt moved to Helton near Lowther, to the one at Hackthorpe. From there, at the age of twelve, he graduated to the grammar school at Appleby.

During these lonely journeys to and fro between bare, rugged hills (to be reflected in his own bleak and lofty manner when an adult), he enjoyed long periods of undisturbed thought. When walking he wore clogs, but superior ones which were envied by fellow pupils at Appleby for their brass sides. When he rode, it was on a chestnut pony and often at the gallop, red hair streaming in the wind. He thus became a practised horseman at an early age, and exercise on horseback was to remain one of his few relaxations.

The great good fortune of his boyhood was the proximity in this secluded rural area of a well-established school with excellent teachers. Appleby was the leading town in the county, boasting a castle with a fine Norman keep, formerly the main seat of the Cliffords. A chantry school had been founded there in the thirteenth century, and this had become a grammar school in 1478. The headmaster for thirty years from 1838 was the Rev. John Richardson, an Oxford graduate and an able teacher with a reputation for classical scholarship.

While attending this school Percival may have moved to the house of another uncle and aunt, Robert and Elizabeth Percival, who farmed at the hamlet of Drybeck, conveniently close to the town.[10] In winter he sometimes stayed with friends in Appleby itself. It was at Drybeck that he lost the third and last of his nearest and dearest. There his sister died in 1851 at the age of fourteen and, as a sixteen-year-old, he must have joined the mourners and attended the funeral when her body was taken back to Brough to be buried near their mother.

At the grammar school his promise as a a brilliant scholar was quickly recognised. Avid for learning, he became soundly grounded in the important subjects of the day: Latin, Greek and mathematics. His time at the school lasted, unusually, for nine years. Towards the end he was probably paying his way by working as an usher, teaching the younger boys while continuing his own studies. In 1855, at the late age of twenty-one, he won an open scholarship to Oxford and went up to the university as a taberdar (scholar) of Queen's College (now styled The Queen's College).

Queen's was an ancient foundation and one of the larger of the colleges, occupying a prominent site at the heart of the city. In an extravagance of early eighteenth-century grandeur its medieval buildings had been demolished and replaced in the classical style by a pupil of Wren. Its frontage, displaying the statue of a queen over the main entrance and effigies of philosophers and graces on the roof-tops, formed a majestic centrepiece to the curving sweep of the High Street.

There was justification for this pretension. The college had lived under the patronage of the Queens Consort of England for the past five hundred years. It also claimed the Black Prince and Henry V as alumni, although on somewhat slender evidence.

Such was the daunting gateway to the great world open, improbably, to the rustic youth of Cumbria. The founder (in 1341) was Robert de Eglesfield, confessor to Edward III's 'Good Queen' Philippa and a rector of Brough. His family held the manor of Eglesfield under the lordship of the Honour of Cockermouth, and he stipulated that, in elections to the college, preference should be given to those 'distinguished in character, needy, and apt for the study of theology' who were natives of Cumberland or Westmorland: 'on account of the waste, impoverished and illiterate conditions of that region'.[11]

The Cumbrian connection had been maintained down the centuries in accordance with the founder's wish, and Percival qualified on all counts (although he was not to take his degree in theology). As Balliol was founded for the Scots, Exeter for West Country men and Jesus for the Welsh, so Queen's offered a home from home to the brightest of young male northerners.

Here, in one bound, Percival's scholarship had transported him to the intellectual power-house of the nation and placed him on the threshold of a career among the greatest and most gifted in the land. For this he was indebted to no outside agency except the benefaction of a long-dead royal chaplain and the rigorous instruction of John Richardson, himself a former taberdar at Queen's.

Idleness and pleasure-seeking were the chief undergraduate preoccupations of the Oxford of Verdant Green in the 1850s, but John Percival is the most unlikely of all students to have indulged himself in dinner parties or drunken frolics or to have wasted his time in boating or billiards or riding to hounds. He was fond of a game of cricket until an injured knee prevented him from playing. That apart, the record of any distraction from work is understandably bare in the case of a student so austere. His mind was fully stretched, and his body, starved of recreation, became the shell of a workaholic. At Oxford – and throughout the rest of his life – a relentless spirit drove a weakened body to the limit of endurance and sometimes beyond.

His daily routine is likely to have resembled that of Frederick Temple, the man who was to become his mentor. Sixteen years earlier Temple had been a similarly hard-working scholar from a poor home, living frugally at Balliol on £80 a year. He rose before dawn and worked in his room from 5 a.m. to 3 p.m. with breaks only for chapel, breakfast and lectures. At 3 he went out for some fresh air until dinner at 4, after which he took another break until chapel at 5.30. He would then walk in the garden or shop in town until 6.30 or 7, when he would return and work until he could no longer stay awake.[12]

For Percival the rewards of his intense study were a Junior Mathematical Scholarship, a Double First in Classical and Mathematical Moderations after one year, and another in Finals two years later. Not satisfied with all this, he took the Honours School in History and had reached the standard of a First in two of the Finals papers before collapsing under the strain. Unable to continue, he had to be content with a pass.

Consumption was diagnosed. His doctor warned him that he would be an invalid for life, never able to do a day's work again – a professional opinion which he was to prove as wrong as could be. It was yet another paradox of Percival's extraordinary individualism that he was among the most energetic and long-lived of invalids.

On doctor's orders the winter of 1858–59 was spent in the Pyrenees recuperating at Pau. This may have saved his life, and more good fortune was in store for him there. In the heady mountain air he not only recovered his health, but also made the acquaintance of a Miss Holland, another invalid, in whom he developed a romantic interest.

From Pau he returned to Oxford, where his college had rewarded his successes in the Examination Schools by electing him to a Fellowship. In 1860, as custom and his own strong inclination demanded, he was ordained deacon in the Church of England and admitted to priest's orders the following year.

While studying for his degree and for ordination he also read more widely. The mid-nineteenth century was a period of intellectual ferment. Foremost among the thinkers and poets who inspired him and his generation Percival numbered Bentham and Mill, Carlyle and Ruskin, Wordsworth, Shelley and Tennyson. Browning was a star just rising above the horizon, as were Herbert Spencer and Charles Darwin. It was an age of giants.

Religious faith remained strong, but the Church was soon to be forced to come to terms with disturbing discoveries in science. Far from being dismayed by Darwinism, Percival welcomed its challenge to believers. He was among the first to appreciate the benefits which science and technology could bring, but lamented the inhumanity of 'Satanic mills' in what he called the 'vast and greedy geographical expansion' of industry and commerce.[13]

Life as an Oxford don seemed to be his lot in the foreseeable future when, after only two years as a Fellow of Queen's, he received an unprompted invitation. The headmaster of Rugby had offered a teaching post in classics to a man abroad and was despairing of hearing from him in time for the coming term. Percival was invited to Rugby as a temporary substitute. Before coming to a decision he sought the advice of the head of his college, who told him that it was a very nice thing which could not fail to do him good. Although doing himself good was not his ambition in life, it was these reassuring words from the godly Provost Thomson (a future Archbishop of York) which launched Percival on his destined career as a schoolmaster.

At that date Rugby enjoyed the highest reputation. Had Percival applied for the post he would almost certainly have been rejected on the grounds that others were better qualified. Thanks to an emergency, he now arrived by the back door. A similar and more remarkable appointment by chance was to follow before long. By most observers these would be seen as examples of serendipity, but Percival himself would have been in no doubt that they were divinely inspired.

CHAPTER 2

The Influence
of Arnold and Rugby

It was the Industrial Revolution which created the public school system in Victorian times, and it was the British Empire on which it thrived. In the England of the nineteenth century there rose to influence for the first time a middle class: wealthy and articulate, riding on the crest of Britain's prosperity as the world's most powerful industrial, commercial and imperial nation. This was the class which was to fill the swelling ranks of the professions – clergy, lawyers, doctors – and meet the challenge of an ever rising demand for civil servants at home and men who would administer and police vast territories overseas.

The public schools evolved at a prodigious rate in response to these demands. Theirs was a dual role: to turn the sons of the socially ambitious middle class into gentlemen and to fit them for leadership. It was of crucial importance that the headmasters of these establishments were men of the highest intelligence and integrity, for the education and training of those who were to become the rulers of a world-wide empire would affect, for good or ill, the lives of millions.

The term 'public school' had first come into use during the eighteenth century. Traditionally, the nobility and gentry had employed tutors to instruct their young at home. Later it became the fashion for university graduates, usually clergymen, to offer tuition to half a dozen or so young gentlemen who would come and board with them. Those were private schools: fee-paying and boarding, but on a very small scale.

The grammar schools, by contrast, catered for local day boys only. They were endowed by benefactors to provide a free education, but the endowments often proved inadequate. Having no other source of funds, many fell on hard times, unable even to afford qualified teachers. Others, not restricted by the terms of their benefaction from charging fees, expanded by adding boarding facilities and attracting custom from a wider catchment area. These so-called Great Schools – neither private nor any longer exclusively local – took the medieval foundations of Winchester and Eton as their models. Together they became known as 'public schools'.

Most prominent among them were Rugby, Shrewsbury and Harrow and the leading London schools. All were destined for success and fame, but in the early years of the nineteenth century they and their two prototypes earned a reputation for educational stagnation and moral decadence. They were Great only in number of pupils. Not until the 1820s and 1830s did agitation for reform herald the truly great age of the public school.

This dawned in the 1840s with the first clutch of Victorian foundations: Cheltenham and Marlborough, Rossall and Radley. By the end of the century more than fifty such schools had sprung to life as centres of excellence and nurseries of leadership. Their specialities were religious instruction, character formation and dedication to a spirit of service. Almost exclusively, they were the feeders for Oxford and Cambridge. They became national institutions, housed in grand buildings which proclaimed their pretensions. There the old and new ruling classes, upper and middle, came together and grew up on equal terms.

In these developments Rugby School, founded in 1567, played a crucial role. Thomas Arnold, headmaster from 1828 to 1842, was the acknowledged champion and pioneer of reform. He set the pattern for all when he decreed that his pupils were to be taught to be not merely gentlemen but *Christian* gentlemen. Strict adherence to the doctrines of the Christian religion, as interpreted by the Church of England, was the driving force behind every Victorian headmaster. Nearly all were in holy orders, and many moved on to become pillars of the hierarchy as deans and bishops and even archbishops. Yet consciousness of the overriding importance of their mission in moulding the minds and characters of the governing classes was such that a later headmaster of Rugby accepted a bishopric with the parting words: 'Let no man speak of my promotion; they cannot promote the Headmaster of Rugby.'[1] Men like Arnold and Percival would have made statesmen of stature, but they regarded schoolmastering as a higher calling.

When Percival took up his post there in 1860, he thus began his

career in the most highly regarded of schools. The pre-eminence of
Rugby was firmly established, thanks largely to the enduring magic
of the name of Arnold, who had been dead for nearly twenty years
but whose reputation as the charismatic initiator of the reformed
system remained very much alive.

Another contributory factor was a happy chance. A significant
development behind the growth of the boarding school in Victorian
times was the building of the railways, and it so happened that the
London to Birmingham line passed through the town of Rugby.
Completed in 1838, it was for some years the only line connecting
the north and south of England.

Most of all, however, Rugby's high standing sprang from the
superlative quality of its teaching staff. This left Winchester and
Eton, both at a low ebb, far behind. Percival was not exceptional
in preferring an assistant mastership at Rugby to the Fellowship of
an Oxford college, and the results obtained from recruiting men of
his calibre were impressive indeed. In classics at Oxford during the
decade between 1852 and 1862 Rugbeians won forty-one Open
Scholarships, gained thirty-five Firsts in Moderations and twenty-
two in Greats, and were elected to nineteen college Fellowships. In
1857 they won virtually all the Open awards at both Oxford and
Cambridge. The Royal Commission on Public Schools which
reported in 1864 found Rugby's teaching of classics 'absolutely
unsurpassed'.[2]

Although the influence of Arnold's reforms on his own and other
schools was considerable, their novelty and extent have been
exaggerated. Rugby had already been subjected to significant
reform when a new constitution in 1777 changed its status from
that of a grammar school. This required the boys to be instructed
in 'the Principles of the Christian Religion, Morality and Good
Manners'.[3] It was implemented, together with other innovations
(the tutorial system, praepostors and fagging), by Thomas James
DD, the first headmaster under the new dispensation, who came
from Eton the following year bringing Etonian customs with him.

The generally accepted statement that 'Thomas Arnold's original
contribution to educational theory had been ... to make the
training of Christian gentlemen his first priority'[4] therefore requires
some qualification. His moral influence on Rugby and the new
public schools was certainly great, but he was treading in the
footsteps of James, who had already transformed Rugby and raised
its standards and standing.

Over the school curriculum, too, Arnold was less of an innovator than is usually supposed. Most of a narrow syllabus inherited from James was left untouched, even though it was already under attack for being 'little beyond formal and arid exercises in two dead languages'.[5] Arnold passionately believed that no culture could be compared to that of Greece and Rome in classical times and that nothing made for clarity of mind so much as the study of their languages. To him Greek was also the best language for expressing new or profound ideas. He claimed that Coleridge's philosophy would have been more intelligible to him if Coleridge had written in Attic Greek.

It was this commitment to the classics which brought generations of Rugbeians so many successes at the two ancient universities, where classical studies still reigned supreme – to the dismay of the next wave of reformers, headed by Percival. It was not Arnold who led the way in adapting a standard public school syllabus to the circumstances and needs of a changing world. At Rugby the first steps were taken by his successors.

Arnold's innovations in Rugby's timetable went little further than one hour's history a week and a similarly grudging allowance of French. Outside the classics, there were few specialist teachers. The study of science Arnold refused to countenance on the grounds that it might become absorbing. 'Rather than have it the principal thing in my son's mind,' he wrote, 'I would gladly have him think that the sun went round the earth.'[6]

This revealing remark provides the strongest evidence that Arnold did not 'change the face of education all through the public schools of England'.[7] That was the prediction of Dr Hawkins, later Provost Hawkins, of Oriel (Arnold's college at Oxford), endorsed by Dean Stanley, Arnold's disciple and biographer. Through constant repetition it is a judgment which has achieved the status of a truth universally acknowledged. Yet Arnold was no revolutionary. He respected tradition and, so far as the curriculum was concerned, his influence served to perpetuate the typical education of his time which was soon to become out of date and out of touch.

Neglect of scientific subjects combined with social attitudes to separate the public schools from the creation of wealth, the very thing which brought them into being and sustained them. Some captains of industry and commerce sent their sons to schools like Rugby, but others preferred to continue training them in factories and counting houses rather than send them away to become proficient in Greek and Latin. Young gentlemen at public schools learned to despise trade, and this unfortunate gap between the best available education and the enterprises on which the prosperity of the nation depended was one which Percival later sought to close on both social and economic grounds.

What Arnold did change, permanently and for the good, was not the face but the heart and soul of the public school. Where he did broaden the teaching syllabus was in a greater emphasis on religious instruction. It was because he considered knowledge of moral issues all-important that he feared the distractions of science. The chapel became the centre of school life, and war was declared against vice. When he came to Rugby, the public schools had not yet thrown off their unsavoury reputation as dens of licenced barbarism and (in the words of the Rev. Thomas Bowdler) 'the very seats and nurseries of vice'.[8] New boys were the unprotected prey of predators. 'What I want to see in the school,' declared Arnold, 'is abhorrence of evil,'[9] and he set about replacing the bully rule of the strongest boys by the prefect rule of the cleverest.

But Arnold did not invent the prefectorial system, as is often supposed. There had been prefects at Winchester since the fourteenth century and at Eton since the sixteenth before James introduced them (named praepostors) at Rugby itself. Arnold's important innovation was to convert them from assistant ushers – the role probably performed by Percival at Appleby – into instruments of self-government: 'My greatest desire is to teach my boys to govern themselves.'[10]

For this purpose he allowed them responsibilities (judged to be useful in later life) as well as limited powers. They were chosen to be champions of righteousness in a fight against the forces of evil. The sinks of viciousness were to be cleansed, not by masters, but by sixth-form boys. This reform failed in its purpose of putting an end to bullying and immorality, but at least some form of regulation was introduced and a pattern for improvement set. In the case of two ordeals suffered by small boys at Rugby, as described in *Tom Brown's Schooldays*, tossing was abolished but roasting continued.[11]

Abolition of brutal corporal punishment was not on Arnold's agenda. It continued unabated. Although not in the same class as Keate of Eton, who once (mistakenly) flogged a whole contingent of candidates for confirmation, Arnold was himself no mean flogger. Holding to the belief that boys were innately wicked and the evil must be thrashed out of them, he fought a grim but inevitably losing battle against original sin. His declared purpose was to form Christian *men*: Christian *boys* he could not hope for, because in the naturally imperfect state of boyhood a low standard of morality was only to be expected. With the eye of a zealot he saw the Devil constantly at work among his charges, and threats of dire punishment were a regular feature of his sermons. From the pulpit he warned ominously that 'the spirit of Elijah must ever precede the spirit of Christ'.[12]

This low regard for the morals of his boys sometimes had an unfortunate result. According to Arnold's creed, lying was among the gravest of sins in a Christian gentleman. He once flogged a boy with an unprecedented fifteen lashes for persisting in a lie when, as it afterwards transpired, what the boy had been maintaining so doggedly was the truth. The flogging was so savage that the victim had to be taken to a sick-bed to recover. The local press got wind of the story, and the news travelled rapidly up the line to London where it flared into a national scandal and Arnold was seen as an ogre.

An intense concern for morals and souls being his real legacy, it was not inappropriate that before the century was out there were three successive Archbishops of Canterbury who had served as masters at the school he had so ardently Christianised. A. C. Tait, Arnold's immediate successor, was succeeded as Primate by Edward Benson, who had gone from Rugby to become the first headmaster of Wellington, and he in turn by Frederick Temple, the headmaster who recruited Percival and was to advance him along the path of his career.

Temple was the greatest single influence on Percival's life. Like Percival, he had taken Firsts in Greats and Mathematics at Oxford and become a Fellow of his college. At Rugby he built on Arnold's success and made up for some of his deficiencies. He enlarged the staff by employing more specialists to broaden the teaching of history and French and English and introduce music and a smattering of science into the syllabus.

Not that anything was allowed to make much headway against the classics. Temple regarded mathematics, for example, as a university subject and not one to be taught in schools except at an elementary level. When asked by the maths master for an extension of maths lessons to three hours a week, he refused with a quip:

Mathematics will flourish, and x, y and z
Will dethrone Greek and Latin and rule here instead.
Ye Mathematicians, so this is your plot:
Catch a weasel asleep, but asleep I am not.[13]

Temple, like Percival, has been undervalued. So far from being
'pale shadows of Arnold', as one historian has judged,[14] both may
more justifiably be numbered among Victorian headmasters as
peaks in a mountain range. Temple's influence spread, as Arnold's
had, through a cultural colonisation of the world of public schools.
Rugby's assistant masters were appointed headmasters of other
schools in astonishing numbers.

Three of these bearers of the sacred flame went to Clifton, two
each to Cheltenham, Marlborough, Haileybury and Bedford, and
others to Wellington, Charterhouse, Fettes and Dulwich. At Marlborough, Wellington and Clifton disciples of Arnold and Temple
were the founding headmasters. When the Prince Consort founded
Wellington it was natural for him to apply to Temple for a nominee
to launch the school.

The influence of this colonisation was not only educational. It
was religious and political too. Despite their high positions at what
might be thought centres of orthodoxy, Arnold and Temple, and
after them Percival, were very far from being establishment men. In
religion all three were Broad Churchmen, held by the dominant
High Church hierarchy to be teetering on the brink of heresy. They
were stern unbending Liberals, afflicted with throbbing social
consciences and motivated by determination to make the world a
different and better place.

It was, moreover, against the nature of men such as these to keep
quiet about their convictions. They trumpeted them, regardless of
the effect on their careers. Arnold was one of the most unpopular
men in England when he died in 1842, denounced for his advocacy
of ecclesiastical reform and denied a bishopric. Temple encountered
a similar storm with his contribution to a controversial volume of
Essays and Reviews, published in 1860. In his case his career was
rescued by Gladstone, who offered him in turn the deanery of
Durham, which he refused, and the see of Exeter, which he accepted
in 1869 after completing twelve years at Rugby. Percival also was
destined to become no stranger to political and ecclesiastical
controversy.

About Rugby he had reservations. 'Notwithstanding the veneration due to the great name of Arnold,' he wrote in 1903, 'I cannot say that Rugby, as I remember it in 1860–62, was a perfect school.' He recalled it nevertheless as 'a fine, strong, healthy, rough and vigorous, self-centred and supremely self-confident society'. For Percival nothing less than perfect would do, but the tribute he paid to Temple after his mentor's death was unstinting:

> I should have been quite unfit to attempt the not altogether easy work of building up such a new school as Clifton College but for the lessons I had learnt and the experience I had gained under Temple at Rugby, whether in the schoolroom, or in the Close, or in familiar intercourse with a rare band of distinguished colleagues, among whom I was but a child; or, above all, in the chapel, Sunday by Sunday; for Temple held fast to the Arnoldian tradition that the Headmaster should speak to the school from the heart every Sunday.[15]

When he visited the school in Arnold's day, Thomas Carlyle had found Rugby 'a temple of industrious peace', but that is not how others had experienced it. In this respect Arnold's Rugby did not differ from Temple's, which Percival described as 'a nursery of the strenuous life'; and that is what he took for his model. 'Peace' was too closely allied to sloth. Boys (so he believed) had to be taught that, if God's will were to be done, life needed to be strenuous.[16]

Percival spent no more than two years at Rugby, building on his early acquaintance with schoolmastering at Appleby. But, as his own acknowledgment makes clear, they were crucially formative years. From that brief apprenticeship he emerged fully armed, settled in his opinion what to adopt and what to discard and confident in the knowledge of how to apply his principles in practice.

He had learned to be eagle-eyed in observing boys so that he could read their characters at one piercing glance. He had absorbed the Arnoldian principle that the prime responsibility of schoolmasters was to awaken their pupils' intellect. ('You come here, not to read,' Arnold had told his boys, 'but to learn how to read.')[17] He had subscribed to Arnold's belief that character and morals were even more important than ability and academic brilliance. He had seen what could be achieved by employing a first-class staff committed to a school's ideals, and he had understood the need to pay them well and raise their status, as Arnold had done.

But the most valuable lesson which he had learned from Temple was the need to analyse and examine in detail how best to organise a school and implement changes to effect improvement. His mind was clear about Rugby's imperfections as well as its virtues, particularly in the matter of the curriculum.

Thomas Arnold, it has been said, stood 'on the threshold of change'.[18] John Percival was to cross that threshold.

CHAPTER 3

A New School for Bristol

Bristol had long been the largest and most important town in the West of England. During Plantagenet times it ranked third in the kingdom. In the sixteenth century it ousted York from second place, following the discovery of the mainland of North America by John Cabot and his sons, who sailed from the port in 1497. For the next three hundred years, until the rise of Liverpool and Glasgow, Bristol was Britain's main gateway to and from the New World. The West India and Virginia trade in sugar and spices, tobacco and slaves, brought immense wealth and made it the centre of thriving businesses, culminating most notably in the manufacture of chocolate by the Frys and cigarettes by the Wills family.

Thanks to the affluence of the merchant venturers, there were thriving schools too, notably Queen Elizabeth's Hospital (1590), Red Maids' (1634) and Colston's (1708). But Bristol Grammar School, founded by royal charter in 1532, never developed into a national institution as other grammar schools had in much smaller places like Rugby and Shrewsbury.

Indeed, by 1800, when the population had reached 40,000, it had no more than a handful of pupils, and for much of the first half of the century, while headmaster and ushers continued to draw stipends, there were no pupils at all. The grammar school had become a victim of local politics. It 'sank into disrepute' with the connivance of a corrupt Corporation.[1]

Merchants and professional men who could not afford the boarding fees of public schools elsewhere or wanted a more relevant training for their sons than the study of dead languages sent them to private schools in the locality. The headmaster who refused to enrol pupils at the grammar school was not idle. He was profitably engaged in providing private, fee-paying tuition instead. By law, grammar schools were not obliged to teach any subject except the classics, and he was therefore within his rights in refusing to include even elementary arithmetic in the syllabus.

Reforming legislation in the 1830s transferred control of the school from the Corporation to Charity Trustees appointed by the Court of Chancery, but it took a series of lawsuits lasting until 1845 to eject the 'no-pupils' headmaster. So the school had been empty for nearly twenty years when it finally reopened in 1848 with a new headmaster, a broad curriculum and nearly two hundred boys. All seemed set fair, but boarders – a crucial source of revenue – were not permitted, the teaching staff were underpaid, and the lessons were no longer free. The entry fee of £6 and an annual fee of the same amount were affordable by the mercantile class, but not by the poor for whom grammar schools were intended.

Paucity of funds soon precipitated a crisis, and the recovery proved short-lived. In 1860 the headmaster was forced to petition the Master of the Rolls for permission to take boarders, only to be refused on the grounds that boarding schools were for one class in society and day schools for another, and the two must be kept separate – a ruling which, incidentally, accorded with the preference of Thomas Arnold, who had tried to have Rugby's day boys removed to a separate school.

Meanwhile two attempts had been made to establish in Bristol the new kind of fee-paying school, open to all, which was beginning to flourish in other parts of the country. Bristol College made a promising start in 1831. It educated Walter Bagehot and some other notables. But when the sons of Nonconformists were admitted and excused from attending instruction in the doctrines of the established Church, it fell foul of the bishop and clergy, who declared it to be godless.

The Church then gave its support to the launch of a competitor, named Bishop's College, which opened in 1840. This resulted in the closure of Bristol College the following year. Twenty years later the new school was in as serious financial straits as the grammar school, and it closed in 1861.

Thus the need was evident but the precedents were not encouraging when some leading citizens met in April and May of 1860 under the chairmanship of the mayor to plan yet another school.

The first meeting was a private one, attended by some fifteen like-minded gentlemen. The second, held in the Clifton Subscription Rooms, was an open meeting. There it was formally resolved to establish a first-class public school for the education of the sons of gentlemen who were members of the Church of England. The site this time was not to be inside the unhealthy, over-crowded city, but in the salubrious residential suburb where they were meeting.

Perched on a height between the city with all its amenities and the deep gorge of the Avon running between downs and woodland with the unspoilt countryside of Somerset beyond, Clifton was, and has remained, among the most agreeable of suburbs. Here the mayor had his official residence, surrounded on the fringes of the downs by the detached and semi-detached palaces of the merchant princes. It was a first-class situation for the first-class school for the sons of gentlemen, who were to be provided with 'a thoroughly good and liberal education at a modest cost'.[2]

Winchester had been founded by a bishop; Eton by a king. In the post-Reformation period it was wealthy tradesmen who assumed the role of benefactor. Rugby owed its existence to a grocer. Appropriately in the climate of the Victorian age, Clifton College was founded by a joint stock company. Like the other newly founded public schools, it chose to be known as a College, adopting the medieval nomenclature still in use at Winchester and Eton, rather than a School, the more common name retained by former grammar schools such as Rugby and Harrow.

The capital of the Clifton College Company Limited was £10,000, divided into four hundred shares of £25 each. More than three hundred were taken up within eighteen months, producing a capital of some £8000. Shareholders never received a dividend. Holders of the privileged Class A shares enjoyed the right to nominate a boy to the school, but that was the sole benefit. This was not intended to be a profit-making business. It was in the nature of a corporate benefaction or, as aptly described at the time, 'nothing more than a philanthropic speculation'.[3]

The first step was the purchase of ten acres of farmland in open country between Clifton village and Durdham Downs. Then, when these appeared likely to prove inadequate, a further seven were added. Apart from the recently opened Bristol Zoo, there were no buildings within half a mile; nor were there any roads. The present Victorian suburb was developed around the school, following the

opening of Brunel's Suspension Bridge in 1864 and Clifton Down
railway station in 1874, which provided a connection with the
centre of the city.

A condition of the purchase of the original land, as phrased in
the deed of conveyance by some legal wit, stipulated 'that no
noisesome or offensive trade or business (except that of a School
for boys or girls) may be carried on therein'.[4] The provision for
girls at that date was far-sighted. More than a century was to pass
before the school became co-educational.

Charles Hansom (brother of the inventor of the Hansom cab)
was appointed architect, and his splendid range of Gothic Revival
buildings in locally quarried limestone remains an enduring testimony to the excellence of that choice. An unusually fine colour
effect was contrived by contrasting the red limestone with windows
and cornerstones in white Bath stone and roofing it with Welsh
tiles in shades of red, blue and purple.

The cost of the initial buildings, consisting of Big School,
classrooms and School House, amounted to nearly £11,000, and
when this was added to the £13,500 paid for the land it left the
company heavily burdened with mortgages. It was as well that
investors expected no dividends, for the creation of the school was
soon seen to be a very considerable act of faith.

The most crucial step of all was the appointment of a headmaster,
for on his performance the success or failure of the whole enterprise
would depend. Here again the Council elected by the shareholders
exercised sound judgment. They applied to Dr Temple at Rugby
and, after exhaustive inquiries elsewhere and visits to other schools,
settled on his nominee, the Rev. Charles Evans.

The composition of the Council which made these all-important
decisions represented, for the most part, a judicious blend of God
and Mammon. Devout clergy contributed the greatly needed faith.
Hard-headed bankers arranged the funding and necessary loans.
All had impressive qualifications.

The chairman was John Guthrie, a canon of Bristol cathedral
and a tireless worker in good causes. A fellow cleric, Canon
Moseley, was not only one of the Queen's chaplains but also a
Fellow of the Royal Society, a professor at King's College, London,
and an Inspector of Schools. Among the bankers were the mayor,
John Bates, and a former sheriff, Joshua Saunders, who was the
Bristol agent of the Bank of England. The professions were repre-
sented by Henry Wasbrough, a solicitor, who had hosted the first

meeting, Nonus Budd, a barrister experienced in conveyancing, and Dr John Addington Symonds, the most eminent physician in the West Country.

Charles Evans, their choice as headmaster, was an outstanding scholar and experienced schoolmaster. At Cambridge he had won the Craven Scholarship and the Senior Chancellor's Medal and been elected to a Fellowship at Trinity. He had served as an assistant master at Rugby for thirteen years. His appointment at Clifton dated from January 1861, and a prospectus was published announcing that the college would open under his headmastership in August of the following year (later amended to September). But when August 1862 came, Evans went.

His untimely desertion was reported to have 'occasioned the Council more anxiety than they can adequately express',[5] as well it might have. At a meeting on 20 August it was minuted:

> That the Revd. Charles Evans having been for some months past engaged to the College as Head Master, and the School having been advertised both by him and the Council to be opened on the 9th of September next under his Superintendances, the Council have heard with the utmost surprize a few days since that Mr Evans has now become a Candidate for the Head Mastership of Birmingham School.[6]

The start of their brave new venture seemed destined to be a drama of *Hamlet* without the Prince, but Canon Guthrie moved at commendable speed to negotiate the appointment of a suitable replacement in the event of Evans being successful in Birmingham. He again applied to Rugby, where Temple, that seasoned supplier of headmasters, was at no loss for a second nominee. He immediately volunteered another of his assistant masters and sought to overcome any qualms about this much less experienced candidate with the confident promise that he would do for Clifton what Arnold had done for Rugby – an extraordinary prediction, but one which happened to come true.

Shrewd assessment of character is one of the attributes of a successful headmaster, and Temple's judgment in recruiting and assessing Rugby's teaching staff was as unerring as Percival's was to become at Clifton. On this occasion his instinct was uncanny, for Percival had not been an unqualified success as an assistant master. He did not enjoy teaching fourteen-year-olds (his fate as a junior master). He took no part in games, had no hobbies and made no close friends among the other masters. Although always prepared to be sociable if required, he kept himself to himself and gave an appearance of donnish remoteness. The consensus among his colleagues was that he ought to abandon schoolmastering and return to Oxford.

The most delicate part of the new candidate's interview with the Council has been succinctly described in these words:

> One member of the Council observed, 'You are very young, Mr Percival.' 'And ummarried,' added another. 'A few years will correct the former,' replied the candidate, 'and a few weeks the latter.'[7]

The Council, presented with no credible alternative at such short notice and probably impressed well beyond their expectations by the maturity of the young man's presence and self-confidence, duly earmarked him for appointment should Evans fail to reappear. As the candidate's admiring godson later recorded without exaggeration: 'The place of Clifton among the great Public Schools was from that moment secure.'[8]

Behind Percival's brilliant career lay the wisdom of those who launched it, for here was a man without money, class, experience or wife. The credit must be shared between Temple and Clifton's Council, although the catalyst was Evans the defector. So far from being a disaster, his departure proved a stroke of remarkable good fortune for the school. Whatever his qualities, it is hard to believe that any other man's Clifton would have equalled his replacement's. And however perceptive the Council members, it is hard to believe that they would have appointed this raw young northerner except in the emergency which confronted them.

Evans's letter confirming his resignation was read at the next Council meeting, held on 4 September. He had been offered and had accepted the headmastership of his old school, King Edward's, Birmingham, but promised to 'take a warm interest' in the progress of Clifton College. 'In the high reputation and ability of my successor,' he wrote, 'you have a certain guarantee of success.'[9] Whether these sentiments mollified the Council is not recorded, but from that day Evans was all but written out of the history of the school. He became the headmaster that never was, and it is John Percival who has been remembered and honoured in chapel prayers by successive generations of Cliftonians as 'First Headmaster'.

Before finally making the appointment the Council had considered and pronounced satisfactory the testimonials received in Percival's favour. Time had been so short that, most unusually, there were only two; and one of these came from Temple himself. The other was from William Thomson, the former Provost of Percival's Oxford college who had advised him to go to Rugby. At Oxford Thomson had reformed Queen's, a task Percival was to attempt at Trinity. In the Church Thomson ended his career as Archbishop of York, an office which, many years later, Percival was led to believe would be his. They were like-minded liberals with parallel lives. For a short period during 1861 and 1862 Thomson had been, by a happy coincidence, Bishop of Gloucester and Bristol, and his endorsement of Temple's recommendation will have weighed heavily with Canon Guthrie.

The name of the new headmaster was made public at the Annual Meeting of the Company on 20 September, when his 'career of almost unsurpassed brilliancy at Oxford'[10] was stressed to counter any criticism of what might be seen as an over-hasty and risky decision.

One of the earliest commitments of the school's founders had been to remunerate the headmaster generously in order to be sure of attracting the very best available talent. Thus from the arrangements already concluded with Evans Percival inherited a handsome salary of £800 per annum plus a capitation fee of £2 per boy when numbers rose above two hundred – an incentive which was to bring him unforeseen wealth, much of which he returned to the school in benefactions for buildings and scholarships. He was required to repay £250 of the £800 as rent for School House, but this could be turned into profit from the fees of up to fifty boarders. All this was a substantial advance on the £100 per annum which he had been receiving at Rugby.

Moreover, his position as an employee of the company was protected by a resolution of the Council passed the previous November in favour of his predecessor: 'Resolved that Mr Evans is not removable from the office of Head Master save and except for such grave reasons as a majority of a Committee, formed of the President, the Vice-Presidents of the College, the Chairman of the Council and the Bishop of the Diocese for the time being, shall consider just.'[11]

Reminiscing at a Commemoration Dinner fifty years later, Percival gratefully acknowledged the forbearance of those who had appointed him: 'The main business of a Council is to elect a Head Master and then give him unswerving support, and as free a hand as possible. This has happily been the policy of the Council of Clifton College from the first.'[12]

Thanks to Guthrie and Temple, the crisis precipitated by Evans's departure was reduced to a quickly forgotten hiccup. The school opened before the end of September, just three weeks later than advertised. In the meantime Percival had moved one step further towards a more acceptable age by celebrating his twenty-eighth birthday.

During the following month the second of the Council's objections was overcome. From Canon Guthrie's house he married Louisa Holland, the lady he had first met four years earlier at Pau, where they were both recuperating from illness. Presumably they had corresponded warmly since, but she must have been surprised by the suddenness of his proposal. In her he was fortunate enough to acquire not only the requisites of a headmaster – a hostess and a mistress for School House – but also one who became a deeply loved and loving wife.

However warm his feelings towards her may have been when they married, Percival was not the man to waste precious time in taking a bride away for a honeymoon, most especially in fraught circumstances. For him the distraction of romance could never be permitted to interfere with duty. Two days at Clevedon, a few miles distant on the Severn estuary, were all he could spare Louisa during the school's first term. Gratifyingly, on their return boys from the school were waiting to unharness the horses, get between the shafts and pull their carriage for the final stretch to School House amid cheers.

The opening ceremony on 30 September had been a service in Big School attended by the first batch of pupils, numbering no more than sixty-nine (although seventy-six had enrolled). Also present to mark the historic occasion were parents, shareholders and other well-wishers. The choir from the cathedral came up the hill to lead the singing, and Percival preached the first of his many Clifton sermons. In this he set out his Christian credo and revealed some of his thoughts and principles with characteristic directness. God came first. The school would be in His hands. 'Neither is he that planteth any thing, nor he that watereth; but God that giveth the increase' was his chosen text.[13] Then:

> This day is the beginning of a union, the effects of which will last through all our future life ... I trust that there is no one whose life is beginning today in this place, but feels himself from this moment to be one with those who are around him. We met as strangers but we are strangers no longer. We are standing now at a starting point in life, and for the future we must walk hand in hand ... There is a heavy responsibility laid on every one, whether master or pupil, who enters a place like this, which has no tradition, no history, to guide us ... If you desire to belong to a place of which you may be justly proud; if you wish to hear this College spoken of as one that bears a high name; as a place where truth and uprightness and purity and all Christian virtues are held in honour; as a place where all that is base or unworthy is hated and despised, then – remember that it rests with you to give it that name.[14]

Those unable to attain intellectual distinction were not to be discouraged, he continued: 'The only really great thing upon earth is *goodness*, and this, thank God, is within the reach of all of us.' A number of exhortations followed: Resolve to be truthful. Beware of the insidious sin of idleness; whatever you do, do your work. Banish all impurity; the air of Clifton is not to be tainted. Keep watch over your tempers. Be patient. Be forgiving. Eschew malice and cruelty. Aim at manliness. Do not be ashamed of prayer. 'You are being trained not only to be industrious, active, successful men, but to be soldiers of Christ.'[15]

There was little to surprise in this address, except for the fervour of the underlying ambition and sense of destiny. In so far as Clifton College was dedicated to the education of Christian gentlemen, it was to be just another public school in the tradition of Arnold, but the methods employed were to be Percival's very own, and he was determined that the resulting products should be different and superior.

The years of tradition which inspired the long-established institutions at Winchester, Eton and Rugby were impediments to change. With roots embedded in the past, it was hard for them to respond to the demands of a rapidly changing world. Yet it was the general practice of the new public schools to borrow the prestige of the past by imitating the older foundations and adopting their traditions.

Clifton adopted some Rugbeian names and customs, but so far as essentials were concerned, that was not the path for Percival. Always forward-looking, he positively welcomed the absence of traditions. It enabled him to create them for himself in tune with modern ideas and his own ideals. Presented with the blank sheet of a foundation with no history, offered a free hand and the ready support of a liberal-minded governing body, he seized a Heaven-sent opportunity.

Years later he was to make the claim that 'our life has not been a mere copy of life in other places'. It had been 'distinguished by encouragement of the newer learning, whilst not neglecting the old'; by 'a ready and unprejudiced adaptability to changing wants'; possibly by 'better methods of instruction, of economy of time, and a pervading spirit of industry'.[16] In Clifton, he believed, a new spirit, a fresh character, a very special ethic of Work and Duty had been born.

An account of his creation may suggest how far this was true, how far self-delusion.

CHAPTER 4

New Teachers, New Teaching

In the pulpit Percival was in his element, as Arnold had been. In the classroom his performance was less impressive. It depended on the subject and the boys. His classes in classics for young scholars could not be bettered, but he did not have the knack of teaching dullards. Nor, despite his own academic brilliance, did he possess what was generally considered a proper regard for pure scholarship. What mattered to him about education was its practical application. He saw it, not as an end in itself, but as a necessary step towards doing the will of God by making the world a better place.

Not a born teacher himself, he made it his business to employ only those who were, and in recruiting assistant masters of the highest quality for Bristol's new school he was at his most ruthless in hunting them down and refusing to listen if they demurred.

The first prey in his man-hunt was H. G. (Graham) Dakyns, a Rugbeian who lived at Rugby, from where Percival determined to uproot him. In his case, with the school due to open in a few days, even agreeing to answer the summons was not enough. The following exchange was reported:

This tornado of a Headmaster said, 'When can you begin, Dakyns?' 'Oh, quite soon,' Dakyns replied; 'in two or three days at most.' 'There's a train in an hour's time,' said Percival; 'they are rather hard pressed down there. I think you had better take that.'[1]

And Dakyns did, followed not long afterwards by three other Rugbeians: E. M. Oakeley, C. W. A. Tait and W. O. Moberly (a nephew of Temple). In due course all four became housemasters and were to spend the remainder of their working lives at Clifton.

At Oxford a recommended don was interrupted in the middle of a tutorial by the appearance of a stranger who identified himself tersely as 'Percival of Clifton'. When the undergraduate had left, Percival announced: 'I want you to come and be my sixth-form master.' It was a command, not an invitation, and to make the point he declared his intention of remaining seated in the room until his victim agreed. It was useless for the man to protest that he was planning to leave Oxford to take up parish work. With Percival immovable after an hour and a half, he was forced to concede defeat and agreed to come for a year as an experiment.

By this means the Rev. W. M. Furneaux was introduced to his vocation in schoolmastering. From Clifton he went on to teach at Marlborough and become headmaster of Repton before ending his career as Dean of Winchester. 'You would have made a very bad parish priest,' Percival informed him later, when approving his move to Marlborough.[2]

At Cambridge T. W. Dunn, another future housemaster, was stalked and trapped on his staircase in college while still an undergraduate. Enticed into coming to Clifton to teach a low form for a term, he stayed for ten years, graduating to the sixth form and then to a headmastership in Bath.

Recruiting from Rugby was playing safe, but in targeting other men of exceptional ability, such as Furneaux and Dunn, Percival paid little heed to prudence or convention. Most of those he appointed were said to be 'vividly individual'. Sir Arthur Quiller-Couch, recalling his time as a schoolboy at Clifton, remembered them as a 'queer crew': 'Great wits . . . were frequently allied . . . with eccentricity, to say the least.'[3] Nor was physical disability a bar. Evelyn Abbott, who taught at Balliol and returned to a Fellowship there after a spell at Clifton, was crippled from the waist down and unable to walk. W. W. Asquith, brother of a future Prime Minister, had been dropped by his nurse when a child and was never fully grown.

The epithet most favoured by reminiscing Old Cliftonians when describing these masters was 'unforgettable'. Percival, aloof himself, encouraged his staff to be on friendly terms with the boys. Provided discipline was maintained, informality was the order of the day. Clifton was not to be a stuffy school and nicknames flourished. The odd appearances and idiosyncratic methods of instruction and punishment of men like 'Charlie' Tait, 'Daddy' Phelps, 'Buffer' Wiseman and Wollaston 'the Woolly Bear' made an indelible impression on the young.

Graham Dakyns became known in school folklore as the heroic hurler of dictionaries from his habit of propelling a Greek lexicon at the head of the inattentive in his form. He once sank to his knees in front of a dull pupil and offered a prayer to Almighty God that He would grant him a ray of intelligence. Exasperated by another, he offered a different kind of prayer: 'Would that you were under the green sod, and that I were dancing a can-can on your grave!'

The hairy, sideburned George Wollaston affably allowed boys to address him to his face as 'Old Bear', but he was liable to punish the unruly by locking them in a cupboard. He was Henry Newbolt's housemaster, and what Newbolt wrote about him goes some way towards explaining the school's success under the tutelage of these hand-picked eccentrics. Whatever their individual peculiarities, all were dedicated teachers in and out of class, feeding young minds every waking hour during term-time.

I judge by what he was to me: just the old saying 'a liberal education'. The rest I think I really might have got from books, or from any kind of teachers: but education itself he gave me perpetually – at lunch, at tea, at dinner, in the garden and the drawing-room and the Close, books, poetry, language, pictures, music, travel – every taste that makes life delectable and passionate, and with it a thing more difficult to describe: a kind of way of seeing life and taking it, a continual sense of meaning.[4]

By reason of their total absorption into the life of the school, the names of most of the masters appointed by Percival are unknown outside it. Among the exceptions are those of T. E. Brown, the Manx poet; Alfred Marshall, the economist, who began his career teaching mathematics at Clifton; H. S. Hall and F. H. Stevens of mathematics text-book fame; and a clutch of distinguished early scientists.

The Rev. Thomas Edward Brown (known to his friends as Tom) came closer to Percival than any other person outside his family. Fellow clerics and northerners, they were bound together by the ties of a common background, similar beliefs, rare intellects and a mutual – but not uncritical – admiration. Born in 1830, the sixth child of an impoverished curate on the Isle of Man, Brown was the elder by four years. Like Percival at Appleby, he was fortunate in receiving an excellent free education at King William's College which enabled him to win a scholarship to Oxford. There, as a poor 'servitor' at Christ Church, he gained Firsts in Greats, history and jurisprudence, and this was followed by the highest distinction in the university at that time: the award of a Fellowship at Oriel through competitive examination.

Brown was introduced to Percival after periods as a Fellow of Oriel, Vice-Principal of King William's College (at the age of twenty-five) and headmaster of the Crypt School in Gloucester, this last appointment having ended in an explosive public row with parents. At their first meeting, in Rugby, Brown, a genial humorist and notorious mimic, was given a warning to be on his best behaviour. This he ignored and was said to have completely shattered Percival's gravity with torrents of fun and spirited render- ings of Manx songs. After a second meeting, in Oxford, Percival characterised him as 'volcanic' – a notable instance of the pot calling the kettle black, except that in his own case Percival's iron self-discipline precluded eruption.[5]

'Oh, he'll do,' was Percival's casual acceptance of Oxford's brightest star,[6] but once at Clifton Brown soon won trust and seniority. He arrived in 1863, a year after the school opened, to take charge of one of Percival's most cherished projects: the Modern Side. In the following year he became housemaster of the second boarding house to be opened, and a year later he was appointed Second Master, the headmaster's official deputy.

During the holidays the two men sometimes walked together in the Pennines, where on one occasion Brown noted Percival's fearlessness in broaching a mountain pass during a storm: 'a man of rare dignity and courage' was his comment.[7] But he was less appreciative of his headmaster in the role of slavedriver. 'I'm here at Clifton, grinding at the mill,' one of his poems begins plaintively; and his greeting to Percival's successor was the promise that the staff would work for him 'without the lash'.

During irascible outbursts and bouts of depression Brown would complain of enduring the havoc of pitiless years. As a housemaster he grumbled about being 'much exposed to parents',[8] and his stocky, thick-set figure became a familiar sight taking solitary walks on the downs wrapped in gloomy thought or communing with his muse. Yet for the most part he and Clifton were well content with each other. Boys were enthralled by his history lessons because of his flair for bringing the past dramatically to life. He was one of Percival's born teachers, if at times a reluctant one, frustrated that he could not devote the whole of his life to his poetry.

Brown's stay at the school lasted the same length of time as Dakyns' – twenty-nine years; and he died there of a brain haemorrhage suffered on a return visit after retirement. This occurred while he was giving a talk to some of the boys on the ideals of the school – 'ideals which he himself had done so much to form'.[9]

The headmaster may have kept his staff's noses relentlessly to the grindstone, but no more than he kept his own, and he was loyal to them, cared for them and frequently pressed the Council to increase their salaries. When they stood up to him, as Dunn often did, they were respected for it. His relationship with them and the reason why so many stayed for so long despite his awesome authoritarianism is exemplified by his treatment of Charles Cay, another housemaster and his first senior mathematics master.

Cay's health proved unable to stand the fiery pace which Percival imposed and he became seriously ill. When he was sent to the south of France to recuperate, Percival and his wife followed and spent their holiday looking after him. When he died there, Percival stayed to make arrangements for the funeral and conduct the burial service.

The emotional sermon which he preached afterwards at Cay's memorial service at the school was said never to have been forgotten by those who heard it. This had been the disciple whom Percival loved best. He was that 'singularly pure and chivalrous master whose life burnt out so quickly in the service of our young society, whose grave is on the Mediterranean shore'. Percival extolled a 'spirit which stamped itself so deep and strong in this place as an example of simplicity, earnestness and enthusiasm'. Cay's memory, he declared, was shining in the hearts of Cliftonians like a lamp of sacred flame; Cay had handed on the flaming torch of true life to future generations.[10] (First to take up the torch was Dakyns, who married Cay's widow and took over his house.)

The brotherhood of individualists in the masters' common-room may have employed very different methods in and out of the classroom, but they were tightly bound together by Percival's dominance, a common purpose and shared ideals. To one sharp-eyed pupil observing them at work they appeared 'professional, authoritative, confident in their position and themselves', like officers in an army.[11] But they were also seen more critically as a mutual admiration society and thought to be rather too conscious of their superior talents.

As their joint and several influences took root alongside the headmaster's, Clifton became less and less a colony of Rugby and more and more *sui generis*. In retrospect the Rugby connection became a touchy point. 'Much as we honour and respect Rugby,' one Old Cliftonian's disclaimer ran, 'we never have been and never shall be "the Rugby of the West".'[12]

An unusually high proportion of masters were specialists, and if they were unconventional, so was the syllabus. Percival believed that schools should offer pupils a broad range of educational opportunities to suit varying abilities and inclinations. Here he boldly crossed Arnold's 'threshold of change'. In this respect Rugby was very far from being the model. He was determined to exploit to the full the advantage of being able to construct a curriculum in keeping with the times as they were and as he foresaw they would be, not as they had been in a past honoured for too long.

No public school in the nineteenth century could hope for acceptance, let alone acclaim, if it neglected the classics, and Percival's Classical Side was quickly brought up to a standard where it could rival other schools (but not Rugby) in numbers of entrants and scholarships to Oxford and Cambridge. But in parallel with the Classical Side he introduced his Modern Side, which he intended to be of equal importance and status. This offered a curriculum which included Latin, French and German, mathematics and science, English history and English literature and composition. Although novel, this was not wholly unprecedented. The twenty-year-old Cheltenham College had already decided not to feed its would-be army officers on an exclusive diet of dead languages and mathematics.

In 1871 the practice of purchasing commissions in the army was abolished. In 1873 Percival responded by establishing within his Modern Side a specialist 'Woolwich set' designed to meet the requirements of those aspiring to a military career. Two years later this achieved separate status as the Military and Engineering Side, which reflected Percival's strongly held conviction on the interplay between abstract knowledge and its usefulness in practice: to teach 'the engineers to think scientifically and the mathematicians to convert their formulae into concrete facts'.[13]

H. S. Hall, the first master in charge of the 'M. & E.', was also the first Old Cliftonian to be appointed to the staff. He was a prime example of the rounded man Percival set out to produce. A good cricket and rugger player, he had won a mathematics scholarship to Cambridge, where he was awarded a prize for Latin hexameters. His career as a master at Clifton lasted for twenty-six years, and during that time one hundred and fifty of his pupils passed directly into Woolwich and one hundred and twenty into Sandhurst. Amongst other text-books, he wrote (with W. S. Knight) *Elementary Algebra for Schools*, a primer which held sway throughout the country for half a century and sold a million and a half copies. During his spare time he invented the modern hook used in fly-fishing.

The 'M. & E.' course proved of value not only to the individual, but also to the nation, which was in great need of a modernised army led by better educated officers. But, to Percival's chagrin, his innovative syllabuses did not attract the brightest boys, and the equality between his two main divisions was no more than notional. The best scholars gravitated towards the classics while the Modern and Military Sides tended to be regarded as easy options for the intellectually weaker brethren.

Yet it is as a pioneer in the teaching of the natural sciences that Percival was perhaps most effective and influential. His views on its value were very different from Arnold's and well in advance of Temple's. It was at the forefront of his thinking, for he had been quick to grasp that this was the subject of the future and became alert before others to the ominous implications of Germany's lead in scientific and technological education. A master properly qualified to teach science was therefore one of his earliest appointments.

Science was on the regular curriculum of no other public school at this date. As the Clarendon Commission on the Public Schools reported in 1864: 'Natural Science, with some slight exceptions, is practically excluded from the education of the higher classes in England.' To teach it at Clifton Percival went on to recruit men even more brilliant than most of the galaxy of stars he had assembled for other subjects. Several graduated to university professorships, and four became Fellows of the Royal Society. The first Head of Chemistry was the afterwards famous pioneer of synthetic rubber, Sir William Tilden. By the end of Percival's time at the school, ninety per cent of the boys were studying science, some for ten hours a week. This flying start resulted in a lead which was never lost and manifested itself during the next century in Old Cliftonian Nobel Prize winners.

In the teaching of modern languages, too, Percival's new school took a decided lead over others. Again according to the Clarendon Commission: 'A footing [for modern languages] is now allowed, but always grudgingly. They are still in most cases regarded as impertinent intruders.' Yet at Clifton every boy was taught them in class by specialists, not as the classics were taught, but as living languages. Out of class there were even debating societies in French and German.

As a classical scholar Percival would have been well aware of Plato's emphasis on the benefit of music in the training of young minds. Although not in the curriculum, this subject was not neglected. For the musically inclined piano tuition was available, and as well as the choir there were choral and orchestral societies, concerts in Big School and house glee competitions. These were stimulated by a strong interest in music among the masters, especially Oakeley, who was a talented pianist and organist, and Brown, who led much of the singing in a voice described as 'rich, melodious and thunderous'.

Percival's own interest was concentrated on church music. The compilation of a school hymnal was his personal concern. Contributions to the words from Brown were welcomed. 'Sugary tunes' – foreign to his austere nature – were comprehensively excluded.

A chapel was not among the first buildings at Clifton. When one was built and consecrated in 1867, five years after the school opened, the choir became isolated in the chancel as it had not been during the services in Big School. It was then thought bad form for the rest of the school to join in the singing: a view which did not meet with the headmaster's approval. In a sermon he demanded that the whole school lift up its voice in praise of the Lord. One form responded, no doubt more enthusiastically than he would have wished, with a resolution that anyone not singing in chapel should have his head punched. The singing thereafter was pronounced 'very hearty' – as it has continued to be ever since.

In the very last month of Percival's headmastership the angelic voice of the first of the school's musical stars was heard when the treble solo in Handel's *Messiah* was sung by Harry Plunket Greene. This heralded a long international career as a tenor, punctuated by frequent returns to sing at the school in demonstrations of the loyalty which Percival had sought to instil in all Cliftonians.

Before long, the excellence of Clifton's musical tradition was to become as widely acknowledged as its military reputation, its strength in science and – in the pursuit of Percival's ideal, the rounded man – its sporting prowess.

All these were his legacy, but much more besides.

CHAPTER 5

The Town House
and Other Innovations

Demand for a public school education was rising during the 1860s, and boarding lay at the heart of the system. Yet some parents hesitated to plunge gently nurtured sons into the jungle of boarding school life, especially while others continued to find such places useful as reformatories for their less well-behaved offspring. Despite reforms it was often the latter who set the tone.

Parental anxiety about undesirable goings-on on the boys' side of the green baize door which separated them from their housemaster and his family had deepened since 1858. In that year corruption of the innocent at a boarding school was brought vividly to public notice through the publication of a best-selling novel which appeared to have been written from personal experience and be true to life. This was *Eric, or Little by Little*, which many mothers will have read with mounting dismay.

Fathers who had suffered as boarders themselves sent their sons to suffer in turn not only because they believed it would make men of them but also because the alternative form of public school education was unthinkable. The few day boys at a school like Rugby were the unwanted relics of its origins as a charity school. They were lads from the town receiving a free education by right and on sufferance. Accordingly, they were objects of scorn, despised as 'town-bugs' and forbidden to participate in games or any other extra-curricular activity. Aping their elders, newly founded public schools pursued the same practice. At Cheltenham forty years after its foundation in 1841 no town boy had ever been selected to play for the school at any game.

But at Clifton, from the beginning, Percival offered a full public school education without fear of the moral perils and physical discomforts of life as a boarder. Day boys were brought into the house system and accorded equal status with boarders in every respect. About two-thirds of the initial intake of boys came from homes in Bristol, where there were already well-established day schools, but none which could offer the quality of teaching, the breadth of facilities or the social cachet of a public school.

Some of this first batch of local Cliftonians boarded in School House, where their parents were confident that they would be safe under the watchful eye of the headmaster himself. Those who remained living at home – the so-called Cliftownians – were assigned to Town House. Twelve years later – in April 1875 – when numbers had grown, this was re-organised into North Town and South Town, divided according to whether homes were north or south of an imaginary line drawn down the centre of the chancel and nave of the chapel. At this date there were only five boarding houses, so that the proportion of day boys to boarders was significantly higher than at other public schools, although the balance swung more decisively towards boarding during the last years of Percival's headmastership, when two further boarding houses were opened.

Percival's control over his day boys extended to their parents. Fathers and mothers were not permitted to be away from home at night at the same time without notifying the headmaster. Nor were day boys allowed to leave their homes in the evening except under the same strict conditions as applied to boarders. No other school operated such a system.

The attraction of the town houses was not confined to local residents. Tender-hearted parents elsewhere became interested. Henry Newbolt and his brother Francis were intended for Eton, but their widowed mother decided instead to move house from Norfolk to Clifton so that they could be day boys there. Newbolt wrote of this in his memoirs:

> Clifton had been recommended to her as perhaps the only place where the two contrasted systems of day-school and boarding-school were so combined in one as to secure the advantages of both without the disadvantages of either. If she chose, her boys might sleep every night under her own roof – might escape the barrack life of dormitories – and yet as members of one of the two great 'Town Houses' they would have by day a full share in the Commonwealth.[1]

Newbolt even prided himself that, being resident all the year round, the day boys were more truly Cliftonian than the boarders. Although he refrains from mentioning it, money might also have been a consideration. Tuition and school fees for boarders were £90 per annum. Without boarding they were £25.

Surprising as it may be thought, Mrs Newbolt's preference was shared by both Arnold and Percival themselves. It was one of Arnold's firmly held beliefs that crowding boys together multiplied the evil in them. As he put it himself: 'The amount of evil in the mass is more than the sum of the evil in the individual.'[2] Acting on this conviction, he removed his two elder sons from Winchester (his own old school, where he had not been unhappy) and had them and their younger brothers educated at Rugby, living at home with him in School House.

Percival, without public school experience as a boy, formed the conclusion as a result of his time at Clifton that 'the best education in English life was not to be had in a boarding school, but was obtained by a boy who lived in a good home and attended a good school near his home'. A good school he defined as one 'well organised, well instructed and of high tone'.[3]

The credit for Clifton's town house system is not due entirely to Percival. Special provision for day boys had been urged before his appointment at the founders' very first meeting. Dr Symonds, the respected physician, had then stressed the immense importance to some boys of combining the intellectual culture and training of a school with the influence of home life. There were, he said, public school men sent out into the world 'who hardly knew what it was to have the blessed, purifying, sanctifying influence of home, and the society of mothers and sisters';[4] so it was the doctor's prescription which Percival administered.

If the integration of day boys represented one of Clifton's most radical initiatives, a more startling example of Percival's pioneering zeal was his proposal to make special arrangements for orthodox Jewish boys to attend an orthodox Church of England institution.

The stated objective of Clifton College was the education of Christian gentlemen, and it had been founded, moreover, in succession to another Church of England school which had been forced to close for the somewhat less heinous sin of making special arrangements for the sons of non-conforming fellow Christians. But the college's constitution also stipulated that no boy be refused admission by reason of his religious faith, and this loophole was Percival's window of opportunity.

If Christian boys received instruction in the Christian faith, he argued, it was only right that Jewish boys should receive instruction in the Jewish faith and not be deterred from observing its practices, even if this entailed their being excused normal school lessons and games on their Sabbath. A few boys from Jewish homes were already at the school, but they were scattered throughout the different houses and enjoyed no concessions or facilities for their own religious observances.

Percival's proposal was the result of meetings between himself and Lionel Cohen, a Jewish Member of Parliament. Cohen lived in London but paid regular visits to Clifton to take the waters at Hotwells, located at the foot of the Avon gorge. Percival took advantage of this to solicit his assistance in obtaining a Royal Charter for the school by steering a Private Member's Bill through Parliament. Cohen, evidently impressed by Percival and his school, raised in return the question of admitting Jewish boys to it under a religious dispensation.

At a meeting of the school Council held in May 1875:

> The Head Master reported that Mr Lionel L. Cohen of 9 Hyde Park Terrace, London, with the Revd. L. Berliner, the Chief Rabbi, had called upon him to make some enquiries as to the possible admission of six or eight of the élite of the Jewish body to the College and they were desirous of knowing whether such boys would be allowed to be absent from prayers and would be excused attendance on Saturdays and Jewish Festivals (and evenings before from dusk); in other respects they could conform to the regulations of the College.[5]

At the next meeting the following month a letter from Cohen to Percival was read. During his stay at Clifton, he wrote, he had been struck by the large number of non-boarding pupils as well as by what he flatteringly described as 'the high character of the College under your able management and the enlightened and yet conscientious supervision of its Council'. At this stage he was not proposing a house. Jewish pupils, he suggested, could live with the minister of the Bristol synagogue. At the outset numbers would be fifteen at most.

After what was minuted as a 'full discussion' (the standard boardroom euphemism for prolonged argument) it was unanimously resolved 'that the Council much regret that they do not see their way to make the concessions asked for'.[6] By the members of the Council that decision was understood to be the end of the matter; but to Percival, whose stubbornness in the face of opposition was unyielding, it represented a challenge and nothing more than a temporary setback.

A successful re-consideration took some time. It was two and a half years later when the headmaster was minuted as referring to previous communications and reporting that he had arranged with Mr Bernhard Heymann to receive ten Jewish boys into his house to attend the College.

Heymann was a native of Hamburg who had worked as a private tutor in London for twenty-four years. Percival had now employed him in the Modern Languages department to teach German and Hebrew. His house was to be under the supervision of the headmaster and subject to the discipline of the school, exactly as the other houses were – except that all the concessions requested in the previous communications were granted.[7]

How Percival manoeuvred, and presumably conspired with Cohen, to achieve this volte-face by the governing body is a mystery. Was it the *quid pro quo* for the promise of a Private Member's Bill? The records are tactfully silent, but a clue may lie in what was reported of the tactics Percival employed at a later date to get his way at Oxford. When his proposals were not accepted, it was said that 'he reiterated them at a later meeting with a combination of unruffled patience and unswerving persistence which was peculiarly irritating to those who thought that a proposal was killed by defeat on a division'.[8] It was a policy of erosion by importunity.

Clifton's Jewish house opened under Heymann in 1878 with just seven boys, but when it became Polack's House, run by successive generations of one remarkably able family, it grew to the same size as others. As with the town houses, it pointed the way for other schools to follow. Cheltenham had a Jewish house for thirty years, between 1893 and 1923, and one at The Perse School in Cambridge lasted from 1911 to 1948. Clifton's was not only the first, but has also proved the longest-lived. After a hundred and twenty years it is still serving the Jewish community.

Age span was another example of the school's departure from

the norm, although this may have been due more to economic necessity than a pioneering spirit. At the top end of the range were eighteen-year-old sixth-formers preparing for university entrance or military cadetship. At the bottom end, the school had opened with twenty boys under the age of twelve, two of them only nine, and within a few months Percival was planning a Preparatory School for boys aged six and upwards.

This was another occasion when he encountered opposition on the Council and was forced to bide his time. At first he had to be content with a Junior School for boys between eleven and fourteen, which was neatly accomplished by incorporating an existing private school. To be allowed a Preparatory School took him ten years. It was established in 1873, catering for boys up to the age of eleven. They were then able to move up the ladder to the Junior School for three years before entering the senior school proper at fourteen. Some other public schools had feeders of this kind, but at Clifton the 'Pre.' burgeoned prodigiously. It was closely integrated and contributed to a spectacular growth in overall numbers.

Another enterprise, and one especially dear to Percival's heart, was the concept and inauguration of the Public School Mission. His social conscience agonised over the condition of the poor in the slums of Bristol. When the evangelist George Whitefield preached there, he described how he felt his bowels yearning for the Kingswood colliers. Percival's yearned too and kept him from sleep. He would go out on the downs at night and stand listening to the 'still, sad music of humanity'[9] rising in a subdued murmur of misery from the teeming city at his feet. Being Percival, he determined to do more than preach. The hollowness of the claim by one historian that Arnold was the only headmaster vitally concerned with social issues could not be more graphically exposed.[10]

From the start of the school, offertories were devoted to a variety of religious and charitable causes throughout Britain and abroad, but in 1869 Percival decided to concentrate on funding a single project on behalf of the needy – the spiritually, materially and educationally deprived – near at hand. Here again his mind was running ahead of the times.

Percival did not invent the Victorian mission to the inner city. Spiritual missions to the urban working class had been stimulated by the national religious survey in 1851 which revealed how few of them attended church or chapel. Christian Socialists, too, were already at work. The novelty was for a school not merely to finance but to undertake such work itself. 'There is no doubt,' wrote Canon Wilson, his successor as headmaster, 'that the original conception of a school acting as "Big Brother" to a poor city district is due to Percival.'[11] The only rival claimant to that honour was Thring of Uppingham.

Having reached the conclusion that charitable donations from the privileged to the under-privileged were not in themselves enough, Percival thus made it his business to involve his school directly in the welfare of the bodies and souls of the Bristol labouring class. He began, in 1868, by enlisting the support of teaching staff and the older boys to establish a Ragged School in one of the most destitute areas on the eastern side of the city: the Dings. Within a short time an elementary education was being provided for a hundred and twenty children previously denied any form of teaching.

This school served its purpose for several years, until rendered superfluous by the opening of a Board School under the provisions of the 1870 Education Act. A mission to the slum parish of St Barnabas, Ashley Road was then decided upon and Percival set about selecting a missioner. On this occasion the Rev. Furneaux was not to be bullied into accepting the post, but the headmaster's second choice proved shrewd enough. The Rev. H. D. Rawnsley, who was appointed mission curate, was later to become Canon Rawnsley and achieve lasting fame as one of the founders of the National Trust.

Rawnsley had to battle against insuperable odds. His flock lived either in squatters' huts or in jerry-built houses which flooded; the streets were unpaved and unlit; and the mission hall was attacked with a hail of stones whenever it was opened for prayer. But when he departed in despair Percival did not give up, not even when the mission was reduced to little more than a temperance coffee-house.

The two of them had, however, prepared the way for Wilson and his missioners to develop an astonishing range of activities: a Workman's Club, a Clothing Club, a Provident Boot and Shoe Club, a Penny Bank, Penny Readings, a Provident Dispensary, a night school, a library, mothers' meetings, bible classes, cookery classes, swimming classes, district visiting and excursions. The culmination was the building of a new church and the creation of the new parish of St Agnes.

Initiated, funded and run by the school, its masters, pupils and friends, what had been despaired of as a 'forlorn hope'[12] became the inspiration and prototype of numerous missions launched in the following years by public schools, Oxford and Cambridge colleges and other corporate institutions.

CHAPTER 6

Wife and Family

Louisa Percival, like the wives of other prominent men in the nineteenth century, was not so much self-effacing as effaced by convention and thereby almost lost to posterity. She shared her husband's life and supported him in his career for more than a third of a century, but no more than a few contemporary mentions and household notes have survived to offer glimpses of what appears to have been a character almost as admirable as his and certainly more congenial.

Louisa was neither a fellow northerner nor a member of the intellectual circles in which Percival moved, and only the coincidence of their being invalids recuperating at the same place at the same time brought them together. She sprang from Lincolnshire stock on both sides of the family: her father, James, was a Holland and her mother a Hardwicke. But they lived in the south London suburb of Norwood, where it is likely that her parents moved in a class of society superior to his and she experienced a much different, more affluent childhood.

Percival's instinct in choosing this chance acquaintance to marry proved characteristically sound, for she became a perfect wife, mother, hostess and foil. There can be no doubt that he loved her deeply, and she brought him a lifetime of unselfish devotion. Small where he was tall, cheery and warm-hearted where he was chilly and silent, socially deft where he was gauche, she was not crushed or overawed by his personality and position and made no bones about differing from his solemn, puritanical view that enjoyment of life was a distraction from duty. Her vitality was infectious. In energy she ran him a close second, all the more remarkably because a carriage accident before she first met him had cost her the use of one lung and she suffered long spells of uncontrollable coughing in bed every morning.

This is William Temple's assessment of her contribution to her husband's life and work:

> In everything he relied greatly on Mrs Percival, regarding her as fully a part of himself and in some sense as his interpreter. She was by nature expansive as he was reticent, and he often left her to say what he found it difficult to say. Thus he sought to unbend by proxy. She was the only person on whom he was really dependent, and without her he would have been very different. She was the channel through which he was in touch with the human, as distinct from the official, side of his surroundings. Moreover she did much to make him intelligible to others. She created an atmosphere of intimacy and cordiality in which his shyness relaxed.[1]

Fulfilling the first duty of a Victorian wife, Louisa produced eight children as rapidly as nature would allow.

There were seven boys and one girl: Robert Hardwicke, Elizabeth Ann (Bessie), John Guthrie (always known as Guthrie), Charles, Launcelot Jefferson (Lance), Arthur Jex-Blake, Frederick (Freddie) and William. The happiness of this family was marred by early deaths. Percival was predeceased not only by Louisa herself but also by six of their children. He needed all his faith in God to bear this succession of personal tragedies.

Charles and William died in infancy. Freddie was killed in an accident while a schoolboy. Robert became a permanent invalid and died in his forties. Guthrie suffered an unexpected death from double pneumonia, and Arthur was an army officer killed in action on the point of being promoted to high command. Bessie was one of the two survivors, whose relationship with their father became increasingly close in his later years. She was married to Basil Johnson, the son of a Dean of Wells. He was a music master at Rugby and then at Eton, and she practised as an artist under her married name. The other survivor was Lance, who alone of the large family provided Percival with grandchildren.

Launcelot Percival epitomised his father's ideal of all-round goodness, taking holy orders and playing rugger for England. He became Prebendary of the Chapels Royal and domestic chaplain to King George V, with whom he was on terms of some intimacy. The

king rewarded him with a KCVO, although, being a clergyman, he
never used the title. He married into one of the richest families in
England, the Pilkingtons of glass fame, and his widow adopted the
style of Lady Percival after his death in 1941. Today Percival's only
descendants spring from this marriage. The two who alone bear his
surname are his great-grandson, Lance Percival the actor, and his
son Jamie.

At Clifton Louisa gathered together everyone in the neighbourhood likely to assist in the new school's progress. Playing the
hostess to old and young, she presided over formal evening dinners,
weekly musical parties, summer picnics and festivities at cricket
matches. According to one Clifton resident drawn into her social
set:

> The establishment of Clifton College, and the coming of the
> Percivals to the School House, brought a new element into
> Clifton society, which had been up till then much divided into
> exclusive cliques. Clifton was almost entirely conservative in its
> politics, while Bristol was equally radical in opinion. But at the
> School House dinner-table people belonging to different cliques
> met each other and found they had something in common.[2]

For Percival these social functions were duties to be endured for
the sake of the school. Small talk was not for the serious-minded,
and no one was more serious-minded than Clifton's headmaster.
At his most marmoreal at the formal dinner-table he was prone to
lapse into embarrassingly lengthy silences. It fell to his wife to lift
this dampening pall, and she adopted the ploy of seating specially
invited conversationalists near his end of the table with orders to
keep their host in play. T. W. Dunn, the most outspoken of the
housemasters, became used to being cast in this role.

At her end of the table Louisa had to cope with the most
distinguished of the male guests, whoever they might be. Sometimes
it was an academic eminence as unsociably inclined as her husband,
such as Benjamin Jowett. As one of the housemaster's wives
complained when the ladies had withdrawn to the sanctuary of
Mrs Percival's drawing room at the conclusion of one dinner, the
shy little pink-faced Master of Balliol generated more light than
warmth.[3] On such occasions Louisa was not above keeping her
other guests entertained by telling – presumably out of earshot of
her husband – what Dunn judged to be 'very risky stories'.[4]

Louisa Percival, in short, was fun: always bright and cheerful; an enemy of boredom; a disperser of gloom. Within the school she quickly became a cherished institution. If anyone was ill or needed cheering up, she 'flew to one's bedside or fireside, breaking down all reserve and going straight to one's heart', as another housemaster's wife enthused.[5]

She welcomed newcomers and made visitors comfortable. She mothered the young bachelor masters and acted as hostess for them when necessary. She became a role model for the new housemasters' wives. She supervised the school's two sanitoria, its laundry and its dairy farm. Yet at the same time her private duties as a homemaker could not be neglected. At regular intervals she had to take time-off for childbirth, and, even with the assistance of nursemaids, a growing nursery required her constant attention. But none of these activities and distractions was her most time-consuming occupation.

As headmaster, Percival was also housemaster of School House. Initially, until new houses were built, this accommodated all the school's boarders, and the public school system decreed that, whatever her inclinations or capabilities, whatever the other calls on her time, a housemaster's wife automatically undertook the duties of housekeeper, caterer and mother-substitute. An abundance of servants was available, but they required supervision and sometimes mothering too.

The young bride returning from her two-day honeymoon in Clevedon therefore found herself in immediate command of an army of nineteen servants and charged with responsibility for the accommodation, feeding and welfare of what was soon to become nearly fifty boys exiled from their own homes. Faced with this formidable task, Louisa never faltered. Her solicitude in caring for the boys has been hallowed by tradition. Sightings of a ghost haunting School House are reported from time to time – the ghost, not of Percival, but of Louisa, presumed to be making sure that the boys are still being properly looked after.

The pace of life in the house was hectic. The weekday timetable imposed by Percival was deliberately planned to allow no opportunity for truancy or more than a few minutes' relaxation. Boys had to be up at half past six and washed and dressed in time for morning prayers and roll call at seven. The time remaining before breakfast at eight was assigned to prep, and after breakfast came morning school. When that was over, a second roll call and dinner followed at half past one. The afternoon was devoted to further lessons and games. Lock-up, a third roll call and tea were at half past six, followed by prep from eight to nine, supper at nine, evening prayers at half past, bed at a quarter to ten and lights out at ten o'clock.[6] Even Sunday offered little breathing-space. The hours were filled with chapel services, walks, evening lectures or concerts and other activities thought appropriate to the day of rest.

If the unrelieved daily grind was outside her control, Louisa could at least ensure that her charges were adequately nourished to stand the pace. This was another departure from the traditional norm. In addition to the hazards of brutality and vice, poor living conditions in general and inadequate and unappetising food in particular had been endemic in public schools. At pre-Victorian Rugby and Winchester those conditions had led to rioting so serious that the army had had to be called in to suppress it at bayonet point. At Eton in 1832 Keate overcame rioters without military assistance by personally flogging eighty rebels into submission. At Marlborough as recently as 1851 a full-scale rebellion had raged for a week, and on that occasion it was the authorities who were forced to submit.

In the boom years of the 1860s and 1870s conditions had improved to meet the expectations of parents who entrusted their sons to the care of new schools with better ordered and more strictly controlled regimes. But the quality of food at public schools was to remain a source of grievance for another hundred years. Yet Louisa's surviving weekly bill of fare for the boys in School House during 1874 (menus which circulated among other housemasters' wives) suggests that they were at least as well fed at school as at home. Dinner served in the middle of the day was the main meal, and over the week she varied the menus as follows:

Monday: Irish stew or stewed steak; jam roll pudding.
Tuesday: Boiled leg of mutton; apple charlotte or baked bread pudding (with currants).
Wednesday: Scotch broth; beef steak pie.
Thursday: Roast beef; baked rice pudding.
Friday: Boiled beef; apple pie.
Saturday: Pea soup; roast leg of mutton.
Sunday: Cold roast beef, salad or pickles; hot plum pudding.

Breakfast consisted of coffee with bread and butter and cold meat (ham on Sundays), and there was bread and butter again for tea. The allowance of butter for each meal was half a pound between nine boys. Supper was bread and cheese washed down with half a pint of beer or milk.[7]

For suppers on special occasions the boys were treated to a gourmet, or at any rate gourmand, spread. One such feast offered a choice of roast fowls (jointed and tied with ribbons), fowls boned for galatines, turkeys boned and stuffed with tongue and forcemeat, pheasants, game pie, boned and stuffed loins of mutton, ham, roast sirloin of beef and boiled silverside. These delicacies were followed by hot mince pies, jam tarts, jellies, creams, oranges, apples and crackers. Punch was served to stimulate merriment.[8]

After enjoying the fullest of lives as wife, housekeeper and first lady at Clifton, Louisa continued to have little time for relaxation afterwards in similar roles at Oxford and Rugby and, finally, Hereford. At Hereford she fell ill in the bishop's palace and was taken to a farm-house outside the city to recover in healthier air, but there she died in the summer of 1896. Her death appeared to stun Percival, although it was a miracle that her health had held up for so long. She had been his bosom companion and the prop on which he depended. Openly he bore her loss with Christian fortitude, betraying no emotion, but the wound was deep and left him inexpressibly lonely. As one of his chaplains later revealed:

He showed little of his grief in public, but his household knew that late in the evening he often went to the terrace walk beside the river – a very secluded place – and there he sobbed alone till he could bear to go to bed.[9]

After a decent interval he remarried in January 1899 at the age of sixty-four, probably more for companionship than love. The new bride was Mary Symonds, an old family friend. She cannot have filled the gap left by Louisa, nor did she gain the same affection and admiration among his family and friends, but she was the companion he needed for his old age.

At Clifton, nearly twenty years after she had left, Louisa Percival was well remembered and sincerely mourned. An obituary in *The Cliftonian* recognised her part in her husband's achievements. It recalled her extramural activities: how she had been a power for good in seconding Percival's efforts to improve social conditions in Bristol and the education of girls and the poor. It recorded too how, above all else, her intense interest, her affectionate nature, her watchful care, her ever-ready sympathy had helped to nurse the infant school into an enduring institution.[10]

CHAPTER 7

Growth and Achievement

'Who would have thought that sandy-haired, consumptive-looking young clergyman had so much energy!' exclaimed one astonished observer of Percival's frenzied progress at Clifton.[1] Policy remained the prerogative of the Council, but the influence of the headmaster was strong and he was the chief executive. As well as teaching, he acted as administrative supremo and master builder. Staffing and time-tables; fund-raising for new classrooms, new sporting facilities and new houses; even negotiations with lawyers and architects – all fell within his province.

He did not, of course, work single-handed, but nearly everyone who had to deal with him, even his talented task force of assistant masters, was said to feel *in statu pupillari*. One of his former pupils, reminiscing, thought he would have made a splendid managing director of Harrods. Another commented that that was only half of it: 'He combined the caution and judgment of a sound man of business with the enthusiasm of an Apostle.'[2] Nothing could dim what T. W. Dunn called the 'keen white light of his moral ascendancy and impulse'.[3]

The school was without endowment and Percival had no experience in money matters, yet he assumed the demanding role of financial controller. The sharp eye which he kept on the boys focused no less keenly on the details of routine expenditure. But the school had to be built to last, and necessary building projects proceeded apace with no expense spared despite the shortage of capital.

Authorisation had to be obtained from the Council's Finance Committee, and that repository of corporate prudence also kept watch over budgets and cash flow, but the headmaster was a seldom resistible driving force. His whirlwind career of success from the very moment of appointment disarmed critics. What might at times have seemed extravagant expenditure was soon seen to be justified by a spectacular growth in the number of boys to be taught and accommodated.

A new class-room wing sprang up, and a special building for the teaching of Physical Science 'in a thorough and practical way'. This contained a laboratory, a lecture room for physics and an instrument room, with an adjacent building converted into a lecture room for chemistry. Next came a sanatorium and a range of recreational facilities to augment the playing field: fives courts, a swimming bath (in 1867 one of the earliest in the country) and a 'large and lofty' gymnasium equipped 'with apparatus complete in every particular'.[4] Nothing but the best would do.

A spiritual centre was essential and in 1867 this function was transferred from Big School, the general assembly hall, to a purpose-built school chapel: a gift from Mrs Guthrie in memory of her husband, the founding Chairman, who had died in office. The benefactor who met the cost of a library was Percival himself. In this, as always, he led by example. To him money was nothing but a means of doing good, and throughout his life his name was prominent among subscribers to the school's appeals for funds.

Outstanding work on School House was finished in 1863, the year after the school's opening. As more and more boarders were attracted, other boarding houses were erected at regular intervals along the newly constructed streets named College Road, Guthrie Road and Percival Road: Brown's in 1864, Cay's (later Dakyns') in 1866, Harris's (later Oakeley's) in 1870, Dunn's (later Watson's) in 1874, Wiseman's in 1877 and Heymann's (later Polack's) in 1878, with Preparatory School houses to follow. The school rose from the ground, it was said, 'as by an enchanter's wand'.[5] The wide expanse of the playing field in front of the main buildings was a fine feature of the architectural setting, and an enlightened decision was taken to leave it untouched, even though this meant purchasing more land for the boarding houses.

In the organisation of the boys' lives out of class Rugbeian practices and nomenclature were generally adopted. The senior boys formed Big Side, and their assembly was Big Side Levée which managed all the games (cricket, rugby football, hockey, running, athletics and bat and hand fives). The prefects were named praepostors, and the playing field became the Close.

The structure of appointment and command did not reflect Percival's radical views so far as the adult world was concerned. In true public school tradition the school was run on wholly undemocratic lines. The praepostors were an aristocracy selected by the headmaster, not elected by popular vote, let alone a Soviet of fags. The power of Percival himself was 'regal and absolute'.[6] No resolution of Big Side Levée was valid without the approval and signature of the headmaster.[7]

But, despite his arbitrary methods and forbidding personality, Percival intended his dictatorship to be benevolent – not, though, towards delinquents. He charmed parents, imposed no uniform dress except for an obligatory top hat on Sundays, encouraged friendly relations between masters and boys, and adopted Arnold's policy of a devolution of some measure of authority to the praepostors. They were treated as favoured courtiers and trusted as junior partners, and some took this to extremes. The head boy of one house is reported to have made a speech at an end-of-term supper in which he politely thanked the housemaster for his support in the running of the house during the term.[8]

The head of the school was especially privileged. The first occupant of that position was Henry Wellesley, a great-nephew of the Great Duke. The traditional role of organising games was delegated to him, and much more. He was admired as 'the genius of the school in its young days',[9] and one of the masters later credited him with having 'had a hand in moulding every single feature of the young commonwealth'.[10] Wellesley, unhappily, was destined for a fate which awaited not a few of Percival's élite who were inspired by his vision of Imperialism as an overseas mission. He entered the Indian Civil Service and died in the East at an early age.

Fagging was another tradition which Percival did not discard, but at Clifton it was not considered unduly onerous. New boys were fortunate that there was no inheritance of time-hallowed initiation ceremonies and, reportedly, not much bullying.

Flogging too was rare, although the headmaster was not averse to administering what he called 'a tooch o' the barch' for sins which could even include false quantities when construing. Headmasters like Keate and Arnold who had convinced themselves of the innate wickedness of boys had no compunction in thrashing it out of them. Percival flogged only to punish any serious deviation from devotion to work or duty.

Even though some aspects of his regime ·manifested an unusual degree of liberalism by the standards of the day, the bounds were narrow and discipline was severe. Behaviour was strictly regimented, and any act deemed dishonest or otherwise reprehensible could result in a sentence of expulsion from which there was no appeal. Above all, Percival's brooding presence, so far from radiating benevolence, commanded obedience as much through terror as respect.

The stamp of his personality and the aura of success took immediate effect, so that the school's first years came to be looked back upon, not for the fear he inspired, but as a Heroic Age. The opening of a new house, the winning of the first Balliol scholarship, the first victories over Sherborne and Cheltenham at cricket – each was hailed as a landmark and a stepping stone. 'It seemed to us no less than the dawn of a new age, the creation of something which, while like, was yet unlike any school that had gone before,' wrote one housemaster.[11]

By its founding fathers Clifton had been envisaged as no more than 'one of the many schools that are useful locally, but attain no great rank or reputation';[12] yet ten years after its opening no less an authority than Dr Jowett pronounced it to be already one of the great public schools.[13] Such was the extent of Percival's achievement and the recognition of it.

He was aided by the timing of the school's birth. Clifton was launched on the crest of a wave of optimism and euphoria which swept through the whole nation during the 1860s. A spirit of enterprise welcomed new ventures and new heroes. The best-seller of the decade was Tennyson's *Idylls of the King*.[14] At Clifton admired masters and boy heroes like Wellesley were identified with Galahad and other Knights of the Round Table.[15] There was no room for doubt over who was King Arthur.

More particularly, this was a period of expansion – indeed explosion – throughout the world of public schools. In 1860 their appeal to the professional and mercantile classes of mid-Victorian England was expressed in these words in the columns of the *Saturday Review*:

To the boy and the community alike, the constant reliance upon one another for aid in difficulties, guidance in perplexities, shelter from temptations, fatally weakens the fibre of the character. Boys, like nations, can only attain to the genuine stout self-reliance which is true manliness by battling for themselves against their difficulties, and forming their own characters by the light of their own blunders and their own troubles ... The object of a public school is to introduce a boy early to the world that he may be trained in due time for the struggle which lies before him.[16]

The boom in numbers was huge. Harrow, for example, was a sixteenth-century foundation struggling to survive with only sixty-nine boys when Charles Vaughan was appointed headmaster in 1844. By the time he resigned in 1859 the roll had risen by four hundred. Haileybury, founded in the same year as Clifton (1862), reached a self-imposed ceiling of five hundred pupils within twenty years.

Percival's achievement in growth of numbers was therefore not unparalleled, but the prodigious rate of expansion at Clifton exceeded others, and that despite the proximity of recently established and already prestigious schools at Cheltenham and Marlborough. Numbers quadrupled in two years, and when Percival left in 1879 the original number had multiplied almost tenfold to six hundred and eighty (including forty-one in the newly opened preparatory school). Earlier the size of Rugby had been surpassed: numbers there in 1874 were four hundred and twenty-five, when Clifton's almost touched five hundred.

Perhaps the principal reason for the school's success was the favourable comparison with other schools in the number and calibre of the teaching staff. With fifty masters on the pay roll by the time of Percival's departure in 1879, Clifton enjoyed an unusually high ratio of masters to boys; and, although Clifton was poorly endowed and Eton, for example, an exceptionally rich foundation, the fees at Clifton were little more than half those at Eton.

The quality of the teaching at Clifton also was superior to Eton's. That at least was the opinion of someone who spent six years as a boy at Eton and five as a master and house tutor at Clifton. In *Some Observations of a Foster Parent* (his term for a master at a boarding school) John Charles Tarver wrote: 'Compared with Eton, all other schools, not excepting Winchester, seem to an Etonian mean and inglorious.'[17] Yet, while disclaiming any wish to run down Eton and puff Clifton, he found a comparison between the two, the old and the new, greatly in favour of the new, which had begun life unencumbered by prejudices or vested interests and was blessed with good fortune in its founding headmaster.

Tarver was writing in the 1890s about a period when Percival was no longer at Clifton, but he had no doubt where the credit for the school's continuing success belonged. Clifton was, he wrote, the creation of 'a man of a rare kind of ability, singular earnestness and persistency . . . His creed was not literature, nor science, nor mathematics, nor sacerdotalism; it was work'.[18]

Specifically, Tarver thought Clifton's arrangement of houses, each with a housemaster and house tutor in charge of forty-eight boys, preferable to Eton's tutorial system. At Eton the pupil-room, not the class-room, was the preferred place of instruction, and this reduced lessons in class to what he described as a farce. At Clifton it was the rigour of lessons in class which counted. In Eton's syllabus mathematics, for example, was 'scandalously neglected', whereas:

> The most conclusive testimony to the merits of the Clifton organisation that I have encountered came involuntarily from a mathematical master from one of the old schools. When there was talk of starting a military department in his school, he came down to Clifton, which had a reputation for passing boys direct into Woolwich and Sandhurst, in order to see how it was done. He was entirely ignorant of the size and importance of Clifton, which I think he imagined to be a small Somersetshire grammar school.
>
> It happened that I was told off to show him about. As he wanted to see the mathematical work of the school, I handed over to him all the examination papers – questions and answers – of the previous term . . . I left him with them for an hour, and then returned. 'Yes, this is all very well,' he said, 'but I do not want to see your *special* work; I want to see the ordinary work of the school.' When I told him that he had seen it, he collapsed like the Queen of Sheba, and asked how it was done, and I hope I made such a reply as would not be unduly distressing to a sensitive person. He would have asked the same question had he looked through the classical papers. The secret lay in the fact that the school was adequately staffed, and that there was a simple and effective organisation for keeping up the standard of the average boy.[19]

The disadvantage which Tarver found in the application of Percival's work ethic was that when Cliftonians reached the sixth form they were still too dependent on their teachers. Etonians, allowed more time to spend in the school library and more scope generally for individual intellectual pursuits, developed a greater self-confidence and self-reliance.

Teaching at Clifton was remarkable not only for the 'highest excellence' but also for 'ample breadth', or so the Council felt able to claim towards the end of Percival's reign. Academically, the Classical Side was dominant, with fifty scholarships to Oxford or Cambridge won during the sixteen years of Percival's headmastership. It outnumbered the Modern and Military Sides by two to one, but there was regular and systematic instruction in Natural Science for all and exceptional freedom for older boys to specialise within the curriculum.

Particular attention was paid to preparation for public examinations, traditionally the preserve of crammers, so that the school provided an annual flow of entrants both to Woolwich and Sandhurst and to the home and overseas civil services. (Competitive examinations had been introduced for the Indian Civil Service in 1853 and the home civil service from 1858.)

Outside the classroom a full social life was on offer. There was a Scientific Society and debating societies. In Big School every Sunday evening community hymn-singing and an organ recital were followed by an address or lecture by a master or distinguished visitor. A wide choice of sports and games was available, and it was not long before the school gained a reputation for prowess at cricket and rugby football. In addition to school activities, each house had a range of its own, including house plays and house concerts.

Apart from the teaching and the curriculum, there were other considerations which persuaded parents from different parts of the country to choose Clifton from among so many rival public schools. Here was a modern school in modern buildings with modern ideas, yet one which at the same time adhered strictly to traditional values. The site between city and countryside was both convenient and healthy, offering fresh open air within a cab's ride of Temple Meads, Bristol's main-line railway station.

Prospective parents, moreover, could not fail to be impressed by Percival's personality and high moral tone. In the words of *The Times*, they 'felt the security which was inspired by his moral earnestness'.[20] There was, too, the heady ambience of triumphant innovation and the soaring morale and excitement created as new classrooms and boarding houses rose up in response to a seemingly endless demand. The whole enterprise appeared to lie under a magician's spell as it experienced the power and fervour of the headmaster's will.

CHAPTER 8

Ethos

In the tradition of Arnold's most potent reform, the chapel lay at the heart of school life at Clifton. The most important event of the week was the headmaster's Sunday sermon, when Jehovah-like pronouncements were sometimes delivered from the pulpit. The content was designed to be inspiring, but the delivery was down-to-earth. In preaching, Percival spoke with little modulation of voice and employed no high-flown language or flowery phrases.

Men of Arnold's and Percival's religious and political persuasion did not use these occasions for expounding dogma. Nor were the services solemnised with High Church rituals, which they abhorred. In unadorned acts of worship they preached stark guides to conduct, full of exhortations on the themes of Good and Evil, Heaven and Hell, and dire warnings of the perils of a boy selling his soul to the Devil.

The overriding message conveyed in these weekly clarion calls to righteousness was the inadequacy of a purely intellectual education. Souls took precedence over minds. Arnold had declared cleverness without goodness to be 'almost like the spirit of Mephistopheles' and more revolting to him than 'the most helpless imbecility'.[1] Cliftonians, like Rugbeians, had to be educated spiritually. Consciousness of an ever-present Christian God and what He required of them was drummed into every unformed mind. Percival's ambition was to mould Clifton into 'a very sacred hearth of the higher life of our times'.[2]

The headmaster 'swept us all along, boys and masters together, with a great moral impulse,' recalled Sir Herbert Warren, an Old Cliftonian who, in the course of forty-five years as President of Magdalen College, Oxford, never outgrew the awe he had felt as a

boy for Percival. The influence of a great headmaster is a life
sentence. Leaving the school and growing to manhood, even
eminence, offers no escape. Percival did not intend that the spell
for good which he cast over his charges at a formative age should
ever be broken.

Thus day by day, and from the pulpit above all, he set out to recreate every one of his pupils in his own image. They were to be
serious, liberal-minded and public-spirited. The moral and intellectual duties which he was always heaping on himself he was
determined to heap on them too: to the exclusion of any enjoyment
of the pleasures of life, or so it seemed. He demanded that they
lead an earnest life and a corporate life, for only by earnest,
corporate effort could evils like poverty be overcome. The school's
mission in Bristol was a practical example.

Life had to be simple too, whatever the habits of parents and
society generally. He complained of the 'uphill course in fighting
the battle of simplicity of life against the habits of a wealthy,
luxurious, and self-indulgent age'. 'One of the most important
things we have to do,' he emphasised, 'is to cultivate in our boys
the habit of simplicity of living.'[3] Hampers were forbidden, and
there were strict limits on pocket money.

Because his purpose was to bring boys to reflect on why they
were here on earth and, having reflected, to do God's will, a
shortcoming which he constantly condemned was 'want of true
aim or purpose'. 'Loafing' was an evil. Those guilty of that failing
were reprimanded with what became a well remembered phrase in
the reminiscences of former pupils: 'Dawn't live the life of a
cabbage, maan.'[4]

One Cliftonian remained haunted for life by Percival's quietly
menacing manner of conveying displeasure when his place in form
was deemed unsatisfactory through idleness. The ordeal of his
interview in the headmaster's study on that occasion was vivid in
his memory many years later when he wrote:

> I would sooner have faced almost anything than have gone
> through that ceremony. And yet the voice in which he spoke was
> so slow, so gentle, so almost enquiring, but – and I suppose this
> was the secret – so full of hidden fires and suggestive of terrible
> possibilities.[5]

The boys were not alone in being subjected to the severity of the headmaster's work ethic. The masters were by no means spared, as T. E. Brown complained in a letter to a friend:

> Percival was like an inspired, demonic conductor of an orchestra. He has lashed us into a Bacchic fury – *forte, forte, fortissimo*. At the end of term we sink back on our seats and mop our foreheads and pant. He is divine, but we want rest.[6]

Sir Rowland Whitehead was another former pupil who remembered that slackness was no minor misdemeanour; it represented descent into 'an unutterable depth of infamy'. Strenuousness, robustness of tone and patriotism were the aspects of Percival's Clifton which he identified. Robustness of tone embraced hatred of luxury; contempt for self-indulgence; love of simplicity and naturalness. Patriotism was devotion to the common weal. Percival's own concept of the common weal was not a narrow one, but Sir Rowland recalled that, when a conflict of loyalties arose, 'this feeling burned with a fiercer flame on behalf of our House than of the whole school'.[7]

Work and Duty. If the requirement of a pervading spirit of industry formed one of the reiterated themes of Percival's sermons, another was the demand for a spirit of duty which would infuse the character of every boy and become the essence of the communal life of the school. All those who took the name of Clifton out into the world were to be imbued with sympathy and tolerance in their dealings with others, but not to be wanting in earnestness and enthusiasm. They were to be firm and strong and manly, but not rough or coarse. They were to be distinguished by courage, independence, moral thoughtfulness, religious conviction and freedom from affectation.

Percival echoed Frederick Temple's belief in the resemblance of a great English school to the early Christian Church:

> There is the same community of life – strong, quick, penetrating; there is the same independent life of the separate members, blended into the whole and unceasingly influenced, yet never so lost as to interfere with individual character and individual responsibility.[8]

How a boy's independence and individual character were expected, let alone encouraged, to survive a communal regime and powerful doses of this kind of indoctrination does not emerge. Percival's commitment to the suppression or at least disciplining of self in a worthier public cause sits awkwardly with the nurturing of individualism. But that was a general paradox of the Victorian age, when the cult of the individual ran parallel with emphasis on conformity.

A distinction had to be made between the private and the public man, and this, presumably, was Percival's thinking. He deprecated 'the excessive and mischievous individualism of modern life', but the concept of individual responsibility lay at the core of his Protestant faith, and his claim to concern for a boy's individuality in the realm of the intellect was genuine. That was vouched for by Sir Arthur Quiller-Couch, whose definition of the main characteristics of the Clifton ethos was 'freedom and curiosity of the mind tempered by a severe conscience in all matters of service and obedience to Duty'.[9]

In a sermon published under the title 'Unaccomplished Work of Schools' Percival packed a romantic vision of the fulfilment of his aspiration into two heavily charged sentences:

I think of the time when . . . there shall go forth a new generation of men who shall be characterised, not by some special gift, not by some literary accomplishment, or some varnish of culture, but by a combination of gifts and strength and spirit, which shall stamp them as prominent workers, if not as leaders and prophets, in the next stage of our country's progress. There is abundant room, to say nothing of the crying need, for these missionaries of a new type, who shall be men of cultivated and disciplined intellect, enlightened and strong; who shall be sworn to the new chivalry of personal purity and the suppression of the baser animal instincts; who shall be men of simple and pure tastes, no epicurean sentimentalists, the declared enemies of luxury, whether vulgar or refined; men, again, in whom public spirit and social purpose shall be practical and guiding motives, not vague and intermittent sentiments, who shall feel the call to alter those conditions of life which are working so destructively in all our cities; men who, with all this, are not bigoted, who shall have learned to know that earnestness and toleration are not incompatible, who shall have no respect for that spurious young man's liberalism, which is the child of indifference . . . above all, men whose life shall be guided by a serious and humble and reverent spirit, who may fairly be described as faithful and religious and devout.[10]

These ideals did not differ in essence from those of Arnold or Temple. Percival's particular achievement with his version of public school ethos lay in commanding instant, intense and enduring loyalty to it. Unlike Rugby, the new school had no past heroes to emulate, no body of Old Boys to foster its character and reputation. Yet, according to Quiller-Couch, 'within twenty years the *ethos* of Clifton had rooted itself as firmly as though Clifton had stood for centuries'.[11] Sixty years after the school's foundation this was re-stated by the then headmaster, Norman Whatley: 'At Clifton all that goes back to Dr Percival is now nearly as old as if it went back to William of Wykeham.'[12]

Among the most passionately loyal of Old Cliftonians was that other literary knight, Sir Henry Newbolt, who wrote:

> For though the dust that's part of us
> To dust again be gone
> Yet here shall beat the heart of us –
> The School we handed on![13]

Newbolt's praise in verse for the more robust aspects of the Clifton code is well known. 'To honour while you strike him down The foe that comes with fearless eyes' is but one striking example.[14] Less well known is a more sober glorification of Cliftonian ideals in his autobiographical novel, *The Twymans*.

In this, Clifton features as Downton and Percival is barely disguised as Dr Cumberland: a tall, spare figure with chiselled face and a lofty, remote air. The Newbolt character, the boy hero, is significantly named Percival Twyman. At Downton he learns: 'For information you would purchase a text-book, an encyclopaedia, perhaps a tutor. For education you live in a society.'

The following passages from the novel illuminate the constraints of the school's life, where discipline and conformity dictate the etiquette of manners and behaviour:

[Boys were required] to be in all things decent, orderly, self-mastering; in action to follow up the coolest commonsense with

the most unflinching endurance: in public affairs to be dévoted
as a matter of course, self-sacrificing without any appearance of
enthusiasm . . .

To show any emotion in public, or indeed to show it at all, to
make any sound at a match, beyond a hand-clap, to applaud at
the fall of an opponent's wicket or the failure of his kick at goal;
to wear, even in the holidays, any but a black or undistinguished
dress – all these were grave misdeeds, acts significant of moral
rebelliousness, or, at the best, of moral delinquency.

According to Newbolt's brother Frank, Cliftonians never cheered
a catch nor even a hat-trick by one of the school cricket XI. That
would have been considered impolite to the visiting team and
therefore 'bad form'.[15] Indeed Clifton's spirit of chivalry was such
that it was said to be about the only school in England where good
play by its opponents was applauded. And modesty was *de rigueur*,
even for heroes of the crease and pitch. Repression of 'any tendency
to "side" or swagger' was noted by Quiller-Couch.[16]

Although he cannot be held guilty of overt political indoctrination, Percival's fiercely-held political convictions were part and
parcel of the moral and social values which he proclaimed and
inculcated so tirelessly. To him Toryism was the work of the Devil,
while Liberal principles were the practical expression of Christian
ideals. To him the Gospel story was 'the Magna Carta of all true,
popular and democratic progress'. He wanted all his boys to
become social reformers like himself. These views will have found
a ready response in radical Bristol, but less so among wealthy,
predominantly Tory parents inhabiting the leafy suburb of Clifton;
although to them the success and prestige of their local school was
no doubt a source of pride.

It was only later, when Liberalism had become less acceptable to
the middle class than it had been in Percival's heyday, that there
was talk of 'that horrible Radical school'. In the 1860s the Liberal
Party was regarded as the champion of the middle-class advance
against upper-class privilege. Twenty years later many of the
liberal-minded well-to-do became disturbed by Gladstone's more
extreme brand of politics, which Percival ardently embraced.

In 1885 the *Bristol Times and Mirror* published a letter denouncing the teaching staff at Clifton as a Radical Club, the writer
proposing that its influence should be countered by the foundation

of a rival school on the opposite side of the Avon gorge dedicated to right-thinking principles.

By that date Percival had departed, and a reassuring reply came from Wilson, his successor. In a recent school debate, he revealed, the motion that 'the sympathy of the House will be with the Liberal Party in the coming Election' was defeated by sixty-five votes to twenty-six.

Some Cliftonians who fell most deeply under the spell of Percival's ethos became prominent Liberals – Warren and Newbolt and whole families of Whiteheads, Whitleys and Wedgwoods, for example, most of whom came from Liberal homes. With the majority he would have had to console himself with the expectation that they would grow into Tories with a social conscience.

CHAPTER 9

Games

The worship of games and the hero-worship of athletes was a deep-rooted public school tradition, and one which Arnold had left untouched. It was an inheritance from the ancient Greeks and Romans whose pagan languages, thoughts and practices formed the core of a public school education, despite some problems in reconciling Greek philosophy with Christianity. The original Olympic Games were the antecedent of school sports. *Mens sana in corpore sano* was the justifying maxim.

One stated purpose was to add inches to the chests of the indolent and the soft, the idle and the over-studious. That 'tender plant', the intellectually precocious boy, was deemed to be in particular need of the benefits of physical recreation. 'Round shoulders, narrow chests, stiff limbs are as bad as defective grammar and arithmetic,' wrote Arnold's disciple, Thomas Hughes.[1]

Another objective, important to Percival if not to Arnold, was to provide an alternative to the deadly sin of loafing. By filling the gaps in the time-table, games narrowed the opportunities for mischief and immorality. Surplus energy was drained in healthy and innocent exercise. Arnold had not been troubled by boys' 'unattended hours', believing that the sooner they encountered the evil in the world and learned to master it the better. At Clifton, although games were not at first compulsory, that view did not prevail.

Games were valued also for building character, a virtue which Arnold had rated more highly than ability. According to Henry Newbolt, Percival 'held that athletics were necessary to our moral health'.[2] Self-reliance was developed at the crease and courage in the scrum. Competitive sport stimulated individual effort and prepared a boy for the struggle through life which lay ahead. Team games were especially applauded: they discouraged selfishness. Triumphs against other schools or houses raised spirits and morale. Loyalty and pride in the community were invigorated.

Percival himself was no games fanatic, but he had some claim to athleticism and was admired by the boys as a sportsman. He had been a cricketer in boyhood and maintained a close interest in the subtleties of the game as an informed spectator. During his years at Clifton his own exercise was mainly taken riding and walking, but he also played an occasional game of golf and in winter took to the ice, where he displayed some expertise in skating.[3]

Bodily as well as moral health must have been constantly in his mind. Chronically concerned about his wife's and his own state of health, he would certainly have paid close attention to the physical well-being of his charges. He might even have been expected to move beyond games and embrace the latest ideas in health care, but it was another founding headmaster, Almond of Rossall, who at that time inaugurated the Spartan regime of open windows and compulsory cold baths which was to become such a favoured means of turning boys into men. The unpopular honour of being the first of the public school cold-water and fresh-air fiends would have suited Percival's temperament well.

As it was, in adopting the common practice of organised games he made only one individual contribution to this aspect of school life. It was his policy to combine work and play in harmony and try to avoid any division in the school between intellectuals and athletes. His demand for all-rounders was insistent. Every boy was under pressure to be both, whatever his natural bent or talent: to compose Latin hexameters *and* open the innings; to master scientific principles *and* be a stalwart second-row forward. Every Captain of the XI was expected to win a university scholarship.

Both Gloucestershire and Somerset were sporting counties. In this favourable environment, and with games soon established as an integral part of a Clifton education, the school was quickly launched on a successful career in the world of sport and its heroes were duly worshipped.

The first of the immortals was E. F. S. Tylecote, who made a record 404 not out in a match between the Classical and Modern Sides and met his headmaster's all-rounder requirement with a Fellowship at Oxford too. Another, and perhaps the most wor-shipped of all, was C. W. Boyle, whose bowling was faster than anyone had seen before. Normally he needed two long-stops, but in the school's first match at Lord's against MCC he had three, one of whom caught, not the ball, but the middle stump of one of his victims. Cecil Boyle was head of Brown's house, won blues at Oxford for both cricket and rugger and played rugger for England.

The Close, which Newbolt has immortalised with his 'breathless hush',[4] became the scene of many sporting dramas. Football was played there in the winter – Rugby's version, naturally; athletics were featured in the spring; and cricket occupied the summer months, when the ground was also used for county matches during the school holidays. W. G. Grace, who lived and worked in Clifton as a general practitioner and played for Gloucestershire, could often be seen batting there against the school or another county. His most famous feat on this ground was to make a double century after spending the previous night without sleep at the bedside of a patient.

In the early years cricket was considered far more important than football, which at Clifton bore some resemblance to the Eton wall game until Rugby Union rules were adopted in 1878. A match against Marlborough played in 1864 under an ill-defined code of practice developed into a brawl which proved so acrimonious that the fixture was not resumed until 1891.

Meanwhile the cricket tradition grew so strong that Clifton became one of only eight schools accorded an annual fixture at Lord's. When a rackets court was built, Clifton also joined the élite company of sixteen rackets-playing schools. High standards were reached in shooting, rowing and long-distance running. In one year at Oxford the captains of cricket, rugger and the boat club were all Cliftonians, and all from Brown's house.

Success was infectious, and games fanaticism grew beyond what Percival thought desirable. According to Newbolt, it was 'a mere truth to say that there were very few members of the school who would not have bartered away all chance of intellectual distinction for a place in the Cricket Eleven or Football Fifteen.'[5] In *The Best School of All*, the school song, he put the same sentiment into rhapsodic verse:

> The stars and sounding vanities
> That half the crowd bewitch,
> What are they but inanities
> To him that treads the pitch?

And where's the wealth, I'm wondering,
Can buy the cheers that roll
When the last charge goes thundering
Beneath the twilight goal.

The tradition has been maintained, and more than a century later Old Cliftonian John Cleese chose to record in *Who's Who* that he had been educated at 'Clifton Sporting Academy'.

Standards of play at all games owed much to the coaching and participation of the masters. It was Graham Dakyns, Percival's first appointment, who set balls and runners in motion at the very beginning. Years later he wrote:

The boys of those days had no notion of games or respect for them. I cannot make you understand how difficult it was at that time to create and develop an ardour in all sorts of athletic matters here . . . You will hardly believe that we used to have to persuade the boys in those days, if it were at all wet in the afternoon, to take their coats off and play football or go runs.[6]

T. E. Brown was still being pressed into service late in life, as though his exacting roles as second master, housemaster and Head of the Modern Side were not enough. This poet, who fell and injured himself while playing fives at the age of fifty-seven, struck a more wistful chord than Newbolt. In *Fives'-Court* he wrote:

Sometimes at night I stand within a court
Where I have played by day;
And still the walls are vibrant with the sport
And still the air is vibrant with the sway
Of agile limbs that now, their labours o'er,
To healthful sleep their strength resign –
But how of those who play'd with me langsyne,
And sleep for evermore?

Housemasters like Dakyns and Brown were responsible for much of the significance attached to games. Rivalry between houses made house matches even more fiercely contested than school matches, and playing for the house brought almost as much kudos as playing for the school. This inner loyalty was encouraged by the housemasters, some of whom may have been motivated by more than pride.

They were paid *per capita* for each boy in their house and therefore had a financial stake in success at sport. The glory of being Cock House at cricket or football impressed parents and attracted more boys to the house.

All this was too much for Percival. Before he left, he went on record with a warning that the physical side of school life had been taken too far. 'I, of course, very distinctly recognise the great value of organised games to a school,' he said in a speech at the Headmasters' Conference in 1873, but 'my own feeling is that they engross a great deal too much of the average boy's energy at school.'

He went on to highlight the importance of establishing 'counter-influences', such as libraries and workshops and scientific and literary societies, to encourage intellectual activity out of school and diminish concentration on games:

> It is not so much the amount of time ordinarily given to school games, as the amount of talk which follows upon the time and the impression the games make on the boys' minds, which are absolutely ruinous, so far as many boys are concerned, to intellectual development.[7]

The hyperbolic 'absolutely ruinous' suggests frustration on the part of the creator that this was one aspect of life at Clifton which had escaped from his control.

Games do much to make a boarding school a happy place, and the assistant masters may have set more store by this than their austere head. But in all the arguments advanced in favour of sport in Percival's era it is hard to find any mention of enjoyment.

CHAPTER 10

Clifton or Rugby?

Towards the end of 1869 Percival was nearly lost to Clifton. Frederick Temple was offered and accepted the see of Exeter, and the headmastership of Rugby fell vacant. It seems unlikely that any other place or position would have tempted Percival from Clifton after only seven years. But Rugby was where his career had begun; it was from Rugby that he had gained knowledge and inspiration; Rugby was the mother school of his own; and the vacant post was the most highly esteemed within his profession. Under strong pressure from Temple to apply, he complied with mixed feelings.

The Council at Clifton was dismayed but took the honourable course of supporting his candidature with a handsome testimonial. For this Percival thanked them sincerely:

> If anything could have added to the reluctance with which I yielded to the advice of many friends and sent in my name as a candidate, it would have been such an expression of kind feeling as that [with] which you have thus favoured me.[1]

Tactfully, he went on to express the hope that he would deserve their commendation in the future, as he did not expect his application to be successful.

That expectation proved well founded. He was passed over despite the support of forty-two glittering testimonials. In accordance with the custom of the day, these were printed in the form of a booklet, prefaced by a contents list of those writing to recommend him. Headed by the Archbishop of York and the Bishop of Gloucester and Bristol, they included the Provost of Queen's,

Jowett of Balliol, headmasters of other public schools, assistant masters at Clifton and former pupils.[2]

It transpired, however, that the conservatively-minded majority of Rugby's trustees were not looking for 'one of Temple's men' and, specifically, the one who was the outgoing incumbent's nominee. Temple had fallen into ill odour with orthodox churchmen and they were wary of tainting the school with more extreme liberalism and broadchurchmanship. Percival was therefore held to be disqualified on both political and theological grounds.

Unfortunately for Rugby, the choice which they made instead proved calamitous. After a few years of Henry Hayman's rule one of his assistant masters expressed a general view when damning him comprehensively with the acid comment: 'If a Headmaster can't teach and can't preach and can't organise, he ought to be either a scholar or a gentleman.'[3]

Rugby's loss was Clifton's gain, and the Council made haste to demonstrate its relief and joy by voting Percival an annual grant of £300 'as a mark of appreciation of his great exertions for the College'. He was also presented with a fulsome address such as few headmasters can have received. Engrossed on vellum and bearing the College's seal, the text ran:

We, the Council of Clifton College, should not be doing justice to our own feelings, and to the important trust which we have in charge if, after recent occurrences, we did not in some form convey to you our assurance of the deep interest with which we have watched the crisis through which the College has lately passed.

Public rumours, and the opinion of many persons high in the scholastic world, indicated so decidedly the likelihood of your appointment to the Head Mastership of Rugby, that we greatly feared we might lose the services of one who has done so much to create a large and successful public school in this place.

Notwithstanding our anxiety, we could not but be pleased to hear the probability of your election so favourably alluded to, as this confirmed our high estimate of your character and abilities.

In your testimonials of fitness for the Rugby Head Mastership, it was gratifying to observe seven eminent Head Masters of distinguished public schools speak strongly of your wide acquirements, of your clear insight into character, your independent judgment, and your unvarying courage. Various well-known men of high University standing have cordially acknowledged not only your great scholarship, but also your power of communicating knowledge, and of impartially weighing the educational value of different subjects.

It is very satisfactory to us to find the Lord Bishop of the diocese bearing testimony to your great interest in the religious training of the boys and to the wholesome and Christian influence which you have exercised over those committed to your care.

We are glad that your Assistant Masters value your great power of sympathy, and your just appreciation of the claims and duties of those who cheerfully work with you.

Nor are we less interested in the Testimonials from numerous pupils who have gained University honours, and who speak so lovingly of their old master, of your kindly interest in their welfare and their pursuits.

The Council heartily thank you for the able, unwearied and successful manner in which you have always discharged your duties, and they earnestly trust that for many years the advantage of your valuable services will continue to be enjoyed by Clifton College.[4]

This well-deserved eulogy was evidently designed to soothe any pains of rejection, place on record the high regard in which Percival was held by everyone except the trustees of Rugby School, and dissuade him from applying for any other post.

Percival's method of putting the rebuff behind him and demonstrating that it was to be business as before at Clifton was truly in character. It was warmhearted, generous and severely practical. After thanking the Council in a letter to the Chairman he made the following offer:

As I feel that it would be a great advantage to the College in various ways to have a good room which would serve as Library and Museum; as I feel also very strongly that it is the duty of the Council to spend nothing but what is absolutely necessary on buildings and to concentrate their funds on the payment of Assistant Masters, to [sic] attracting some boys of ability, if possible by means of scholarships; and as I have some other feelings in the matter with which I need not trouble you at present, I should like the Council to look at the accompanying plan, and, if they approve, to make the school a present of the Library and Museum.

The plan involves also 4 Class rooms which I should propose asking the Council to build at the same time, hoping that they may be a necessity for us.

Mr Hansom estimates cost as follows: Basement Floor £240, First Floor £788, Second do./Library & Museum £688, Roof £344, Temporary Staircase to Library £40, Total £2100. I should hope that with possible modifications this might be lowered considerably so that total cost of Library should not exceed £1000 and that of the Class rooms be something less than that.

I only present these as a basis for consideration. If the Council approve of the general scheme, perhaps they will appoint a Sub-Committee to consider details.[5]

The library was duly built at the headmaster's expense and opened less than two years after the offer was made. Known as the Percival Library, it is still in use today. The museum came later and its cost was met by the assistant masters. The Council found the money for the classrooms.

Council and headmaster continued to work in harmony for a further four years until towards the end of 1873, after a series of damaging law suits, Rugby succeeded in ridding itself of the unconscionable Dr Hayman. Applications were once again invited for a new headmaster, and this time pressures on Percival to stand were exerted not only from the bishop's palace at Exeter but from Rugby itself, where a pro-Percival party was headed by the senior assistant master.

At Clifton the Council's letter of appreciation on this second occasion was written in advance in an attempt to forestall Percival's application, which it believed would alarm parents, boys and masters. A unanimous resolution resulted in a private and confidential plea to him to stay. This ran (in part) as follows:

For some time past every succeeding year has been marked with a success for the College which has excited the admiration not only of all interested in the Institution but of the scholastic world and elicited from those best qualified to judge expressions of astonishment at the brilliant achievements which your ability and indefatigable exertions found means so quickly to attain.

In fine under your rule the College is fast taking root as a great

Public School and we state with confidence our belief that in a very few years under your guidance it will take root as a permanent institution.

Under these circumstances we cannot as a Council thank you too much for your exertions in the past or express too earnestly our hopes that they will still be given to us in the future.

We venture to suggest to you that the building up of an English Public School is no unworthy object of a high ambition and that fair as the prospects of the College now are a change of the Head Master must be a source of grave anxiety and peril to so young an institution; pardon us if we add our belief that your stay with us a few short years will suffice for you to gratify that ambition and to avert that peril.

In endeavouring to set before you in the strongest manner our estimation of your services to the College and the importance we attach to them we are acting in the simple discharge of our duty but we should fail to do justice to ourselves if we did not say that it affords us the greatest pleasure individually and collectively to thus express ourselves to one whom we all regard personally with such warm sentiments of esteem.[6]

The plea failed. Once again Percival expressed his reluctance to stand but was eventually prevailed upon to do so. On this occasion he held back because it would mean competing with an old and highly regarded friend (after whom one of his sons was named). This was Dr Jex-Blake, who had been a colleague at Rugby and become Principal of Cheltenham College.

They became the leading contenders and Jex-Blake was narrowly the winner by seven votes to five. Some of Rugby's trustees appear to have believed that, having rejected Percival previously, it would be a confession of failure to elect him now. Others continued to distrust his fiery radicalism and preferred the prospect of a more tranquil life for the school under the regime of a well-qualified moderate. Perhaps decisively, Jex-Blake was an Old Rugbeian.

When the appointment was announced, the Council at Clifton formally recorded its 'utmost gratification' that Percival's services would be retained. His loss had seemed so probable that names of possible replacements had been discussed and a Public Advertisement drafted. There had been good reason to suppose that Rugby would take him. The thirty-seven testimonials supporting his candidature this time included fulsome praise from those best qualified to judge: the headmasters of Eton, Winchester, Harrow, Shrewsbury, Christ's Hospital, Uppingham, Repton and Sherborne.[7] Jex-Blake's could hardly have rivalled that.

The Bishop of Exeter declared himself mortified by Percival's rejection and the masters at Rugby were greatly disappointed, but Jowett, now Master of his college, wrote from Oxford to console the loser with his considered opinion that it was better for him to remain at Clifton. When he became tired of the place he ought to return to Oxford as Provost of his old college, Queen's. 'These headships of colleges, although not very distinguished positions,' wrote the Master modestly, 'are good places in which to grow old.'[8]

At Clifton it was not only members of the Council who rejoiced. As second master, T. E. Brown wrote jubilantly on behalf of all the teaching staff, while the Sixth Form formally notified their headmaster that 'they have not words to tell their thankfulness that he is saved to Clifton and themselves individually, bound as they are by ties of respect and affection'.[9]

Such warm expressions of relief may be thought surprising, but now that the school had taken root and success seemed assured, Percival had won the loyalty of at any rate the most senior of those whom he ruled so autocratically. He in turn had begun to mellow. Occasionally he was even seen to smile, and tensions were eased by familiarity as his subjects grew accustomed to his ways and came to recognise their value. Each new generation of boys grew less fearful of his god-like figure, and comradeship with his hard-pressed staff developed. In the words of one of his housemasters (T. W. Dunn):

> We discovered that he had a sense of humour and even of fun, and that he could not only awe, but attract and attach. The granite peak to which we had looked up with distant awe glowed in the sun as we got a little nearer it.[10]

In public, as the years passed, geniality sometimes broke through the crust of solemnity on formal occasions such as Commemoration; yet there was no letting-up in chapel. In the headmaster's sermons home truths continued to be spelt out in a voice which conveyed messages of inspiration and expressions of confidence in tones of despondency. The memorable north-country burr was arresting, sometimes spell-binding, but the quiet, cold delivery suggested few tidings of comfort or joy.

On closer acquaintance the great man's forbidding air of aloof melancholy had come to be understood and accepted. It was attributable to self-repression. Percival's emotions were strongly felt, and he bottled them up inside himself out of fear that they would deflect him from the path of duty. He possessed an innate affection for boys and an instinctive ability to understand and influence them, but his nature shied away from intimacy. Some appreciated this; others, while coming to terms with it, still found him impenetrably chilly.

Frank Newbolt, for example, recalled a cheerless interview with his headmaster during preparation for confirmation: 'I remember entering his study, and seeing his grave, stiff attitude as he sat at his table. His face was worn and ascetic, and he did not smile as he motioned me to a chair.'[11]

The experience of the favoured sixth-formers was different. Their feelings were expressed by the future Sir Herbert Warren, who was at the school from 1868 to 1872, in much the same terms as Dunn. A praepostor who became head of the school and remained close to Percival in later life, he was one of those who, like the masters, were privileged to glimpse the sun peeping out from behind the clouds:

> Yet gradually, I can honestly say for myself, and I think for our generation, we came by and by not only to respect and admire but more and more to love him. 'Praise seldom' was his practice, but when it came the praise was additionally sweet. When he warmed into affection it was like the sudden glow of sunshine on one of the rocky peaks of his native countryside.[12]

So the further 'few short years' hoped for by the Council were granted amid general satisfaction. Percival's founding headmastership was extended to a full period of sixteen years and two terms, and his stamp on the school became ineradicable.

In 1862, 1869 and 1874 Rugby had done Clifton a succession of inestimable favours: first by sending Percival to take charge of the new school and then by twice refusing to take him back.

CHAPTER 11

Constitutional Reform

At his interview with Rugby's governing body in February 1874, Percival was asked about his relations with the Council at Clifton (a question which he considered an impertinence). In reporting this to the Council on his return, he stated that he had felt proud to be able to say that 'we had never had any difficulties'. In making this response he was, presumably, referring to personal relationships. In that sense there may have been no *difficulties*, but *disagreements* there certainly were, and not only over the issue of a Jewish house. The most notable was one of some magnitude concerning the school's future status and constitution.

The Endowed Schools Act of 1869 aimed at reforming and reorganising endowed schools throughout the land. Bristol's plea to be excused was rejected, and its worst fears were confirmed when Mr Fitch, the local sub-commissioner, proposed the virtual abolition of three of its long-established charity schools – Colston's, Red Maids' and Queen Elizabeth's Hospital. Their endowment income was to be diverted to new schools more in keeping with the times.

These new schools were to be divided by age into third-grade for the youngest, second-grade for the middle range and first-grade for the oldest in a system calculated to benefit all Bristol's children. It would provide them with a structured ladder to higher education, whereas the existing charitable foundations were unco-ordinated and their benefits confined to a limited number of families – and, remarked Mr Fitch, 'those perhaps not the most deserving'.[1]

Bristolians were outraged at this interference with their affairs and threat to their institutions. The proposals were vigorously contested, and when the plan was published, only a single voice was raised in its favour: that of the headmaster of Clifton College.[2]

Percival was motivated by a combination of principle and self-interest. Not only did he believe wholesale reform to be desirable, but one provision in the Commission's scheme involved what was indignantly described as 'crippling if not degrading the Grammar School, in order, as Mr Fitch avowed, that it might not interfere with the development of Clifton College'[3] – a denominational class school belonging to a joint stock company.

It was the intention of the Commission to establish a first-grade school in Bristol charging fees of not more than £25 a year, preferably 'in union' with the college, but by other means if necessary. If the college chose to be involved, money from the Bristol Endowment Fund would not be handed over unconditionally. The Council would have to accept that it could not continue running the college on its existing lines as part of the national scheme. If agreement on new arrangements could not be reached, a rival school with lower fees would be established in Clifton.

Faced with this alternative and eager to join hands with the state system, Percival opened negotiations by informing Fitch that his Council was 'very ready to consider any fair proposal from the Commissioners'.[4]

At a special Council meeting held in June 1870 Canon Moseley reported that the Commissioners were open to a proposition whereby the shareholders, while retaining their independence, would agree 'to receive at reduced fees boys of the class of those who now attend the Bristol Grammar School so that the College might as far as the citizens of Bristol are concerned come in the place of the first-grade school which is proposed to be established'. There seems little doubt that Percival was the author of this compromise agreed with Fitch, and it must have come as a severe rebuff to him when Moseley went on to designate the changes essential to bring it about as 'most undesirable'.

The arrangement, said Moseley, would entail the existing average fee becoming the maximum; the abolition of social distinctions; and acceptance of a new conscience clause which would breach the company's Articles of Association. What, he asked, are the views and feelings of the people of Clifton, for whose advantage the college was established? In what estimation would first-grade schools of the Endowed Schools Commission be held socially?

Probably as some kind of Citizen School. 'But it was distinctly not as a Citizen School that Clifton College was established, but rather as a school of the class of Marlborough and Cheltenham or even Rugby (if possible) or Harrow.'

Moseley went on to argue that competition was not to be feared. The funds at the disposal of a rival school would be insufficient to attract a good headmaster and under-masters. The Commission would not succeed in raising the grammar school's educational standards merely by moving its location out of the city centre to new buildings in Clifton.

Canon Moseley's speech is recorded at length in the minutes of this meeting. Percival's reply occupies no more than a single sentence: 'The Head Master stated the reasons which induced him to consider that it would be exceedingly inadvisable to refuse to negotiate with the Commissioners.'[5]

The 'exceedingly' plainly reveals his strength of feeling. Persistent and persuasive as always, he obtained permission to continue negotiations, even though his room for manoeuvre was restricted by the need to take Moseley's reservations into account.

It took six months of discussions with Fitch before Percival felt able to return to the Council table with counter-proposals which he believed might prove acceptable to both Council and Commission. These did not take issue with the Commission's plan to move the grammar school to Clifton, where it would have three hundred boys paying fees of between ten and fifteen guineas a year. But Percival wanted it to remain a second-grade school with a leaving age between sixteen and seventeen. University material from this and Bristol's other second-grade Endowed Schools for boys would be admitted to the college at ages between fourteen and seventeen at reduced fees. The Commission would top up these fees at the rate of ten guineas per head per year for a maximum of one hundred and fifty boys.

The Council approved this scheme as a basis for further negotiation despite reiterated reservations about the social consequences. A haggle about money formed the next hurdle. The Commission wanted to know why the cost of tuition for a boy at Clifton, then £30 a year, was £8 dearer than at Cheltenham, and how this could be justified to the citizens of Bristol who would be paying the subsidy. The Council accordingly fell into line by agreeing to admit one hundred and twenty boys at a total cost of £22 a head (fees and subsidy). The Commission then responded positively, conceding that this arrangement contrived by Percival was an improvement on its own scheme in view of the undesirability of having rival schools.

At the next special Council meeting, held in March 1871, Percival gathered the support he was seeking. It was minuted that: 'The Council clearly feel on their side that Clifton College does not provide for Bristol what it may fairly ask, and they therefore propose to alter their constitution in such a way as may meet the wants of the residents.' The *quid pro quo* would be a firm assurance that the Endowed Schools Commission would not establish any other school in Bristol for boys over the age of seventeen.

This elicited a warm response: 'As far as the Commissioners can see, your Council are now addressing themselves to the problem of public education in Bristol in a very generous spirit and with an eye to the interest of the whole community.'[6] But this harmony achieved by Percival's persistence was shortlived.

Agreement in principle had been hard enough to reach; the difficulties involved in putting it into effect were to prove insuperable. The parties were bound by conflicting duties and obligations, so that freedom of action was subject to constraints on both sides. The legal obstacles were formidable; pecuniary problems were to rumble on unresolved; and when the Council had at last brought itself to the point of formally resolving that the special-entry boys be admitted without social distinction, misgivings surfaced only two days later when it was recorded that a minority was opposed to the removal of social distinction 'to any greater extent'.[7]

At this critical juncture Percival enlisted the aid of his colleagues, and the Council received a letter signed by every one of the assistant masters in favour of opening the college to boys of all classes. The Chairman replied with an assurance that the Council was giving 'earnest consideration' to opening the door of admission more widely to 'boys of talent without reference to their social position', but went on to warn that the Council represented a large body of shareholders whose views could not be altogether ignored and whose support the Council needed in meeting the Commission's terms.[8]

The very success for which Percival himself was responsible militated against change. The school was booming. During the previous year (1870) numbers had risen above four hundred. Why change a winning formula in favour of a move towards the kind of local community institution from which nationally acclaimed schools like Rugby and Harrow had emerged so triumphantly? What might suit the citizens of Bristol did not appeal to the residents of Clifton.

Negotiations dragged on for several more months amid growing doubts and exasperation on each side. Finally they petered out, so that the charitably endowed Bristol Grammar School and not the shareholder-financed Clifton College became the city's first-grade school, with substantial funds forthcoming from the Commissioners for the purchase of land and the erection of an imposing building in Tyndall's Park no more than a mile or so from the college. The effect of this nearby subsidised competition for day pupils was to shift the emphasis at Clifton more towards boarding.

Although never one to display bitterness, even when the will of God was at its most inscrutable, Percival must have felt deeply depressed and wounded by this defeat. Like many another would-be reformer, he had been beaten by the class system which ruled English society.

Money was at the root of the matter. Although Clifton had been founded for the sons of gentlemen, the school was wholly dependent on income from fees and in practice open to any boy who could pass the entrance exam and whose parents, whatever their social status, could afford to pay. The classless, humbly bred Percival would never have turned away a boy on grounds of class. But the money barrier effectively ensured that the school was an exclusively middle-class institution, and that was what the shareholders wanted it to remain.

Had Percival succeeded in forming a viable partnership with state education, other public schools with liberal leanings might well have followed suit, with consequences for the divisions in society which can only be conjectured. But this was one of his pioneering ventures which was doomed to failure. His far-sighted anticipation of the assisted places schemes of the next century proved too advanced for mid-Victorian times.

It was not until 1940 that another headmaster of Clifton introduced bursaries to enable boys from Bristol's elementary schools to attend the college, and then the average number permitted by the funds available amounted to no more than three a year. It was 1944 when the Fleming Report recommended, in vain, that at least a quarter of public school places should be reserved for pupils from grant-aided primary schools, their fees to be paid from public funds.

In 1874, shortly after this setback, the disappointed headmaster was elevated in status. He became Dr Percival, following the award of an honorary LLD degree from St Andrews University (in spite of the Professor of Divinity registering his dissent).[9] This unlikely connection between Percival and a Scottish university may be attributable to the influence of Dr Lewis Campbell, the university's famous Professor of Greek. He had been Percival's tutor at Oxford.

In the autumn of 1876, with this handle to his name, Dr Percival is reported to have accompanied the Chairman and another member of the college Council to the Privy Council office in London for a meeting with the secretary to the Duke of Richmond, Lord President of the Council. Their purpose was to take soundings about the college's eligibility for a Royal Charter.

This was an act of presumption on the part of so young an institution. Nevertheless, after their visit they were notified of the duke's decision that, if an application for a Royal Charter for Clifton College were made, 'the circumstances were so exceptional that it would be favourably entertained'.[10]

Council and headmaster had been at one in growing nervous about working under a constitution which contained no safeguards or guarantee of permanency for the school. A Special Resolution passed by shareholders could change the rules of management at any time. Surplus revenue could be applied to the payment of dividends instead of school endowments.

If so minded, shareholders could even capitalise on success, wind up the company and divide its considerable assets between them – even though they had contributed only about ten per cent of the total of between £70,000 and £80,000 spent by this date on land and buildings. There was no suggestion that any such move was contemplated, but the Endowed Schools Commission affair had exposed where ultimate power lay.

After the Lord President's nod of approval, a Special General Meeting of the company was called. As befitted the importance of the occasion, the Earl of Ducie was in the chair. Lord Lieutenant of Gloucestershire, a Fellow of the Royal Society and a former Liberal Member of Parliament, he was the college's rarely fired big gun, serving as President from the very beginning in 1860 until his death more than sixty years later.

At this special meeting, as a further deterrent to objectors, the President was supported by the Mayor of Bristol as well as by the Rev. James Heyworth, Canon Guthrie's successor as Chairman of

Council. But only forty-one shareholders chose to attend, and these included other members of the Council.

There being no opposition, the three resolutions before the meeting were passed without dissent: the first to dissolve the company voluntarily and appoint a liquidator; the second to transfer all property and rights to a chartered company to be constituted and incorporated by Royal Charter. The third was a personal tribute: 'That the best thanks of the Company be given to Dr Percival for his great zeal and ability and untiring perseverance which have made the College so great a success.'[11]

In the Annual Report for 1877 shareholders were thanked for their forbearance and public spirit in surrendering their pecuniary interests and for their cordial support given to the Council in its endeavours to obtain a Charter. Their sole reward was to become Life Governors, with the right, as a body, to appoint the members of the Council. Their right to nominate boys to the school was removed. Only two shareholders asked to be reimbursed for the cost of their shares.

A Petition had already been presented to the Queen. It explained that the Council as the governing body felt that the position of the college as a joint stock company was fraught with great danger. What was suitable for a company formed for commercial purposes was now seen to be altogether inappropriate for an institution established for the purposes of education and without any view to gain.

The Royal Charter was duly granted three months later when, on 16 March 1877, Queen Victoria signed a warrant authorising the affixing of the Great Seal. This transformed Percival's thriving academy from the quasi-commercial enterprise of its infant years into the fully established and grandly named 'Body Politic and Corporate by the name of Clifton College' with the privileges of a perpetual succession and a common seal. Under the provisions of the Charter the college was to provide education of the highest class on moderate terms. The religious teaching was to accord with the doctrines of the Church of England, but a renewed conscience clause allowed any pupil to be excused religious services or lessons at the request of a parent.

However valuable as a safeguard, this development represented no departure from previous practices. Yet there was one formal change in which the hand of Percival may be detected. Under its new constitution Clifton College was to be a school for boys and young men, no longer one for the sons of gentlemen as announced in the original prospectus.

Doubtless contrary to the wishes of the radical headmaster and his liberal-minded team of assistant masters, however, any effect resulting from this official abolition of social discrimination was never discernible. More than half a century later the school's historian was to comment: 'Any social bar hitherto existing was thereby legally removed, but it may be safely affirmed that the post-Charter Cliftonian and the pre-Charter Cliftonian are of exactly the same type.'[12]

In other ways the Royal Charter was a change in substance as well as form. It conferred prestige, reinforced the reality of the school as a charity and brought the desired independence from the original investors.

The whole credit was not due to Percival. In this successful petition he enjoyed the lead of the Chairman and the full support of the other members of the Council. The contribution of Heyworth (Chairman from 1868 to 1880) to decisions on such matters of policy was said to be 'wise and matured judgment'.[13] Yet there could be no room for doubting that it was the headmaster who was responsible for creating the circumstances which the Privy Council's Lord President had judged to be 'so exceptional'.

In yet another tribute to yet another triumph the school's Annual Report for 1878 expressed satisfaction at the grant of the Royal Charter, 'which, without the marked success of Dr Percival's Head-Mastership, would have been impossible of attainment'. It was the crown of fifteen years' achievement.

CHAPTER 12

Two Rebels

The imposition of conformity has been the cause of enduring criticism of the public school system. Whatever their natural bent, boys have been purposefully shaped into the same pattern of manners and outlook. At Clifton Percival diversified the curriculum but intensified the ethos. 'The corporate life is decidedly fatiguing and not always compatible with the development of the individual life,' the school's historian acknowledged;[1] and A. A. David, a later headmaster of both Clifton and Rugby, similarly conceded that 'the schools have demanded a sacrifice of individual development'.[2]

It had not always been so. This cramping influence was a logical consequence of Arnold's reforms, and it increased inexorably after his time. At Rugby in the 1830s boys were allowed ample time and opportunity for independent activities. After class they were left largely to their own devices, which included fishing, birds-nesting, poaching – or merely loafing.

Tom Brown's Schooldays paints a vivid picture of this carefree aspect of boarding school life, but it also reveals the mischief resulting from lack of supervision. Satan found work for these idle hands, and it was for that reason that headmasters like Percival adopted a policy of organised games and other means of filling the timetable to the exclusion of individual pursuits. Unconventional himself, a rebel against much of the orthodoxy of his time, he nevertheless found no place for nonconformity in matters of correct behaviour and obedience to duty. Properly trained boys would be better qualified to take the right decisions for themselves in adult life. Meanwhile thinking for themselves was encouraged: there was no restriction on freedom of the mind.

For Percival it was an article of faith that the community must take priority over the individual, because communal life represented a higher good than self-expression, which he believed it to enhance. He put it in these words in a sermon:

> Our character as members of a society or fellowship is something different from our individual character where we are living apart or in solitude. There is a latent fire in our souls which does not burn up till it gathers force by the contact of life with life. As we sit here side by side, stirred in some degree by the same impulses and penetrated by the same influences, our spirit moves as it were all together, in something like a rhythmic harmony – for the time, at any rate, if not for all time, our life is a different thing.[3]

This is what Newbolt was echoing when he wrote: 'For education you live in society.'[4] But it is not how the victims of the system have viewed it.

Complaints of life-long traumas resulting from the restrictive routines of philistine institutions have been loudly voiced by generations of aesthetes and intellectuals who have suffered from the unwelcome pressures of the communal life at their boarding schools. How, then, did those Cliftonians who resisted falling into line as all-rounders fare under the iron rule instituted by Percival? What was their attitude towards the school and the system in retrospect? An example from each category may be illuminating.

Roger Fry, artist and critic, was aestheticism personified. As chief art critic of *The Athenaeum*, the leading journal of Victorian culture, he enjoyed an international reputation which led to his appointment as Director of the Metropolitan Museum in New York. On his return to England he became editor of the influential *Burlington Magazine*. There, and in a series of essays and lectures later gathered together in *Vision and Design*, he developed his theory that the only valid criterion for judging a work of art is 'significant form'.

In 1910 he won immediate obloquy and lasting fame by mounting the first Post-Impressionist exhibition in London. Those brought up on *The Monarch of the Glen* and *When Did You Last See Your Father?* were scandalised by his serious treatment of the, to them incomprehensible and ludicrous, works of Cézanne and Matisse. Fry in his own field was as much a pioneer as Percival in his. 'In so far as taste can be changed by one man, it was changed by Roger Fry,' was the judgment of Kenneth Clark (Lord Clark of *Civilisation*).[5]

Fry's advanced views found him a natural home in the Bloomsbury group. Clive Bell admired him for daring to be 'intellectually the freest of men',[6] and after his death his biography was written by Virginia Woolf.

Fry was born a member of the well-known Bristol family of chocolate-making Quakers. His father, Sir Edward, a judge, lived in London, but decided to have his son educated at Clifton. The Bristol connection was one reason, but another, perhaps stronger, was the college's reputation as a new kind of school, where science was well taught and there was little flogging or bullying. Roger arrived at the school in 1881, two years after Percival's departure, but with the regime which he had inaugurated fully maintained by the Rev. James Wilson who, with his gaunt appearance, luxuriant beard and beetling eyebrows, resembled an Old Testament prophet even more closely than Percival himself.

The free-spirited Roger felt crushed by the machine of government established by the founding headmaster and operated so efficiently by his successor. The routine bored him and the terms dragged. He was unmoved by the school's good works and, in a letter home, mocked a missionary's appeal for funds: 'A Mr Johnson obtained £70 for a steamer on Lake Nyanza by an earnest tho' incoherent & rambling address.'[7] In later life his experience of Clifton was held responsible for breeding in him 'a sullen revolt' against 'the whole public school system . . . and all those Imperialistic and patriotic emotions which it enshrined'.[8] Percival's ideal of Christian patriotism was anathema to Fry.

Yet the school catered well and agreeably enough for some of his interests. Science was the main one, and he enjoyed experimenting in the laboratory. The specific gravity of candle grease was the particular object of the future art critic's curiosity – hardly part of a restrictive curriculum. He also contrived to find time to paint flower pictures and botanise on the downs. But what he described as the one great consolation of his latter years at Clifton was the friendship formed with a fellow rebel, Jack McTaggart.

Roger was tall for his age, gangling and bespectacled. Jack was a shambling, dishevelled laughing stock. They became misfits together and shared Sunday evening walks in earnest argument over the headmaster's sermon. Roger was full of Quaker piety. Jack was a materialist.

The colonel who commanded the school's Engineering Corps taught military drawing, which was hardly Fry's kind of art, but Percival also employed a succession of specialist art masters in another of his contributions to an enlightened curriculum. These, however, appear to have made little impact. In his memoirs of school life in the 1870s Henry Newbolt's brother Frank (later Sir Francis, barrister and artist) wrote scathingly that 'the realm of art was as far off as the Sahara, and as little known'. Cliftonians, he declared, were 'Philistines to the last degree' and probably thought Botticelli was a cheese.[9]

So the school failed to detect the young Fry's genius; which may partly explain his virulent hostility. Yet in science, which was the enthusiasm of his boyhood, the school provided him with an exceptionally high standard of teaching and facilities, and this enabled him to win an exhibition in science to Cambridge, where he developed his love of art.

Of Roger Fry's special friend, John McTaggart Ellis McTaggart, it was said by Lowes Dickinson, his biographer: 'Seldom, I suppose, has a boy so gifted and so strange passed the portals of a public school.'[10]

As a small boy, young Jack used to take solitary walks round his village talking to himself. His peculiar sidling gait, keeping his back to walls, was later variously attributed to agoraphobia or a precaution against having his bottom kicked while at Clifton, but it seems to have been his natural mode of progression. To the other boys in the village he was known as The Loonie, and a similar verdict of insanity was pronounced at his prep school, from which he was expelled for arguing against the Apostles' Creed and denying the existence of God.

McTaggart first passed through the portals of Clifton in January 1882, the year after Fry, who first glimpsed him on the football field, 'a limp, melancholy, asymmetrical figure'.[11] Having decided that football was not for him, the boy philosopher simply lay down on the field and refused to get up. This was unprecedented and Authority was nonplussed. When it became clear that it was his unalterable response to participation in compulsory games, he was ordered to take five-mile walks instead and thus able to spend profitable hours on the downs in uninterrupted thought. At cricket his role was scorer, which he enjoyed.

Bullying was inevitable, particularly when he declared himself a republican and publicly regretted that a madman who fired at

Queen Victoria had not been a better shot. For this he was tried by a court of other boys and, in spite of the witnesses being confounded by his cross-examination, sentenced to run a gauntlet of knotted towels. Republicanism made him unpopular enough; his atheism he chose not to parade as Shelley had done so scandalously at Eton. This uncharacteristic restraint sprang from a sense of loyalty to the school as an Anglican institution. He did not believe in God, but he did believe in the Church of England.

Once it was accepted that he would not submit and conform, McTaggart became an institution in himself and the school began to pride itself on accommodating such a physical oddity holding such outrageous opinions. Unlike Fry, he was always good-natured and kind-hearted and never grew embittered; and he later said that the friendships which he had formed at Clifton were among the best of his life.

For *The Cliftonian* he wrote poems and precocious essays on the doctrines of John Stuart Mill and other learned subjects. In the school debating society he argued in favour of radical causes and refined the skills which were to bring him the Presidency of the Union at Cambridge.

McTaggart's genius was more apparent than Fry's and did not go unrecognised at school. When he learned that this extraordinary talent was bound for Trinity College, Cambridge, Percival, then President of Trinity College, Oxford, wrote to the boy's mother urging her to send him to the Oxford Trinity instead. As a bait he held out the promise of a scholarship or exhibition on the strength of his record at school. Wilson too took a particular interest. He urged his star pupil to read political economy at university, because of its concern with humanity. 'I would not wish to see a mind which is capable of dealing with facts and men losing itself in metaphysics, playing to a small audience somewhere in the clouds. I wish to see him in the thick of affairs,' he wrote in true Percivalian vein.[12]

Neither plea diverted McTaggart. He went to Cambridge, and his name stood alone in the First Class of the moral sciences (metaphysics) tripos in 1888. Elected a Fellow of Trinity, he became England's most penetrating exponent of Hegelian philosophy, with works on Hegel's dialectics, his logic and his cosmology. These were followed by *Some Dogmas of Religion* and *Nature of Existence*, in which he expounded his own, peculiarly idiosyncratic beliefs: in immortality but not in God, and in the twin stars of truth and love, love (not duty) being the supreme good.

McTaggart's attitude towards Clifton was the very opposite to Fry's, and Fry wrote of this betrayal by his fellow rebel with sadness: 'There grew up in him not only a deep and lasting loyalty to the institution, but a romantic attachment to the whole public school system.'[13] This included all the aspects of patriotism which Fry detested. Indeed McTaggart's devotion to his old school grew and grew until it reached such a pitch that nothing in his later years was said to have given him more pleasure than his election to the Council. On his death the school was the major beneficiary of his will.

If Clifton was not the most congenial of nurseries for Fry's genius, at least it survived to blossom later. With McTaggart, Percival's creation triumphantly proved that a public school could cope successfully with the oddest of oddities. Yet much of the credit must go to the oddity's own imperturbable inflexibility. The greater triumph was his.

McTaggart's subsequent career and thinking, distinguished as it was, was not what Percival would have ordained. The spirit of Clifton decreed that his talents should have been used, as Wilson had vainly urged on him, not in abstract speculation, but more practically in the service of humanity by advancing the radical causes of the day in which they all three believed.

McTaggart and Henry Newbolt lunched together one day at the Savile Club, when the philosopher sent the poet's mind reeling with the remark: 'I believe, and I think I can prove, that we are all immortal. But of course I don't believe there is any God beside ourselves.' Newbolt left the table to struggle with the idea of a Spirit composed of spirits; of an Absolute realising itself in a community of individuals.[14] Unlike McTaggart, he had entered the school ripe for the stamp of authority, eager for guidance about life's goals and meaning, and he had found them by merging his own spirit into the spirit of Clifton, as Percival demanded. McTaggart had accepted the communal life as an Absolute and fallen in love with the school, but on the subject of God he remained, as Fry did in all things, far removed from Percival's ethos.

CHAPTER 13

Illegimitacy and Impurity

In recent years the name of Percival has been ridiculed for prudery. The incident for which he has become best known is his edict, while headmaster of Rugby, that football shorts must be lengthened to conceal the sight of naked flesh above the knee. But earlier, during his time at Clifton, his puritanism went into action on a much more serious issue and one reflecting on his own family: illegitimacy.

The person responsible for bringing him into the public arena on this subject was George Moore, the fellow Cumbrian who commissioned Watts to paint his portrait. Moore too was the son of a 'statesman', a title which he claimed to be as highly regarded in the north as the Order of the Garter. After leaving school early to serve an apprenticeship in Wigton he came south and made such a huge fortune in London that he was able to build himself a house in Kensington Palace Gardens and dispense large sums in charity. Like Percival, he never forgot the poor or his roots in 'auld Cummerland'. His career was such a notable example of self-help and good works that when he died Samuel Smiles himself, the famous author of *Self-Help*, wrote his Life: *George Moore, Merchant and Philanthropist*.

Moore involved Percival in schemes to improve the education of the poor in Cumbria, but in August 1865 when he invited him to his estate near Wigton to attend a school prize-giving by the Archbishop of York, they had another shared interest to discuss: the prevalence of bastardy in Cumberland and Westmorland.

Earlier in the year Percival had written a letter to Moore on the rate of illegitimacy in the two counties as revealed in the Registrar-General's recently published returns. At more than eleven per cent of all births it was the highest in the country. In neighbouring Durham the rate was little more than five per cent, and in London less than four and a half. The efforts of local clergymen and schoolmasters to mend matters were defeated by the conditions of life, and the fair name of Cumbria was sullied.

Moore gave Percival's letter to *The Times*, which published it accompanied by a leading article deploring such a 'fearful degree of profligacy' and pointing a finger, unknowingly no doubt, at people like the letter-writer's own parents:

> When we remember how common it is among the poor in country districts to defer marriage until pregnancy is far advanced, we cannot take the percentage of births out of wedlock as a fair measure of the prevailing vice. The number of bastards represents, in fact, but a delusive *minimum*.[1]

Percival's letter denounced bastardy as an evil poisoning country districts, an ugly blot disfiguring beautiful hills and valleys. 'One cannot forget,' he wrote from the heart, 'the wretched liability of the poor child to be tainted all through life with this stain of bastardy, which he cannot escape.'

Being Percival, he was at no loss to propose what should be done. His first target was the traditional licence at fairs. He proposed an end to Martinmas and Whitsun holidays, and that farmers and other employers should not allow female servants to attend any kind of merry-making except on condition of returning home before dark. Overcrowding in households and work places was the next target. Steps were urgently needed to improve the dwellings of the poor, where families were so 'huddled together as to outrage all decency'. In such conditions, he wrote, pure morality was impossible.

Other measures which he proposed were instilling a sense of shame and providing young country men with opportunities for innocent recreation instead of leaving them 'a prey to strong passions and sensual indulgences'. Many might enjoy reading but had no reading-rooms and nothing to read. Finally, the country parsons were held to be at fault: 'I believe I might venture to say that many even of the clergy don't so much as know the faces of the majority of the farm servants in their parishes.'[2]

Publication of the the letter achieved Moore's purpose. It created a great stir. Correspondence followed in *The Times* itself and other leading newspapers and journals, including the *Daily Telegraph,* the *Pall Mall Gazette* and the *Saturday Review.* Among the local press the subject filled columns of the *Journal* and the *Examiner* in Carlisle and the *Observer* in Penrith. Overall coverage was so extensive that when all the leaders and letters were reprinted in a booklet, entitled *The Morality of Cumberland and Westmoreland,* they filled more than a hundred pages.

This nation-wide debate must have brought the young head-master and his three-year-old school to wide public notice and enhanced their already growing reputations. At the school itself, however, his concern was directed towards the avoidance of other aspects of impurity.

Prior to Arnold's reforms in the 1830s, the vice and immorality for which the public schools had become notorious included such sins as drunkenness, cruelty, lying, disobedience and idleness. In that pre-Victorian period, when single beds were charged as extras, it must be presumed that some exploratory fumbling beneath the sheets was taken for granted. As a schoolboy at Rugby in the 1840s the good-looking Charles Dodgson (Lewis Carroll) confided in his diary that he was 'never secure from annoyance at night'.[3]

By the 1860s and 1870s the focus was more sharply on sexual misconduct as the dominant vice, with attitudes towards it increasingly censorious. Thus, in guarding against vice among his pupils, the puritan Percival, in common with all other headmasters, was forced to bring his mind to bear on the repellent practices of fornication, masturbation and homosexuality.

In the matter of fornication it had to be recognised that public school boys at the age of puberty were exposed to the danger of seduction by maid servants and boarding-house nurses – even, at Rugby, by prostitutes who found enough custom at the school to make the journey from Coventry worth their while.

Masturbation, usually unnamed, was a furtive malpractice hard to detect. It could be countered only by the direst threats and was therefore alleged by those who warned against it to cause blindness, madness and even death. Thomas Hughes wrote darkly that he 'could tell of souls hopelessly besmirched and befouled by this deadly habit', which he identified as *scelus Onanis.*[4] In 1877 the headmaster of Eton, the Rev. the Hon. Edward Lyttelton, wrote a pamphlet (privately printed) in which he identified masturbation as responsible for pederasty, because all 'dual vice' resulted from 'solitary vice'.

Homosexuality, although rarely so named, could be mentioned openly in those pre-Freudian days provided there was no suggestion of a physical relationship. Close friendships between older and younger boys feature unashamedly in *Tom Brown's Schooldays* and *Eric, or, Little by Little*. In *Eric* no alarm bells were set ringing when two boys 'squeezed each other's hands, and looked into each other's faces, and silently promised that they would be loving friends forever'.

Arnold himself had spoken of having experienced a similar emotional intimacy with a fellow schoolboy at Winchester. When the older boy was acting as protector, that was generally seen as a noble role, although such 'taking up' could become suspect when the younger was a fresh-faced androgyne pampered to excess. With so many masters displaying homosexual tendencies it would have been thought strange if controlled and sublimated homosexuality had been treated as a serious aberration, although the sexual act itself was a criminal offence.

At Clifton, according to one former pupil of Percival, sentimental friendships were 'mildly epidemical' owing to a dearth of female companionship. The headmaster was reported as viewing these idealisations of a younger boy by an older with unease and perplexity. Not having attended a boarding school as a boy himself, he suffered from inexperience as well as being faced with the impossibility of legislating against sentimentality. His unstated rule seems to have been the one generally prevailing: 'Keep within platonic bounds or else . . .' On the rare occasions when these were discovered to have been transgressed at Clifton, it was customary for the offenders to be held guilty not so much of a sin as of a disgraceful example of 'bad form', and to be punished severely on that score.[5]

Percival was not alone in floundering over the burgeoning sexuality of his charges. Wilson, his successor, frankly revealed the embarrassment he and other headmasters felt at being expected to explain the facts of life to boys. Writing on behalf of himself and his colleagues, he declared teaching about sex to be so utterly repulsive to their nature that those of high character and refinement could not and would not do it. There was a consensus that silence was the best course, so that boys might remain completely innocent until marriage.[6] In those circumstances it is scarcely surprising that some should choose to experiment with whatever or whoever was available.

Percival's introduction of a practising homosexual into the life of his boys at Clifton must be attributed to ignorance. John Addington Symonds concealed his sexual orientation and would in any event have been hard to keep away. He was the son of the doctor of the same name who was Physician to the General Hospital in Bristol and lecturer at the medical school. The Symondses had been doctors for six generations, and this Dr Symonds also enjoyed a national medical practice and reputation, numbering Gladstone, Tennyson and Jowett among his patients. More pertinently, he was one of the most prominent founders of the school and among the most involved members of its Council.

Living in splendour in Clifton Hill Hall, a Georgian mansion which is now a university hostel, the Symonds family belonged to the aristocracy of Clifton society, the 'best set' which embraced Percival and his wife in an exchange of dinner parties and other social functions.

The younger Symonds, Percival's junior by six years, was an exceptionally gifted intellectual and stimulating company, but he was not to be trusted with boys. As a friend and neighbour, he became one of the presumably unsuspecting headmaster's riding companions and took long walks in earnest conversation with the two most senior assistant masters: T. E. Brown and Graham Dakyns. In 1869 he edited the testimonials forwarded to Rugby in support of Percival's application for the headmastership. As he explained to a correspondent:

We are busy here about Percival's candidature at Rugby. It gives me a good deal of tiresome small work – and I am made use of to compose people's testimonials or tinker up their English when made. Do not imagine that I correct at will after they have signed! I mean only that bodies of men like the Council and Assistant Masters want a literary assessor and seek me.[7]

When his father died the son who had made himself so agreeable and useful was elected to fill his place on the Council and served on it for ten years (from 1872 to 1882).

As a boy Symonds had been sent to board at Harrow at a tender age. There, in the words of his secret memoirs:

Every boy of good looks had a female name and was recognised either as a public prostitute or as some bigger fellow's bitch.

Bitch was the word in common usage to indicate a boy who yielded his person to another. The talk in the studies and dormitories was incredibly obscene. One could not avoid seeing acts of onanism, mutual masturbation and the sport of naked boys in bed together.[8]

Such coarse behaviour disgusted him, and he took no part in it: 'the inclination for vulgar lust was wanting'.[9] When a friend boasted that he was having an affair with the headmaster and showed him some love letters to prove it, he was appalled. His own kind of homosexuality was aesthetic and romantic, and here was a clergyman in charge of six hundred boys secretly indulging in practices which he denounced from the pulpit as grievous sins. Sworn to secrecy, Symonds broke his word after leaving Harrow. At Oxford in 1859 he informed a professor, who told him that he must show the evidence to his father, and this he did.

Dr Charles Vaughan, the headmaster in question, had been one of Arnold's two brightest pupils at Rugby, and he had married the sister of the other, Arthur Stanley, Arnold's biographer and afterwards Dean of Westminster. Up to that time Vaughan's career had closely paralleled Percival's. Appointed headmaster of Harrow in 1844 at the age of twenty-eight, he had revived a moribund school almost as dramatically as Percival had set an infant one on its feet. The school had not, however, achieved much academic distinction, and he had not been as exacting or, as it appeared, as personally upright in the matter of purity.

He hurried to Clifton in response to a summons from Dr Symonds, who insisted that he must resign his headmastership immediately and agree to accept no further preferment in the Church. On those terms the doctor promised to spare him public exposure, which could have led to a prison sentence.

Vaughan, effectively blackmailed, had no choice but to submit. His wife found the terms too harsh. She, the daughter of a bishop, followed him to Clifton and begged on her knees for a reprieve, but the doctor, a pious Nonconformist, was not to be moved, and Vaughan resigned at the height of a brilliant career to universal astonishment.

Offered in turn the sees of Worcester, Rochester and Ely, he attracted admiration for his Christian humility in refusing them all. Rochester he did, in fact, at first accept, but a telegram from Clifton caused a hasty withdrawal. He ended his career as Master of the

Temple and, after Symonds's death, Dean of Llandaff. Buried with honour, he became revered as Harrow's re-founding father. The truth behind his resignation remained a secret for a hundred years.

It was in April 1860, shortly after the young Symonds's revelation about the sexual malpractices at Harrow, that the first meeting of the founders of Clifton College was held, at which Dr Symonds proposed the establishment of the school. No doubt he blamed Harrow for his son's experiences and would have employed all his considerable influence in the coming years to ensure purity at the new school.[10] The Harrow incident may also account, at least in part, for his preference for schoolboys living at home rather than boarding. A reaction against homosexuality may thus have contributed to the early emphasis on Clifton, not as a boarding school, but as a local school which made special provision for day boys with a Town house.

Once alerted to the nature of his son's sexuality, Dr Symonds prescribed a period abroad and later, at the age of twenty-four, marriage. The young Symonds obeyed and the bridal night in 1864 was a fiasco because he had never before performed a sexual act with another person, male or female, and had no idea what to do. Several years earlier he had enjoyed a long passionate affair with a fifteen-year-old Bristol cathedral chorister, but its climax, in the seclusion of Leigh Woods, was two kisses – in which (so he recorded) he found perfect joy and almost fainted from the rapture of the contact.[11]

After marriage the objects of his desire continued to be young working-class males – a British soldier, a Venetian gondolier, a Swiss sledge-driver – but between such extramarital escapades he succeeded in fathering four daughters. Whether any of his love affairs were consummated with more than kisses is not clear. It seems probable that they were; yet for him passion was fine and noble, sex merely coarse.

It is most unlikely that Percival would have known or guessed at Symonds's role in the Vaughan affair, let alone his mania for passionate male friendships. The cover of marriage probably deceived him. But during their rides together Symonds, who was proud of his part in Vaughan's downfall, sometimes turned the conversation to the evils of homosexuality which he had encountered at Harrow and Oxford. Percival, as he reported to a correspondent:

seemed very ready to discuss and anxious to be informed. I was surprised to find him so ignorant of the real evil which is going on. He was just alive to the fact that boys by herding together acquire coarse and vicious habits among themselves. But he conceived that the more intellectual would, by the energy of their minds, be protected and diverted . . . I found it difficult to express to Percival the exact nuance of the evil in this its most subtle manifestation.[12]

While Symonds believed from personal experience that the most sensitive were the most vulnerable, Percival held to the view that intellectuals were equipped to rise above unnatural vice. When Symonds cited Swinburne and his interest in Sappho, Percival dismissed this 'as a clear case of lunacy'.[13]

Over a period of many years Symonds carried on a heart-to-heart correspondence with Dakyns, Percival's very first appointment and among his most inspired. The two were brought together by a shared interest in Greek literature. It was a subject which Dakyns taught, and he published a translation of Xenophon. He too was excellent company. As an undergraduate he was said to have been the most popular man in Cambridge, and this had resulted in the honour of being chosen as tutor to Tennyson's sons.

Ancient Greek thought and literature, in which relationships between older and younger men were held up for admiration and judged to be something quite separate from, and not incompatible with, conventional marriage, were a strong influence throughout the public school world of the nineteenth century. The preponderance of those studying Greek contributed to the acceptance of homosexuality so long as it stayed in the mind. But John Addington Symonds's experience of gross promiscuity at Harrow gave him an alternative perspective to that of the uninitiated like Percival, who were liable to react too little or too much.

Dakyns was worried by the headmaster's lack of understanding of homosexuality, and they were on one occasion at odds over the treatment of a homosexual incident among boys in Dakyns's house. On a later occasion Symonds wrote to him: 'I scarcely think Percival is quite the fool you take him for . . . Ecce Homo is his Gospel – and a good one, believe me.'[14] From this it would appear that Percival, by instinct and principle the most puritanical of men, preferred to leave well enough alone, but when that was not possible he refused to adopt a liberal policy urged on him by the more experienced Dakyns.

Whatever their differences over what constituted impurity and how best to treat it, it should be added that the mutual trust and respect between headmaster and housemaster was life-long. Percival's loyalty to his highly-prized staff did not end with his headmastership. When Dakyns dropped dead on Haslemere railway station more than thirty years later, Percival did not hesitate to interrupt his duties as a bishop and cross the country from Hereford to Surrey to conduct the funeral service, as he had done for Cay in the south of France.

On 1 December 1868 Dakyns hosted a dinner party to which he invited the then married Symonds to meet some sixth-formers. The guest was unable to keep his eyes off one of them, who, he enthused, 'could have made a fortune as a model'.[15] This was Norman Moor, head of the school, a dashing batsman, a noted wit and the first Cliftonian to win a Balliol scholarship. Symonds was dazzled, 'eager to know the boy better'. Even Cecil Boyle, the 'dear Hero' to whom he had paid homage with the gift of a statuette of a gladiator, was outclassed.

Moor reciprocated and he and Symonds engaged in a sentimental, sensual amour, meeting frequently and openly in the Close and the school library. They spent nights in London together and travelled on the continent, often sharing a bed. Yet, according to Symonds, 'nothing occurred between us which the censorious could rightly consider unworthy of two gentlemen'.[16]

When he came down from Oxford, Moor was taken on the teaching staff by Percival and spent the rest of his life as a master at the school. He was there from 1874 to 1895, when he died in office as housemaster of what had been Brown's house. Some time after his return to Clifton he had written to Symonds that the combined influences of Symonds himself and Percival had cured him of homosexual lust.[17] It can be confidently surmised that those influences must have been brought to bear in very different ways.

Apart from the danger he represented to the virtue of Percival's charges, there was much to be said for Symonds's connection with the school. He was a brilliant scholar, a good poet, a role model as an aesthete, and a sparkling conversationalist. At Oxford he had taken a Double First in classics, won the Newdigate Prize for poetry and appeared settled for life at Magdalen until a homosexual affair cost him his Fellowship. Later he stood unsuccessfully for the Chair of Poetry and probably failed only because it became known that the poetry he was writing, and printing for private circulation, was erotic verse on homosexual themes.

What Symonds was working on, more respectably, during this period of his acquaintance with Percival were his acclaimed *Studies of the Greek Poets* (published in the 1870s and much admired by the young Oscar Wilde)[18] and his classic *Renaissance in Italy* (published between 1875 and 1886 in six volumes).

He also assisted in the revision of Jowett's translation of Plato's *Symposium* and debated with him over the nature of 'Greek love', which Jowett, who held the Chair of Greek at Oxford, said he believed to be a 'figure of speech' for Plato, while Symonds argued that it was 'a poignant reality' and warned that the study of Plato was 'injurious to a certain number of predisposed young men'.[19]

In 1869, while preparing his *Studies*, Symonds suggested to Percival the idea of his giving a course of lectures on ancient Greek literature to the sixth form. This was agreed and they proved a resounding success. Half the *Studies* were based on them, and they came to be cited as a prime example of Clifton's enlightened curriculum.

When an adult, one of the boys who attended them innocently remembered 'the sudden stimulus conveyed by that extraordinary active brain, with an impact which I still recall as almost physical'.[20] Another, Herbert Warren, went so far as to describe Symonds as 'one of the chief determining influences of my life' and Percival's employment of him as a sixth-form lecturer 'inspired'. 'Into my world,' he wrote, 'just as the process of intellectual puberty had thoroughly set in, suddenly came Symonds with an influence novel, potent and thrice welcome.'[21]

So there was much satisfaction on both sides. While the boys admired the wit and style and intellect of the lecturer, the lecturer was enchanted by the physical charm of the boys. The course 'brought him into frequent and delightful companionship with masters and boys alike, many of whom became his lasting friends'.[22]

The headmaster and his handsome presence had made a deep impression on Symonds and, despite the narrow gap in their ages, he seems to have looked up to Percival as a father figure much more appealing than the real one who had led him into a deeply unhappy marriage. In one of his letters to Dakyns he wrote: 'We went to the College today. Percival was magnificent: he spoke well:

and inner enthusiasm and care for the School and love even (I thought) for the boys came out.'[23]

There can be no doubt that Percival's kind of love for his boys was pure. The moral question posed by Symonds's involvement in the school is whether homosexuality was to be considered impure in itself or whether that was dependent on the form which it took. For an answer to that, Percival would surely have looked to the Bible, not the classics.

CHAPTER 14

The End of a Reign

The reign of a headmaster, however successful, is best not prolonged. 'Remain for fifteen years or till you feel no emotion on
receiving a new boy' had been Arnold's dictum, and after fifteen
years at Clifton Percival told a colleague that he was only deferring
his resignation until he could make sure of the right man to succeed
him.[1]

In his case health was the deciding factor. As early as 1869
Jowett, his Oxford correspondent, was writing: 'I hear from several
persons that you are seriously injuring your health. They tell me
that nothing can be better for the success of the College, but they
also think that it is quite impossible that you should go on much
longer in your present way of working.' Jowett warned him against
burdening himself with drudgery and recommended a holiday for
six or twelve months.[2]

The hectic pace of the school's growth created problems, physical
and financial, and it took a man of Percival's resolve to maintain
the momentum. Almost inevitably, the supply of new buildings and
facilities was constantly lagging behind demand. Class-rooms were
too few. In the Close a boy at cover point in one game of cricket
might have to jostle with another at square leg on an adjoining
pitch. In the overcrowded swimming pool a boy drowned
unnoticed. It was small wonder that, despite his triumphs, the
headmaster often appeared jaded as worries accumulated and he
piled more and more duties on himself and others.

Yet it was nearly nine years before he could bring himself to
accept Jowett's advice. For the previous three he had been suffering
from nightmares and, in the words of one of his housemasters, 'his
exhaustless energy seemed even to his own sanguine spirit some-

what impaired'.³ At the age of forty-three his sandy hair was already turning grey.

In January 1878 the Chairman was told confidentially by another member of the Council that the headmaster was seriously ill and his doctor was urging him to spend the remainder of the winter and spring resting in the south of France. Percival himself was intending to apply for only two or three weeks' leave of absence instead of the four months recommended.⁴ When alerted, a sympathetic Council acknowledged 'a serious strain upon his mental and bodily strength'.⁵

The cause of the strain and nightmares may be readily conjectured. Percival was both an idealist and a perfectionist, and the school which he had created was becoming blighted by imperfections which he was finding impossible to remedy. Success he was accustomed to take in his stride; failure when everything depended upon him was hard to bear. His nature forbade him to share the burdens of command and responsibility with others; his upbringing in the solitude of remote dales had taught him self-reliance. The achievements which attracted so much general admiration fell short of his own aspirations. Whether it was praise or censure, he was 'singularly unaffected by the opinion of those about him'.⁶ Instead, his mind became tortured by self-criticism; by his own feelings of frustration and inadequacy.

There was plenty to trouble it with self-questioning in the small hours. The number of boys in the school was still climbing and now approached seven hundred. New class-rooms were desperately needed, but how were they to be built? More land had to be found for games to relieve the congestion in the Close, but how was it to be acquired? A rising income from fees covered rising running costs, but there was no surplus for capital expenditure. Founded without endowment, the school had exhausted available funds. Worse, it was heavily burdened with debt from borrowings.

Then there was the quality of the teaching staff. Maintaining it was crucial, but recruitment had reached a critical phase. All the housemasters and other senior staff were still young, and this meant little prospect of promotion for deserving juniors or ambitious newcomers.

And what of the mould-breaking Modern Side? Although well taught and flaunting honours boards listing innumerable admissions to the military academies, it had fallen below expectation and become regarded as the very thing its originator had sought to avoid: a haven for the second-rate, the unambitious, the lazy. The cherished School Mission, too, had proved a disheartening venture. One curate in charge after another had resigned in despair, and its future, if it had one at all, looked bleak.

Too over-stretched and broken in health to cope with all these difficulties, even after a long summer break, Percival resigned himself to moving on. A timely offer from the Fellows of Trinity College, Oxford to become their President was accepted. It took effect from October 1878, but he agreed to the Council's request to stay at Clifton until the following Easter to allow time for the appointment and arrival of a successor. On this occasion no pressure was put on him to change his mind.

In December, in one more gesture of appreciation, the Council appointed him a Life Governor and voted him the fifty pounds necessary to qualify. It also resolved to remit, while he remained, the fees for the three of his sons who attended the school and to waive the fees for a further five years in the case of the one who would be staying to board after he had left. But the amicable parting was not without a hint of friction.

A disappointment which still pained him was the rejection of his plan for a hundred and fifty boys from poor homes in Bristol to attend the school, paying little or nothing, in the tradition of foundation scholars in the former endowed schools. Half the fees would have been remitted by the school, the other half met by a special fund or subscription.

His protracted struggle to broker a deal between the Council and the Endowed Schools Commission along those lines had run into the sand. He had set his heart on making the finest education in Britain open to all, but it was still being denied to those who could not afford it, however talented, however deserving. This had rankled for seven years, and he could not refrain from a parting shot in writing to the Council.

Had the changes in the Constitution which I advocated some time ago, including the abolition of social distinction, been carried out, nothing would have induced me to exchange Clifton for any other school as that reform would have given me the one educational opportunity which I coveted, and the loss of which I can never entirely cease to regret.[7]

Percival was a Gladstonian Liberal, and the abolition of barriers to individual opportunity and achievement was a Liberal objective. It had been one of the main threads running through the reforms of Gladstone's administration between 1868 and 1874. Percival's belief in the social justice of a good education regardless of ability to pay also went hand in hand with another article in the Liberal creed: the nation's need of a meritocracy, for which he was training recruits.

What may well have stirred his resentment over the stillborn proposals for assisted places at Clifton was the recent loss of a chance to achieve a similar objective elsewhere.

George Moore, his rich friend, was as keen on the provision of a good education for clever boys from poor homes as Percival himself, and he decided to use some of his wealth to that end in Cumbria. Percival was consulted and worked out for him a practical scheme to avoid pitfalls and deploy his intended endowment fund most effectively. After many meetings and consultations with other educationists, including Frederick Temple, a draft plan was drawn up and printed with the co-operation of the Education Department.

The large sum of twelve thousand pounds was set aside by Moore to meet the initial cost, and one day in November 1876 he asked his wife to write to Percival to arrange a final meeting. He then drove to Carlisle, where he was knocked down in the street by a runaway horse and died a few hours later.[8]

The project was partially revived as a memorial to him when more than eight thousand pounds were raised by public subscription to fund scholarships and exhibitions, but Percival's more ambitious plan, probably seen by him as a model for the rest of the country, was never realised.

To succeed him at Clifton Percival confidently nominated James Wilson, a former colleague at Rugby and at that time a housemaster there. Wilson was another gifted member of the circle of intellectuals from the north-west. He too was descended from a line of Cumbrian 'statesmen', and it was he who had urged Percival to appoint another member of the circle, the Manxman T. E. Brown, to his staff at Clifton. Wilson's father had been the first Principal of King William's College, Isle of Man, where he and Brown had both been at school.

This school off the Cumbrian coast was remarkable for nurturing talent not only in education and poetry but also in science. Another pupil who became a headmaster was Frederic Farrar, who used the school unflatteringly as the setting for his best-selling tear-jerker, *Eric, or Little by Little*.[9] Farrar became Master of Marlborough, where – as a friend of Darwin and T. H. Huxley – he appointed the school's first science master.

Wilson had been allowed to introduce the occasional science lesson into the curriculum at Rugby, and he was called as an expert on the teaching of science to give evidence to the Clarendon Commission on the Public Schools and the Commission on Scientific Instruction. But that was not his main subject. At Cambridge he had gained a First in mathematics and was Senior Wrangler in 1859. When Percival summoned him to Clifton he had spent twenty years teaching mathematics at Rugby, although, as he later confessed: 'I did not know what first-rate mathematical teaching was till I went to Clifton in 1879 and saw the work of Watson and Hall and Stevens.'[10]

In the autumn of 1878 Wilson's wife had just died and he was about to abandon schoolmastering, take holy orders and devote himself to parish work. So, when Percival's letter arrived stating that the governors of Clifton College had asked him to recommend a successor and that if he put forward Wilson's name his appointment was sure, Wilson responded with an unhesitating refusal. He explained that life as a schoolmaster had become distasteful to him, and that in any event he was not suitably qualified because the duties of a headmaster included the teaching of sixth-form classics and, except as an occasional relief duty, he had taught none for twenty years.

On his usual principle of never taking no for an answer, Percival at once set to work to reverse Wilson's decision. T. E. Brown's persuasive charm was enlisted, and the wisdom of Bishop Temple, Wilson's and Percival's former headmaster at Rugby, was invoked. Weakening, Wilson agreed to consult the bishop, who, no doubt suitably briefed by Percival, duly informed him that it was his duty to go to Clifton.

No sooner had Wilson accepted this advice and the appointment been agreed than one of the housemasters, E. M. Oakeley, in writing to congratulate him, added somewhat tactlessly that some people had hoped for an open competition; in which case it was believed that C. G. Bell, the then Master of Marlborough, would have been the successful candidate. This led Wilson to consult his conscience and take what he considered the only honourable course. He immediately resigned, but with the proviso that if the appointment were thrown open to competition he would apply in the normal way.

Members of the Council were embarrassed and irritated by what appeared to them an over-sensitive reaction to rumour. They were forced to go through the whole procedure of placing advertisements and assessing testimonials, well knowing that, with Wilson's hat still in the ring and Percival still determined to have him, it was all for nothing.

What was even more riling was that Oakeley had been misinformed. Bell was not among the applicants and had never intended to be. Wilson and, for form's sake, one other were interviewed; after which, in Wilson's words: 'Early in December 1878 the Governors met again and elected me, under the strong persuasion of Percival.'[11]

Clifton without Percival was a step into the unknown. The school was about to be orphaned. The departure of the father-figure was an occasion for both sadness and apprehension. Some feared a sea change with a Senior Wrangler instead of an Oxford Classic, a man of science instead of a theologian, and a widower with no consort to replace the much loved Mrs Percival.[12] Looking back in old age, Henry Newbolt remembered the loss of his headmaster as more of a shock than the death of Queen Victoria.

Reassuringly, though, the appointment of Percival's own choice seemed a promise of continuity, and Wilson, when he made his first public appearance, was judged to have a very kindly face (as much as could be seen of it beneath the whiskers). The same could never have been said of Percival, whose very look could inspire terror.

Yet masters and boys had in the end come to detect a kindly disposition beneath the outward severity of that 'tall, masterful, completely arbitrary'[13] figure with its fearsome driving power and its white-hot moral fervour perpetually at boiling point. Behind his back boys were by this time daring to make fun of him and imitate his accent in characteristic pronouncements, such as 'Arl these things pynt to a higher life'. Their nicknames for him were Jumps and Perkeye.[14]

In surveying his headmastership two surviving letters offer insights. They were addressed to W. D. L. Macpherson, an unsung contributor to Percival's achievements. He was appointed college secretary in May 1864 and held that post of chief functionary for forty-eight years, servicing the requirements of Council and acting as the headmaster's general manager and assistant financial controller. Percival was one of his own executive arms; Macpherson, the forerunner of the modern bursar, was the other.

On a letter to him from a mother complaining that the headmaster had done her son on the Modern Side a great injustice by not promoting him, because (so she alleged) Percival viewed the Modern Side unfavourably, Macpherson wrote: 'The only unkind letter I have found about Percival.' This is all the more revealing because later in his career Percival was to provoke unkind letters in shoals.

The other letter came from a prospective parent: 'I learnt from Mr Percival that not only is the system of fagging allowed in the College, but that senior boys are even permitted to inflict corporal punishment upon the juniors. To both practices I have an insuperable objection. I am, therefore, compelled to abandon the idea of placing my sons at the College.'

Percival's reputation for creating a different kind of school was well deserved but, as indicated here, he disappointed some of the most liberal-minded by not carrying his reforms far enough. On this letter Macpherson wrote rhetorically: 'To what other Public School could the boy[s] go?'[15]

What then was Percival's vision of a new type of public school, the vision which Wilson shared? Many years afterwards, at a Jubilee Commemoration Dinner in 1912, Wilson identified it as 'a nursery or seed-plot for high-minded men, devoted to the highest service of the country, a new Christian chivalry of patriotic service'. 'That vision,' he claimed, 'has affected all the other public schools of England.'[16]

Even if the vision had become endangered by the practical defects which Wilson inherited, Percival had bequeathed to him one priceless asset in preserving it: a loyal staff of rare ability united in commitment to his ideals. Together with Percival's nominee as the new headmaster, they made certain that it survived.

The respect and even affection of those who rose to the top in Percival's autocracy is understandable, but a collective sigh of relief at the prospect of a black cloud lifting might have been expected from the rest. That the mourning at his departure should have been all but universal was a symptom of the enchanter's magic, and it affected parents and masters as well as boys. Parents, in particular, had good reason to be content with his regime, for when Wilson took over he was reported to have found the boys intelligent, industrious, modest and well-mannered.[17]

The ceremonial farewell took place in April 1879. In the library which he had donated Percival was presented with an address by former pupils ('Steadfast as is our loyalty to the name of Clifton, it is yet true that much of that loyalty arises from a personal attachment to yourself, upon whom we look as the real Founder of the School . . .'). This was followed by the gift of a silver service so huge that one lady condemned it as a white elephant ('He will have to keep an extra footman at Oxford simply to clean it').

In reply Percival voiced his faith that Cliftonians would grow up with a vocation of service to their fellow men, coupled with the realisation that they were not born to live selfish or sensual lives. Whatever the occasion, his message was always 'duty, not pleasure'.

A supper in Big School followed in the evening. Five hundred boys and eighty Old Cliftonians sat down to the meal, and the gallery was afterwards packed with the rest of the school and visitors who came to hear the speeches, toasts and songs. A tribute from the local Member of Parliament included the remark that Bristol was now sometimes known as the place where one got off the train for Clifton College. When Percival rose to respond he was 'greeted with the wildest enthusiasm. Thunders of applause and tornadoes of cheering rent the air.'[18]

On the next day the departing hero, while preaching his farewell sermon in chapel, broke one of his own rules by indulging for once in the 'bad form' of boasting:

Today we may say without fear of contradiction (and why should the false pride that apes humility prevent us from saying it and drawing our lesson from it?) that there are few schools more widely or more favourably known throughout our kingdom and its dependencies; that there are few, if any, that possess a fuller, more varied, more active, and, let us thank God for it, purer life. Had our age been three hundred instead of sixteen years, I do not know that for all essential and highest purposes it would have been very different with us . . . Do I speak as if I claimed for us something more than an ordinary place among schools? I certainly feel we may fairly claim it.[19]

With that epitaph the creator left Clifton for his new, less onerous life in Oxford. He was only forty-four. Ahead stretched nearly forty more years of active, working life. But this was the peak of his success and popularity.

It was to be *au revoir*; definitely not *adieu*. The following January, as soon as a vacancy occurred, he was elected a member of the Council, and to the end of his long life he would return to the school, his first and dearest love, again and again and again.

In death he lies there still.

CHAPTER 15

Ex-Headmaster

He had left but not left. At Clifton the ex-headmaster was ever-present as a brooding spirit and made constant reappearances in person at Council meetings and other functions. In arranging for James Wilson's appointment as his successor he had intended to ensure continuity for his creation and was making certain of it.

He was not disappointed. Wilson greatly admired Percival. When they were assistant masters together at Rugby, he was the senior, although two years younger, and his opinion had been sought about the suitability of Percival's appointment to Clifton. In the course of his tribute to the school's founder at the Jubilee Dinner in 1912 he recollected how he had commented on Percival's youth at that time.

> That was a mistake. He never was young, and none of you will live to see him old. We knew him then as a man of great latent force, very reserved, of white-hot moral enthusiasm, wide intellectual outlook, great originality and self-reliance, immense industry, and the power of exacting it from others. But none of us could then foresee his capacity for creating, his daring but wise finance, his insight into men, and, above all, his new ideals for a School. It was a new ideal he set before this College, not only of simplicity, seriousness, modesty and industry, but of devotion to public service. He saw visions which we did not see.[1]

It was Wilson who reported Frederick Temple's assessment of Percival as the greatest educational force since Arnold, and who himself predicted that Percival's name would live beside Arnold's in history.[2] He did not believe that Percival's doctrine of self-denial was spiritually or intellectually repressive. The great man's ideals as interpreted and endorsed by his successor were Freedom and Responsibility – personal freedom fired by a sense of responsibility to country, humanity and God.

On arrival at Clifton Wilson inevitably found Percival a hard act to follow. Rigorously high standards had to be maintained despite the parlous state of the school's finances, which showed more signs of daring than wisdom. So it was that his own eleven-year tenure under the watchful eye of his predecessor became a period of consolidation. He brought the peace and calm which follows the passing of a hurricane.

Although like-minded, the two headmasters were very different in temperament. The sternness and melancholy of Percival's ascetic personality had given the impression that he was for ever striving against the wickedness of boys ('tainted as our nature is with the infection of Sin').[3] In this, if more hopeful about the outcome of the strife, he might have been seen as Arnold's heir. Wilson, on the other hand, was 'convinced of the essential goodness of heart of mankind – including boys'.[4]

Percival rarely displayed emotion. Kindness lay hidden in his heart beneath layers of shyness and outward severity, while Wilson's kindheartedness was to be seen on his face and sometimes ran out of control. It was unthinkable that anyone outside his family should ever see Percival weep, but the misery of a boy or even a particularly affecting passage in the New Testament could reduce Wilson to tears in public.

What 'astonished and uplifted' him when newly arrived was 'the magnificent and helpful spirit of masters and boys', which he contrasted with his experience at Rugby after Temple's departure. 'I cannot exaggerate this,' he wrote. 'It was a splendid staff of masters some of whom were of quite exceptional ability. This devotion of masters and boys to the school [was] the creation of Percival's personality.'[5] Such indeed was the loyalty of the staff that, when Wilson himself left, nearly all the housemasters and other senior masters whom he had inherited from Percival were still in place.

The new headmaster tackled the crisis over finances and facilities head-on by energetic fund-raising to add more buildings and buy more land. The money came in the form of donations from masters, boys and friends of the school, but above all, in accordance with the precedent established by Percival, from the headmaster himself. The Wilson Tower is his monument.

As Percival had foreseen in promoting his appointment, Wilson

broadened an already liberal education with an expansion of the
science curriculum. He also took holy orders during his first term
(later becoming Canon Wilson) and rescued the school mission in
Bristol. In his sermons he emulated Percival in efforts to lift the
soul of the school 'above the heavy mists of indifference, sloth and
self-complacency' and in a determination 'to awaken every one of
the young souls before him to their possibilities as children of
God'.[6] From the pulpit too, and better qualified for this than
Percival, he argued the case for reconciling the recent findings of
science with Christian faith.

In Wilson Percival had once more made an unerring choice, and
when his successor resigned in 1890 to become Archdeacon of
Manchester he was again poised for masterminding a new appointment from the vantage point of a seat on the Council. Herbert
Warren, intellectually his most distinguished pupil, was pressed to
accept the vacant post, but could not be prised out of the President's
lodgings at Magdalen. The Rev. H. A. James, Principal of Cheltenham and a future headmaster of Rugby, was the next choice, but
he withdrew his acceptance under pressure from Cheltenham.

The name of George Wollaston, the housemaster of North Town,
was then proposed. Like Wilson a religious scientist, he was the
master who had so impressed the young Henry Newbolt. The post
was offered to him, but he refused it in spite of strong pressure,
exerted most especially by Percival.[7] The appointment went instead
to the Rev. M. G. Glazebrook, High Master of Manchester
Grammar School, who was said to be the first (or second) Englishman to clear six feet in a high jump.[8]

Glazebrook was able but disliked and under him numbers began
to fall for the first time. Four years after he took office Percival
became Chairman of the Council, an appointment which he held
from February 1895 until December 1917, thus keeping Clifton
firmly in his grip to within a year of his death.

With morale as well as numbers sagging, Glazebrook twice
offered to resign, only to have the offer refused by the Council. As
a matter of principle Percival did not believe in headmasters
subjecting themselves to governing bodies, but he did require them
(at Clifton) to respect the school's (that is, his own) traditions.
Glazebrook therefore stayed but was frustrated when he proposed
to make what he considered necessary changes. The school suffered
accordingly, and not until he had resigned for the third and final
time did numbers begin to rise again.

Glazebrook had been an outsider, but the Rev. A. A. David, the next incumbent, appointed in 1905, was once more Percival's man and entirely to his satisfaction. David was an Oxford Double First who had taught at Rugby and become a Fellow and Dean of Percival's old college, Queen's. The headmaster who had appointed him to Rugby was none other than Percival himself. Unfortunately, David's talents were too much in demand, and after only four years he returned to Rugby as headmaster. While there, he refused three offers of bishoprics before accepting a fourth.

There were five candidates to succeed him at Clifton. One of them was, even more than David, a man after Percival's heart. This was his godson and former pupil at Rugby, William Temple, who was another Fellow of Queen's and the son of Percival's own mentor at Rugby. Temple was an early socialist who made no secret of his belief that the public schools contributed towards the perpetuation of class divisions, and that this was something he hoped to change. Later he was to write critically of the public schools' responsibility for 'a cleavage in the educational and social life of the country'.[9]

This point of view no doubt explains a resolution, proposed at a Council meeting held to consider the appointment, that his name be excluded from the list. An amendment to consider all five candidates, supported by Percival from the chair, was defeated by eight votes to six, and the resolution was then passed by eight votes to five.[10]

This was thought to be the first time that Percival had failed to get his way on the Council since his setback over reaching an accommodation with the Endowed Schools Commission, and the reason was the same: the preservation of class distinction. It came as some consolation that the successful candidate was a former pupil: Dr J. E. King, Headmaster of Bedford Grammar School and a former High Master of Manchester Grammar School. He was an Old Cliftonian who had begun his career by returning, briefly, to teach at the school.

William Temple's appointment would have been an interesting one. He became headmaster of Repton instead; and there, in an isolated village instead of the neighbourhood of a great city, he was both unhappy and unsuccessful. He had wanted to follow in the footsteps of his godfather, whom he revered, and the disappointment rankled. Most of the teaching staff at Clifton had favoured his candidacy, or so he claimed. Wilson too had encouraged him and tempted him with talk of the 'multifarious' outside interests available at Clifton: he had only to walk down Park Street to be in the thick of them.[11] In a letter to his brother Temple hinted at a coup against Percival by the less radically-minded members of the Council: 'There are some odd things I will tell you one day about the Clifton election, but as I am not supposed to know I won't put them on paper now.'[12]

Many years later Temple joked with an acquaintance that he was still headmaster of Clifton, because he had been informed of his appointment and never notified that it had not been confirmed. It would not be hard to guess the name of his informant. Percival was evidently still taking it for granted that his writ would run. But, in his mid-seventies in 1910, he had lost the power to force his will upon recalcitrant majorities.

Temple's veneration for his godfather found expression in his *Life of Bishop Percival* written soon after Percival's death. Meanwhile, with the succession at Clifton denied him and Repton unsympathetic, he proved himself a true apostle by pursuing Percivalian causes in Church affairs and voicing similarly outspoken demands for social reform.

At the summit of his career Temple reached Canterbury, as his father had done: nominated for the primacy by a reluctant Winston Churchill. As Bishop of Manchester (from 1921) and archbishop, first at York (from 1929) and then at Canterbury (from 1942 to 1944), he crusaded relentlessly against the evils of slums and profiteering. Since his death he has been hailed as the outstanding British religious leader of this century.[13] His was a career which might have been Percival's, and his godfather and former headmaster would have been proud of him.

Percival was in his eighty-fourth year when he resigned the chairmanship of the Council, and even then he remained a member until his death the following year. His involvement with the school during the long years since his resignation as headmaster had not been confined to the appointment of successors and other Council business; and there were further reasons for frequent visits to Bristol, where he found it convenient to establish a second home. As a Canon of Bristol Cathedral from 1882 to 1887 he was obliged to spend three months of each year in the city, and his presence was also required at University College meetings and meetings of the governors of two girls' schools.

At Clifton enlargement of the chapel claimed his attention. It had been built in the usual public school style: long and narrow. With great boldness Percival proposed to tear the fabric apart and recreate it to provide seven hundred seats. In 1908 he wrote to a meeting of Old Cliftonians to enlist their aid in funding a spacious design for which there was no precedent in a school chapel: 'I confess a strong desire to see a fine central lantern tower built with suitable transepts – a tower that would have an uplifting effect, and give the chapel a nobler character.'[14] Work began the following year and was finished two years later.

The hexagonal tower of wood sheathed in copper, modelled on that of Ely cathedral, then became the most striking feature of the wide vista of stone buildings on view across the expanse of the Close. Percival had set a crown on the spiritual centre of his foundation, and it was fitting that his full-size effigy should be placed high above the congregation on one of the six niches of the interior. He may be seen there today, in the colourfully painted company of five other heroes of learning: King Alfred, King Henry VI, William of Wykeham, Dean Colet and, most appropriately, Thomas Arnold.

In the same appeal to former pupils Percival urged the purchase of more land for playing fields and the endowment of more scholarships – not this time for the poor:

The importance of such scholarships arises from the fact that unless you have them all the cleverest boys from the upper and professional classes will be attracted to such schools as Eton, Winchester and Rugby, and the College will not be adequately represented in the life of the nation.[15]

His own benefactions to the school continued long after the end of his headmastership. When members of his family died, he chose to perpetuate their names through the foundation of prizes or scholarships. In 1899 he founded Louisa Percival prizes for knowledge of the New Testament in memory of his first wife. In 1910 he gave more than two thousand pounds to found three scholarships for day boys: the Louisa Percival, the Frederick Percival (in memory of perhaps the most loved of his sons) and the Robert Hardwicke Percival (in memory of the eldest). A further benefaction of a thousand pounds followed in 1915 to mark another family tragedy: the Arthur Percival Scholarship, founded in memory of the soldier son who was killed in action.

That the former martinet came to attract enduring affection as well as loyalty and respect was demonstrated at the emotional Jubilee reunion in 1912 when Wilson delivered his eulogy. At that ceremony he was presented by the President of Magdalen ('always your attached friend and pupil') with an address signed by a hundred and thirty-four of the Old Cliftonians who attended:

> We, the undersigned, who were boys at Clifton during your Headmastership and are now met to celebrate the Jubilee of the School, wish to say how glad we are that you have been spared to see after fifty years the great results of your work for the School, and to express to you our deep personal gratitude for all that it has meant to us to have been at Clifton under you.[16]

In 1908, while planning the enlargement of the school chapel above ground, he also turned his attention to the crypt in preparation for his own death; although in the event this was not to occur for a further ten years. The Local Government Board and the Board of Education had both to be consulted about the legality of a vault which would contain his body.

Because the chapel was not licensed for burials the responses were discouraging, but old age had not sapped the strength of his will and Percival rose to the challenge like a veteran campaigner. Arnold's body lay in the chapel at Rugby, and Percival was not to be deterred from having his similarly entombed at Clifton.

In 1910, after much correspondence, Counsel's opinion was sought. This confirmed that any such burial would appear to contravene the terms of the Public Health Act of 1875. At the same time, however, it opened two possible loopholes. The prohibition applied to places of public worship in urban areas. Was a school chapel to which the public were admitted private or public? And was Clifton's in an urban area? It stood among school buildings in a suburban oasis: surrounded by streets of houses, yet bordered by playing fields and with Bristol Zoo immediately on the other side of the nearest road and downland beyond that. There was scope for argument.

This continued for a further four years until officialdom was finally harassed into submission and surrendered.[17] Work on the vault then began. Percival had won his last battle. Until the Day of Judgment his body was to lie beneath the altar at the school which was his monument and legacy to posterity.

CHAPTER 16

Percival's Men

The privilege of a Clifton education must be paid for by service to the community. That was Percival's most potent message. Every Cliftonian left the school with insistence on public service and Christian duty ringing in his ears.

For combining the exercise of these virtues with a life of adventure a vast field of opportunity lay open to public schoolboys in the nineteenth and early twentieth centuries. Before them stretched the British Empire. Strange as it may seem today, Percival was thus cast in the role of a high priest of Imperialism. But if Liberal Imperialism sounds paradoxical to modern ears, to Percival and many of his contemporaries it was by no means a contradiction in terms.

Old Cliftonians abroad were designed by him to be missionaries. They were to go out into the world to bring to the under-privileged the blessings, not only of Christianity, but of its practical application in the form of enlightened government. It was a noble ideal, if sometimes impaired by arrogance, and they and their fellows from similarly-motivated schools justified the faith of their masters by proving themselves sound administrators and reliable keepers of law and order.

Good government was seen by Percival to be desirable both in itself and as a step towards the goal of self-government for which his disciples were to prepare those subject peoples. Yet, unhappily, few in the territories of the former British Empire have enjoyed a better life since the end of Pax Britannica and the withdrawal of administrations which were both efficient and free from corruption. Percival would no doubt have condemned it as 'bad form' to draw attention to that regrettable fact. Certainly he would have applauded independence unreservedly as the fulfilment of his former pupils' mission.

In his farewell sermon as headmaster an eloquent passage was devoted to a vision of the missionary spirit which he had implanted and now detected stirring the life of Cliftonians. Already they were answering its call both at home and overseas:

> in every quarter of the earth, on the Afghan hills it may be, or on the plains of India, in the plantations of Ceylon, or the sheep-walks of Australia, or the antipodean homes of New Zealand, or in the New World of the west, or close at home at their various posts of work and duty.[1]

The raw material for the high-minded Old Cliftonians whom he envisaged was drawn from the upper-middle-class stock of professional and military families and prosperous merchants and manufacturers. Among the well-known names of those who came in tribes were Bonham Carter, Fry, Wedgwood, Wills and Young-husband. Blue blood was neither sought nor attracted. A future Duke of Portland left after one term.[2] Because only Anglican forms of Christian worship were permitted, there were no Roman Catholics, but Bristol's Nonconformist families found nothing objectionable in the chapel services and were strongly represented.

Until the grant of the Royal Charter in 1877 shareholders had the right of nomination. This limited the school's power to select only the most able, but all were trained to be leaders and winners. Failure or shortcomings of any kind were unacceptable to the grim presiding mould-maker and those who sustained his tradition. To fall short of what was expected, whether in class or on the playing field, was morally indefensible. 'Our deepest and truest needs are above the second rate'[3] and 'The second rate in matters both moral and intellectual always go closely together'[4] were two of his dicta.

More than fifty of Percival's former pupils thus indoctrinated were knighted, but the majority will have led useful but probably humdrum lives as solicitors or vicars or teachers or managers in local communities in England. Among others 'close at home' and destined to rise to notable distinction within the academic world were some eminent fellow liberals. As well as Jack McTaggart at Cambridge and Herbert Warren at Oxford there were men of the intellectual calibre of Charles Firth, Charles Cannan and Arthur Quiller-Couch.

Sir Charles Firth held the Chair of Modern History at Oxford. Charles Cannan became Dean of Trinity College, Oxford and, as Secretary to the Delegates, head of the Oxford University Press, with responsibility for publications such as the Oxford English Dictionary and the Oxford Classical Texts.

Sir Arthur Quiller-Couch crowned a literary career as 'Q' with the editorship of the *Oxford Book of English Verse* and the Chair of English Literature at Cambridge. In his last year at Clifton he had been in competition with Henry Newbolt for the English verse prize, when T. E. Brown had adjudicated in his favour. For inclusion in the *Oxford Book of English Verse* he selected Newbolt's 'He Fell among Thieves', a poem about an ex-public schoolboy far from home facing death courageously.

But it was Sir Herbert Warren, above all, who represented the cream of Clifton scholarship. The son of a Bristol alderman, he came to the school in the last year of Percival's headmastership and went up to Oxford as a scholar at Balliol. There he took a First and won both the Hertford and Craven scholarships as well as the Gaisford Prize. In the tradition of Renaissance man, he was also a published poet and a champion fives-player.

President of Magdalen for forty-three years and Vice-Chancellor of the university for four, Warren was as distinguished a Liberal and staunch a churchman as his old headmaster could have wished for. The admiration was mutual. His own for Percival, who 'had the paramount gift of making us enjoy our lessons',[5] was frequently expressed and life-long. For many years they sat together on the school Council, and it was Warren who succeeded Percival in the Chair.

In the army, as a result of Percival's inauguration of a Military Side, Old Cliftonian officers proliferated. In the First World War they included seventy-five generals and two Field-Marshals. The latter were commanders of unusual intelligence. Haig's school career had been undistinguished, but he took a degree at Oxford before going on to Sandhurst. Birdwood became head of a Cambridge college: Master of Peterhouse.

One morning in December 1922, four years after Percival's death, four gentlemen met in a reserved first-class railway compartment at Paddington station. All of them had been educated at Clifton and all had become members of the Council. They were travelling to Bristol together to attend an important Council meeting.[6]

One of the four had succeeded the Earl of Ducie as College

President, and during the journey he sounded the views of the others on the business of the day: arrangements for the appointment of a new headmaster and a discussion of the merits of the candidates. On arrival at Clifton he conducted his part of the meeting with his usual courtesy and brisk decisiveness, so that they were able to catch an early fast train back to London in a relaxed mood for more general conversation.

The literary member of the quartet took the initiative. This was Henry Newbolt, the bard of Liberal Imperialism, whose verse had brought him fame and fortune and whose name would for ever be associated with the school through *Clifton Chapel* and that 'breathless hush in the Close'. *Admirals All*, his first volume of collected verse, published in 1897, had been so enthusiastically received by reviewers that some booksellers ordered five hundred copies at a time and twenty-one editions were sold out before the demand for it was exhausted.

Past fifty when the First World War broke out, Newbolt had regretted being too old for active service. He had, however, found war work as a civilian at the Admiralty, and he mentioned this now, with diffidence, as an excuse for turning the conversation to the President's experiences during the war.

The President spoke without bitterness of his troubles with mutinous *poilus* between August and November 1918. In the face of a German push Pétain had refused to make a flank attack and ordered a retreat instead. The President knew from what had happened the previous year that once the *poilus* left their trenches they would desert *en masse*. He had therefore persuaded Pétain's chief of staff to say '*Non, mon Général*' and refuse to transmit the order. He had then squared Foch and contrived to save Amiens with his own British forces unaided.

This was Field-Marshal Earl Haig, the victorious commander-in-chief of an army of two million men, the largest British fighting force ever assembled (before or since). Later, when the terrible British casualties on the Somme and at Passchendaele became more vividly remembered than his triumphant breach of the Hindenburg Line, his name was abused and ridiculed. But in the 1920s he was a national hero, accorded equal stature with Marlborough and Wellington.

Schooled in modesty at Clifton, Haig never boasted of his part in the Allied success. Percival had enjoined that Cliftonians should feel pride in their achievements but never show it, and Percival's rules were never to be broken. On that railway journey Newbolt, similarly schooled, noted approvingly that the President was modest to perfection. Listening to him, he thought, was like reading Caesar's *Gallic War*, in which the author never used the first person and only once mentioned himself. Yet it was plain that in the crisis precipitated by Pétain's defeatism it was the British commander-in-chief who had held the Allied line and saved the day.

Another of their travelling companions was then drawn into the discussion by Newbolt. J. H. Whitley came fresh from dealing with trouble of a different kind. As Speaker of the House of Commons, he had been hard pressed to bring to order some 'wild men' in the House during the most recent session of Parliament. He had succeeded in quietening them by delivering a lecture on constitutional law from the chair and persuading them in private afterwards of the proper function of Parliament in a Parliamentary Monarchy.

During the whole journey the fourth member of the party remained silent. He sat hunched in a corner, staring at the others thoughtfully through what Newbolt described as 'large coal-black eyes'. This was the man who many years ago had broken into a sprint at the finish of a seven-mile cross-country race to overtake Newbolt and beat him to the winning post in Clifton's Short Penpole. This was a man who had won fame while the other three were still unknown. Even before Newbolt spread the gospel of the spirit of Clifton from his desk, this was the man of action who had taken some of its precepts out into the world and practised them:

> To count the life of battle good,
> And dear the land that gave you birth,
> And dearer yet the brotherhood
> That binds the brave of all the earth.[7]

Colonel Sir Francis Younghusband, soldier, explorer, administrator and mystic, had indeed taken 'the road that only rumour knows' and honoured while he struck them down the foes that came with fearless eyes. In an unrivalled feat of endurance he had travelled through unknown territory in Manchuria and then from Peking to India across the Gobi desert and Chinese Turkestan. From there he had made his way over the Pamir mountains and the even higher Karakoram range down to the vale of Kashmir through a pass in the Himalayas never before attempted by man. Newbolt felt as humble in his presence as in Haig's:

Frank Younghusband [he had written] was one of those men
who do their stay-at-home friends the great service of fulfilling
their romantic and humane ideals for them ... he has kept the
heroic dream of service alive in a host of less adventurous
fellows. It was with no ordinary admiration that we who were at
school with him followed his steps in our fireside imaginings.[8]

And in verse, in an 'Epistle' to Younghusband, he wrote:

> The victories of our youth we count for gain
> Only because they steeled our hearts to pain,
> And hold no longer even Clifton great
> Save as she schooled our wills to serve the State.

ending ruefully:

> So passed our greeting, till we turned once more,
> I to my desk and you to rule Indore.

As a leading actor in the Great Game played out on the Roof of
the World between the empires of Britain, Russia and China,
Younghusband had followed his epic journey by taking a force of
British and Indian troops to the border of Tibet in a show of
strength to protect British interests. In defiance of orders from the
Commander-in-Chief in Simla (an apoplectic Lord Kitchener) and
to the fury of the Foreign Office in London, but with the tacit
connivance of the Viceroy (Lord Curzon), he crossed the border
and fought his way to Lhasa.

There he outmystified even the ruling council of lamas and concluded with them a treaty which opened Tibet to the world for the
first time. This enterprise was not appreciated by officialdom. In
dire disgrace with the British and Indian governments and the army
high command, he enjoyed the compensation of becoming a popular
idol and the best-selling author of his own hair-raising adventures.

Clifton had not only nurtured Younghusband's courage and
sharpened his wits. Like Roger Fry and Jack McTaggart, he had
escaped from the discipline of conformity and learned from Percival's personal example to think and act for himself. By the date of
the railway journey he had taken to consorting with philosophers,
exploring the world of the spirit for the meaning of life. Unlike
Rudyard Kipling, he believed that east and west could meet in a

universal religion, and he was to realise that belief by founding the
World Congress of Faiths.

Two passages from Younghusband's writings illustrate an interpretation of a Cliftonian's role of leadership in the world which
Percival could scarcely have visualised, even in his prophetic
reference to Afghan hills. Both refer to events which occurred on
the Roof of the World in 1889.

> We stood together for a long time round the fire, a curious group
> – rough, hard, determined-looking Kanjutis, in long loose wool-
> len robes, round cloth caps, long curls hanging down their ears,
> matchlocks slung over their backs, and swords bound to their
> sides; the timid, red-faced Kirghiz; the Tartar-featured Ladakhis;
> the patient, long-suffering Baltis; the sturdy, jovial little Gurkhas;
> the grave Pathan, and a solitary Englishman, met together here,
> in the heart of the Himalayas, in the robbers' stronghold.[9]

The next passage describes Younghusband's approach to the
Himalayan state of Hunza for the first formal meeting between the
Chief and a representative of the British Raj:

> Hearing that Safder Ali wished to receive me in state on my
> arrival at Gulmit, I put on my full-dress dragoon uniform, and
> the Gurkha escort also wore their full dress. We had to cross a
> nasty glacier at Pasu, and I did not find spurs and gold-laced
> overalls very appropriate costume for that kind of work. Then,
> as we neared Gulmit, a deputation was sent by the chief to say
> that I must not be frightened when I heard guns being fired, as
> they were intended for a salute, and not offensively.[10]

There were shades of difference between the imperialism of
Percival, Younghusband and Newbolt. It is most unlikely that
Percival approved of the foray into Tibet, but Younghusband once
wrote to Newbolt in words which could have been their headmaster's own:

> I have the greatest possible faith in our race and in its high
> destiny ... I have become convinced of nothing more strongly
> than that if we are to do any good in the world we must have
> religion. I have no faith in a man without religion; and it is just
> as necessary to a nation as to an individual.[11]

Imperialism in the spirit of religion was the doctrine Percival had taught. The army as a force for maintaining law and order had his full approval; militarism did not. There is much in Newbolt's effusions on which the headmaster must have frowned. The two men took opposing views on the Boer War.

Although a Liberal in politics, Newbolt was a conservative with a small 'c'. He was a romantic overcome with admiration for the manly virtues of the ancient world and medieval chivalry. To Newbolt patriotism, courage and loyalty to a brotherhood were virtues in themselves. Percival extolled them only as instruments in the service of God, and he did not see the fighting in South Africa in that light. In its aftermath he moved close to outright pacifism.

Newbolt was, in his own words, 'an Imperialist who was a little sensitive about the views and utterances of some of my fellow Imperialists'.[12] The chief offender was Kipling, who derided the linking of war and school games as an expression of immature romanticism.

Warfare in verse broke out between the two militant civilians when Kipling poured scorn on 'the flannelled fools at the wicket or the muddied oafs at the goals' and Newbolt returned fire in a satirical poem in which Kipling is depicted unflatteringly as 'the Indian drummer'.[13]

The criticism of Kipling's kind of imperialism made by Percival was more measured but no less severe. He detected in him little real sense of the brotherhood of man and denounced him at a Peace Conference in Boston in 1904 as an exponent of strife and violence, even brutality: 'His ideals are those of the barrack-room ... he voices the baser elements in human life. His influence is downwards.'[14]

When the railway journey in 1922 ended at Paddington, the four Cliftonians went their several ways, looking forward to meeting again on their next visit to the school to which they were bound inseparably for life. Such was the sense of loyalty instilled by Clifton's creator.

'Henceforth the School and you are one.'[15]

PART II

REFORM AND CONTROVERSY

CHAPTER 17

A University for Bristol

Nursing the new school at Clifton through its prodigious infancy would have absorbed the whole attention and all the nervous energy of a normal man, but Percival's capacity for hard work and reserves of energy seemed inexhaustible. Even extraneous activities like campaigning to reduce illegitimacy in Cumbria and lobbying for alterations to the requirements for university entrance were not enough to satisfy his appetite for Work and Duty. Education for all was his objective, and that meant the provision of schooling beyond primary school level for women and at all levels for the poor. 'All who were shut out from the fullest opportunities of mental growth'[1] commanded his sympathy, and he responded with decisive action.

In 1868, after six years at Clifton, he founded a local Association for the Promotion of the Higher Education of Women. This was followed a year later by an Association for the Promotion of Evening Classes to meet the needs of 'the clerks, shopmen, artisans and other young men in business'. A year after that he was appointed to the School Board charged under the 1870 Education Act with providing every boy and girl with primary education. His attention then focused on higher education. He had created a public school for Bristolians; now he would give them a university.[2]

A committee was formed in 1876 to bring into being what became University College, Bristol and developed, after thirty-three precarious years, into the University of Bristol. The first committee meeting was held in April. Formal incorporation followed in August, when the committee was re-formed as the Council. In October the college opened its doors to students. It was the first institution of higher education in the country to admit both men and women from the beginning: initially a hundred and seventy-three men and a hundred and sixty-four women, with women predominating in the day classes and men in the evening.

Percival did not himself take the chair at Council meetings (he had proposed Jowett for that honour), but he was active not only on the Council itself but also as a member of the Preliminary Arrangement Committee and the Local Executive Committee which supervised business in detail. Lewis Fry, the Liberal MP, who was the Council's first Vice-Chairman, 'was quite of the opinion that they owed the foundation of the College – as far as that statement could be made of a single person – to Dr Percival'.[3]

Important though this enterprise was in itself, to Percival the visionary it was also a springboard from which to revolutionise the whole nation's higher educational system. To this end he had earlier, in September 1872, addressed from Clifton an open letter to the governing bodies of all the Oxford colleges and published it as a pamphlet entitled *The Connection of the Universities and the Great Towns*.[4]

At that date there were just two modern universities in England, Durham (1832) and London (1836), and of the 'great towns' in the provinces only Manchester had even the embryo of one – in Owens College (1850).

Percival's letter began by stressing 'the sense of loss suffered by provincial city communities with no centre of higher education'. To many of the 'most influential workers and residents in our chief commercial and manufacturing communities' Oxford and Cambridge were, he believed, little more than geographical names, and he questioned whether 'this divorce between the great gathering-places of commercial population and the higher intellectual life is indeed necessary and inevitable, or whether it is not in the power of the universities to put an end to it'.

He asked the colleges to consider a remedy for this separation, arguing that 'any reform which might succeed in this would not only be the means of raising the general life of the commercial classes to a higher level of cultivation and taste, but would, at the same time, open a comparatively new sphere of usefulness to the universities themselves, and give them a fresh hold upon the mind of the nation'.

Anticipating the question 'Cannot the towns do it themselves?' he replied that, if left to their own devices, all they would provide would be technical or professional training. Only a direct connection with the old seats of learning would produce 'a liberal culture'.

That was what distinguished a university and what wealthy trading communities required 'above all things'.

Percival's solution envisaged what later became familiar as University Extension. He wanted Oxford and Cambridge to plant in the largest towns branches or faculties which would be an integral part of the parent university. Being Percival, he moved on from generalities to set out a practical scheme in detail. Well aware of the conservatism of the bodies he was addressing, he sought to persuade them with the assurance that this would involve no initial outlay, no hazardous expenditure, no draining of resources, no radical change, no interference with present work, nothing at all revolutionary or destructive ('unless the re-organisation of the sinecure non-resident Fellowships can be so designated').

Under the Percival plan two or more non-resident Fellowships at the wealthier colleges would be converted into professorships to be held at towns such as Birmingham, Bristol, Leeds and Liverpool. It would be a proviso that the town must make suitable buildings available without charge and contribute £200 a year for each professor to supplement his income from college and student fees. With this contribution a professor's total remuneration ought to be sufficient to attract men of the highest calibre who would be expected to live and teach in the town for at least six months of the year.

To ensure a full university curriculum, a complement of nine would be required, offering instruction in mathematics, chemistry, physics, physiology, Latin and Greek, ancient and modern history, law and political economy, moral and metaphysical philosophy, and logic. Students completing a course and passing the examinations would be entitled to a university degree.

The first function of these higher educational outstations would be to instruct young men who had left school at sixteen or above and were embarking on commercial, industrial or professional careers. Most lectures would therefore be held in the early morning or in the evening. The second function – 'and by no means the least recommendation of such a scheme as this' – would be to bring the essentials of a university course to young women so that they might acquire a good education, 'hitherto monopolised by their brothers'. This, so Percival asserted, was not only a matter of principle. It was also sound economics, because their inclusion would help to raise income from student fees to an acceptable level.

His proposals were coolly received. From Balliol Jowett reported that 'there was great jealousy about taking college funds out of Oxford',[5] and only two colleges responded positively to his specific appeal on behalf of Bristol as the pioneering project. These were Balliol itself and New College, both of which offered sponsorship and financial assistance (£300 a year, guaranteed for five years) on several conditions, all in line with Percival's thinking. The first insisted on a curriculum which included the humanities as well as science and technology. Another stipulated that these disciplines be made available to 'those of modest means' through evening classes. A third was the admission of women on equal terms with men.

A move was already afoot in Bristol to expand and transform the existing Bristol Medical School into a Technical College of Science, but pressure from Percival and the two Oxford colleges won the day for their more ambitious project.

In June 1874 a public meeting was held in the Victoria Rooms in Clifton to promote a 'College of Science and Literature for the West of England and South Wales'. In the chair was the President of the British Association, and Frederick Temple, at that time Bishop of Exeter (where he had made Percival an examining chaplain and prebendary of the cathedral), attended to lend support. The theme of his speech was the necessity of employing 'the good teacher', so that students might catch 'the infection of his example'. Percival and Jowett both spoke in favour of 'Literature', arguing that physicians and scientists would benefit from a broader culture and that the tedium of urban industrial life must be alleviated by the enlightenment of a liberal education.

They had two categories of student in mind: those who were too poor to afford to go away to a university, and those who were working and could study only in the evenings or early mornings. 'Was it not almost denying a man bread to deny him knowledge if he had a wish for it?' demanded Jowett.[6] If those aspiring to be students could not get to a university, then a university must be brought to them.

The University College which opened two years later was located at a short distance from Clifton College, conveniently under the ever-watchful eye of the headmaster. His influence could be detected when the economist, Alfred Marshall, who had taught at the school before moving to Cambridge, was appointed to be the first Principal. It also came to be seen most visibly when Charles Hansom, who had designed the school buildings, was chosen as the architect for the first new building. But Percival's most valuable contribution was the forging of the link with Oxford through the involvement of the like-minded Jowett, whose proclaimed mission was to 'inoculate England with Balliol'.

There being no entrance qualifications, academic standards were inevitably low, and the early years saw an almost impossible struggle against financial odds despite the generous support of the two Oxford colleges and a contribution of five hundred guineas a year from the Clothworkers Company in London. 'The good teacher' was hard to recruit and keep when staff salaries went unpaid for months. Perpetually on the brink of insolvency, the college's growth was slow and its impact on the community slight. To Bristolians 'the College' continued to mean the well-known school, not the struggling attempt at a university.

Never a quitter, Percival was one of those who saw this second infant of his through a series of crises. His leaving Clifton made no difference: he remained on the Council for more than thirty years despite a heavy load of commitments elsewhere. When other sources ran dry, he and Jowett gave money out of their own pockets to keep the college going.

The first President was Percival's friend, Gilbert Elliot, Dean of Bristol. When he died in 1891 and Jowett succeeded him, Percival took over the President's role of chairing the Annual General Meeting of Governors; and when Jowett died after only two years, Percival became President and retained that office for the remainder of the University College's life (1893–1909).

It was not an untroubled time: the financial problems were chronic. 'There were jealousies between Bristol and Clifton, and the College lacked general support,' wrote one of the earliest students in her reminiscences.[7] In 1887 Percival was moved to write to the *Bristol Evening News* in response to criticism. 'It is incumbent on the citizens,' he wrote, 'to support the council in their efforts by subscribing the money which is required ... and I hope they will forgive my adding in all frankness and sincerity that it will be a lasting blot upon their civic patriotism if they fail to do this.'[8]

There was more of the headmaster than the diplomat in this appeal. It did not inspire the citizens of Bristol to demonstrate civic patriotism, and the following year the college's Treasurer reported that it was an institution 'marching on the high road to bankruptcy'.[9]

In 1906, as President of the college, Percival was invited to

attend a public meeting in the Lord Mayor's parlour in Birmingham
to witness how that city was raising funds for its university.
Through the solicitation of individual subscriptions, culminating in
that meeting, a sum of £95,000 was raised. This put Bristol to
shame, and Percival wrote to a member of his Council to urge a
similar campaign soliciting subscriptions of £1000 or £500 ('not
less'). 'If we can only stir Bristol pride & patriotism to its depths,
general support should not fail us,' he added with unfailing
optimism.[10]

Financial stringency had not deterred him from advancing, at the
Annual General Meeting in 1901, the idea of an autonomous
institution, a Bristol and the West of England University, instead of
a college which had indeed progressed from issuing certificates to
awarding degrees, but only the degrees of another university:
London BAs since 1883. Eight years later his pleas and prayers
were answered. A munificent donation of £100,000 from H. O.
Wills, the tobacco magnate, enabled the college to qualify for a
Charter and become, triumphantly, the University of Bristol.

One of the professors present at the dinner held to celebrate the
announcement of this gift recalled the impression made by Percival
on that occasion:

> The speeches had been a little disappointing; they dwelt rather
> too much on the material side of things, and the spiritual note,
> as sometimes happens, was wanting. Then, almost at the close,
> Dr Percival was called on and everything seemed to be put right
> in a moment. I remember just where he stood and how he
> looked, and the sound of his voice – so unlike our West of
> England voices. His was a very noble and beautiful figure to look
> upon in his old age – an old man 'of a ruddy countenance',
> venerable, with the fine white hair which added so much to the
> natural dignity of his earlier days, drawing himself up to his full
> height and speaking to us, like a prophet, about our city, the
> 'lantern of the West', and his dream for it, and the sense that he
> had of a warfare accomplished, and a work that he left to us,
> who were present there that night, to carry on in the old spirit.[11]

During his speech in the Victoria Rooms thirty-five years earlier
Jowett had claimed that 'many' in Oxford and Cambridge desired
to extend the boundaries of the universities (though 'a minority'
might have been more precise), and he had written to Percival that

the college at Bristol should be 'the beginning of a movement which we must not allow to let drop'[12] – a movement both to enhance the quality of urban life through liberal studies and to provide adequate training in engineering or mining or whatever else the local economy required.

In this cause Percival served as a member of the Council of Firth College, which became the University of Sheffield, and his influence was widely felt when the government appointed him a founder member of the committee established to administer university grants.

The University of Bristol received its Charter on 25 May 1909. By 1910 England could boast six new universities and four university colleges, and this was only a beginning. During the twentieth century universities were to proliferate in response to public demand and need, just as the public schools had in the nineteenth. It is remarkable that one man should have contributed so much to two such important developments.

CHAPTER 18

Educational Reform

On the Relation of the Universities to School Education,[1] published in 1870, was another salvo in Percival's pamphlet cannonade against conservatism in higher education. This was an attack by a frustrated headmaster and social reformer on the kind of knowledge Oxford and Cambridge required from entrants. It accused the universities of failure by defect in demanding too little in some subjects and failure by excess in insisting on what was unnecessary.

Their requirement was for some acquaintance with a select number of Latin and Greek authors and a smattering of elementary mathematics; yet (so Percival argued) parents wanted their sons to be taught modern languages, English literature, history, geography and 'at least the elements of scientific knowledge and method, both natural and economic'. These, he insisted, should form an integral part of all higher education and an indispensable preliminary to university entrance. Within this framework there should be freedom of choice – and, specifically, no compulsory Greek.

His concern about this aspect of university education was partly that of a schoolmaster committed to the introduction of a modern curriculum: 'As things are at present, a school which endeavours to adapt itself to acknowledged modern wants, and mould its education in some degree in accordance with the circumstances of the time, does this at considerable risk of drifting away from its connection with the universities.'

But he was equally concerned on social grounds. He thought it lamentable that English boys destined to become captains of industry and commerce should attend schools which offered no prospect of university entrance. Experiencing 'no breath of academic influence', the business class who directed the life of the great provincial cities would become permanently separated from the national culture. Already there were indications of their inferiority in comparison with German and Swiss businessmen and even, within Britain, with the Scots: in Glasgow Scotland had a venerable and influential university within the country's leading commercial centre. It was, he declared, the duty of Oxford and Cambridge to reform their curricula in the national interest.

Government action on educational reform had already begun and improvement was on the national agenda, but it was encountering staunch resistance. A Royal Commission on the Universities set up in 1850 had resulted in some modest overhauling of the machinery, and this had been followed by official reviews of other institutions, most notably by a Royal Commission on the Poorer Classes (the Newcastle Commission) and a Royal Commission on the Public Schools (the Clarendon Commission).

While welcoming any move at all towards reform, Percival was critical of this piecemeal approach. He wanted the whole system investigated and reorganised as a whole. In his pamphlet he asked rhetorically: 'Has not the time come when isolated reforms and fragmentary legislation should be superseded by the action of some guiding and central hand?'

He proposed a post then unknown in Britain, a Minister of Education, 'whose authority shall extend over every grade of public instruction from our ancient Universities to the primary schools'. Prussia, he pointed out, had appointed Wilhelm von Humboldt to just such a post more than sixty years before. In retrospect it is not easy to appreciate how revolutionary such a sensible proposal was thought to be. Such an invitation to interference in the public interest horrified university academics and public school headmasters.

The Clarendon Commission, established in 1861 and reporting in 1864, was contemporary with Clifton's birth. It was a response to public disquiet, expressed most strongly in the columns of the influential *Cornhill Magazine, Quarterly Review* and *Edinburgh Review*. A disenchanted Old Etonian complained of neglect of pupils, waste, inefficiency and dishonesty at his old school, where the headmaster was an 'undistinguished nobody' paid £6000 a year. According to another correspondent: 'A boy may leave Eton with credit and be quite unable to pass the common tests of the Civil Service Examination.'[2]

The Commission's brief was 'to investigate the Revenues and

Management of Certain Colleges and Schools and the Studies and Instruction given there', and Eton and Rugby were among the nine schools examined. The seven commissioners sat for three painstaking years, studying hundreds of pages of evidence and interviewing a hundred and thirty witnesses. Every aspect of school life went under the microscope: the curriculum, methods of teaching, discipline, the place of religion, living conditions, food, fagging and the role of prefects. Most of the schools were indignant at this 'Ordeal by Commission', especially when it proposed external examiners to test how well the boys were being taught, in particular the average and below-average.

Rugby, understandably, raised no objection to outside examiners, but the headmaster of Charterhouse denounced the proposal as practically an examination of the masters rather than the boys, and the Commission retreated under pressure. The dogmas of the old guard were faithfully represented in the evidence of the headmaster of Winchester (George Moberly), who expatiated on the worthlessness of science as a means of education in schools.

The Commission's Report recommended the reform of statutes, governing bodies and curricula. It was accorded a generally favourable reception in the press but an unfavourable one not only among the public schools themselves but also in Parliament (which was composed of public school men). In the resultant controversy ten different Public School Bills were introduced and debated in Parliament between 1864 and 1873 and seven Public School Acts passed.

There was general agreement that the public schools were important national institutions. The arguments raged over whether or to what extent they should be made publicly accountable and whether they ought to become an integral part of a national educational system, as Percival believed. The outcome disappointed him and fellow liberal advocates of accountability, integration and a modernised curriculum. In summary: 'The Clarendon Commission and the Public School Acts conferred a separate, superior status on the public schools, reformed school government and finance, but left the schools' classical curriculum largely undisturbed for many a year.'[3]

But not every other public school headmaster was rooted in the past, and Percival was not the earliest of mid-century headmasters dedicated to change. That honour belongs to the Rev. Edward

Thring, who was appointed headmaster of Uppingham in 1853 at the age of thirty-two and became involved in the consultations preceding Clifton's beginning.

'There are many names in the last fifty years which deserve to be placed by the side of Arnold,' wrote Oscar Browning, the Eton schoolmaster and Cambridge don, in 1890.[4] He did not specify those he had in mind, but Thring stood close to Percival in innovative achievement and his name, like Percival's, would undoubtedly have been one. Indeed his Victorian biographer claimed that he was 'unquestionably the most original and striking figure in the schoolmaster world of his time in England'.[5] Certainly, in some respects, the careers of the two men ran on parallel lines.

Thring, too, was a radical and a Broad Churchman with a strong social conscience. He was the pioneer of the separate study and the dormitory with cubicles, the school gymnasium, the school concert hall and the school swimming bath. Like Percival, he was continually demanding funds for new buildings and equipment. Initially, Uppingham's growth was as remarkable as Clifton's. In twelve years from 1853 numbers rose from twenty-five to three hundred.

Arnold's Rugby had been a battlefield between good and evil. Thring had a more sympathetic understanding of boys and at Uppingham created a family atmosphere. Among Victorian schools, his was exceptionally 'user-friendly'. He recognised a boy's need for solitude and privacy, and insisted on small classes and small houses to ensure individual attention. At ten houses with thirty boys each – the maximum numbers which he believed could be known personally to housemasters and headmaster – he drew the line. So far from subscribing to Arnold's creed that it was a headmaster's duty to get rid of unpromising material, Thring held that the weaker brethren deserved special attention: the stupider the boy, the cleverer must be the master.

All this impressed the founding fathers of Clifton College. In his diary for 17 October 1860, two years before the opening of the school, Thring wrote: 'I have had much talk with Mr Warborough (from Bristol). I think they will found a really fine school on our system. He seems very sensible, liberal and earnest.'[6] 'Mr Warborough' was Henry Wasbrough, at whose house the first meeting of the founders had been held. He was a member of Clifton's Council from its formation in 1860 until his death in 1892.

The following week Thring recorded: 'Could not help feeling

bitterly, as I was writing to a man today about the proposed Bristol scheme, at the zeal and liberality there contrasted with everything mean, petty and obstructive here.'[7]

In November came the news 'that the Bristol people were going to adopt our system as the best of all the public schools'. Thring then arranged for a 'Clifton College document' which he had obtained to be circulated to his governing body to let them know that in Bristol £13,000 had already been spent on a site, and 'a fine schoolroom' was intended. This, he thought, would reassure some of his frugal governors and frighten others.[8]

What was to become Percival's Clifton enjoyed the advantage of the resources of a thriving city. Thring's Uppingham lay deep in Rutland countryside, and his self-imposed ceiling on numbers inevitably restricted revenue too. There was to be no further expansion equivalent to Clifton's continuing growth.

To what extent Thring's ante-natal influence on Clifton survived the arrival of Percival from Rugby can only be surmised. Despite having much in common, the two reformers did not always see eye to eye. In the matter of the curriculum Thring, like Arnold but a generation later, was no radical. He remained firmly committed to the supremacy of the classics.

In December 1869 he took the lead in launching the Head-master's Conference, an alliance formed to defend the independence of the public schools. Percival attended the second meeting, con-vened at Sherborne a year later. Elected to the committee, he became active in its counsels and eloquent at the annual confer-ences, serving as a committee member almost continuously from 1870 to 1878 while at Clifton and again from 1887 to 1894 while at Rugby. In 1875 he hosted and chaired the conference, when Clifton was the venue. Forty-eight headmasters assembled there, including Thring, and Percival duly acknowledged the honour paid to a school 'so very young'.[9]

At the meeting at Sherborne Percival had seized the opportunity to air his criticism of the universities' authorities at Oxford and Cambridge for not recognising the teaching of modern subjects at schools. He advocated a system of school-leaving exams to include those subjects. This gathered little support. But he also seconded a motion that entrance to the universities be secured, not by college and private examination, but by a public matriculation exam; and this was not only carried but (three years later) received a satisfac-tory response from the universities.

At subsequent meetings he urged the abolition of closed university scholarships and a low maximum figure for the open ones 'to prevent large scholarships being heaped on people who did not need the money',[10] and he also supported a motion that the emoluments of scholarships should not be enjoyed by the sons of wealthy men. They could enjoy the status, but the money should be diverted to those who had need of it.

Over the years he continued to speak frequently and forcefully on the teaching of science and modern languages. In 1888 he moved in vain that some knowledge of a modern language and elementary natural science be required for Oxford responsions and its Cambridge equivalent.

He became obsessive in making the case for school science to be part of the regular curriculum instead of an optional extra: 'Merely to introduce Natural Science for the benefit of boys who cannot do Latin and Greek verse seems to be only playing with the subject.'[11] At Clifton, he pointed out, science was compulsory in the lower forms of the Classical Side, and it was a subject which included botany and physical geography as well as chemistry and physics.

The Conference's reports reveal the vigour of Percival's debating style. They include such phrases as 'wholly opposed to', 'entirely opposed to' and 'distinctly of the ópinion that'. In 1876 the two autocrats clashed memorably when Percival spoke in favour of making Latin verse optional for university entrance and Thring met the challenge with an equally emphatic response, beginning with the words: 'I rise as an upholder of Latin Verse.'[12]

The breach continued. Two years later, when a motion supported by Percival to make Greek an optional subject for a degree appeared on the agenda, Thring demonstrated the strength of his opposition by resigning from the committee of the organisation which he had founded before the item was even discussed.

But Percival's concerns about education were by no means confined to the privileged worlds of public school and university. Twenty-five years after the Endowed Schools Commission of 1868 had exposed the chaotic state of secondary education and involved him in controversy at Clifton, he delivered a paper in Oxford on *The place of the First Grade School, Classical or Modern, in a complete system of Secondary Education.*[13]

The Commission had proposed three grades of school above the Elementary level, but this had come to be seen as over-differentiation and current policy was to dispense with the Third Grade. Under this system, said Percival, 'we may hope to see in every populous place the First Grade School educating from thirteen upwards all who are to stay at school till eighteen or thereabouts, the Second Grade School educating those who are to leave school at about fifteen or sixteen, and the Elementary School'.

He recommended that promising pupils should be transferred to First Grade Schools at an early age, and that these schools must not be regarded as a luxury or a monopoly of the few and rich. His experience of rural Warwickshire while at Rugby had turned his attention to country districts, where he noted that the number of First Grade Schools was being reduced. This was putting a First Grade School education 'practically beyond the reach of all but those who are sufficiently wealthy to send their children to a boarding-school'.

If a reduction in the number of country schools was unavoidable, he argued, then it was the Second Grade which should go; and if good teaching staff were in short supply at the senior level the railway network should be used 'to establish an order of peripatetic masters in certain subjects of study' along the lines of University Extension lecturers. He insisted that there should be First Grade Schools all over the country at intervals of not more than ten miles, 'so as to open a career to every boy of talent'. In this he had in mind the families of the poorer clergy and professional classes and those of farmers and tradesmen.

The second half of his address harked back to the well-worn theme that the higher education syllabus at schools was dictated by university examinations and schoolmasters were fettered. Happily, he thought that the universities were now generally more ready to meet necessary wants, although scholarships and exhibitions still demanded too early and too much specialisation. Never at a loss to prescribe specific remedies, he suggested four ways to improve relations between universities and First Grade Schools.

First, scholarships should not be confined to a single department of knowledge, but awarded for 'proficiency in such a combination of studies as is admitted to constitute a fairly complete system of liberal education'. Secondly, this whole range of subjects should, similarly, form part of the universities' entrance requirements. Thirdly, the universities must open their gates to those trained by the First Grade Schools in modern and scientific studies. These were virtually excluded by the requirement of 'a modicum of elementary Greek to which they still cling somewhat tenaciously'. The fourth proposal was a plea specifically on behalf of those preparing for a professional career or going into business or industry at eighteen or nineteen. To cater for them, there must be medical and engineering colleges attached to universities.

In the next decade, when he had left schoolmastering and become a bishop, Percival's interest in education became more and more focused on its relevance to the 'the condition of the people' and the needs of the working class.

In August 1903, towards the end of a University Extension summer meeting in Oxford, he presided over a conference attended by representatives of trade unions, co-operative societies and the universities. This voted into existence an Association to Promote the Higher Education of Working Men. It was largely Percival's initiative and persuasion, his scholarship, his persistence, 'his kindly influence', that welded these three elements together into what, a year later, became the Workers' Educational Association (the WEA), which still flourishes today. That acknowledgment of his contribution was made by Albert Mansbridge, the Association's first General Secretary, who wrote:

> The movement of the WEA thus owes to Dr Percival more than can easily be expressed. In my office as General Secretary, I was not only guided and counselled by him, but inspired; and through him our work was commended to the world at large.[14]

In January 1909 Percival prepared the outline of a scheme – part WEA and part University Extension – for the instruction of working-class youths at Durham University. This he 'ventured to commend . . . as one which deserves the sympathy and support of both the University Authorities and all leaders of industry and commerce in the four Northern Counties'.[15]

The prescribed course was to extend over two residential terms of ten weeks each and be rewarded with a certificate or diploma. Every student would be assigned to a tutor who would supervise his studies and his university life generally. The subjects to be taught would fall under four headings, the first two to be compulsory for all students: civic institutions and duties of citizenship; English literature and English history (constitutional, commercial, economic and industrial); natural science and practical mathematics; and laboratory and workshop instruction in the elements of chemistry, physics, mechanics and engineering (this last to be in Newcastle).

The maximum fee would be £2 a term, the additional cost to be met by subsidy, and there would have to be at least fifty bursaries worth £20 to £25 each. As ever, Percival's vision behind these proposals was down-to-earth but also up in the clouds – severely practical, yet idealistic:

> It is indeed hardly possible to over-estimate the good influences which would be diffused by such a stream of young men bringing from their University experience all their new knowledge, their new thoughts and new standards of opinion and duty into the various parts of the people's life or the power of such influences to raise the general levels of intelligence, taste and conduct among the working multitudes.
>
> Such a period of University residence, instruction, study and social intercourse amid the uplifting and ennobling associations of Durham and close to the great industrial activities of New-castle, under the influence of high-minded and inspiring teachers, and at the most receptive period of life, would be to the young working men or the country lads who would come for these Courses, nothing less than the opening of the door into a new world, a world of fresh and higher interests, higher purposes and views of life, and higher standards of personal conduct and duty, whilst the new intercourse thus enjoyed with men of other classes than their own, whether teachers or fellow Students, could not fail to clear their minds of class prejudices and misunderstand-ings, and so help to lessen that cleavage between the classes and the masses which so often proves an obstacle to mutual good will and the general welfare.
>
> And the time is very opportune for the development of Higher Education, as it is, I imagine, now generally recognised that we are entering on a new period of growing democratic influence in the life of the nation, and that the working classes are destined in the immediate future to secure a continually increasing share of influence and power in all public affairs.

Unfortunately, Percival's 'reasonable hope' that employers, trade unions, wealthy landowners, county and borough councils and

Percival at Oxford, aged 23: from a daguerrotype, June 1858.

Headmaster of Clifton, 1878.

Percival with assistant masters at Clifton, 1865.

Clifton College, *c.*1880.

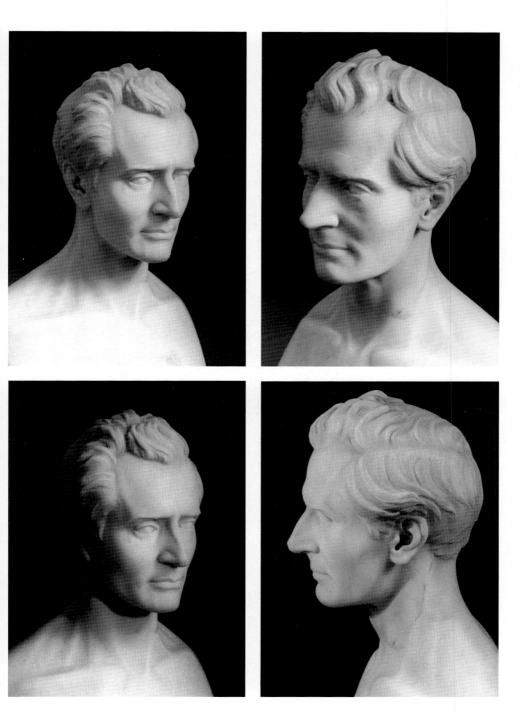

Bust of Percival by Thomas Woolner, R.A., 1880.

Cartoon on Trinity election: Percival crowing over Woods.

PROPOSED NEW QUADRANGLE
T.G.Jackson – Architect
Feb. t. 1880

Design for new quadrangle at Trinity, 1880.

Headmaster of Rugby: portrait by Sir Hubert von Herkomer, R.A.

Bishop of Hereford: portrait by H. Riviere, 1899.

At the gateway of the Bishop's Palace, Hereford.

Feeding the fantail pigeons.

Percival on his eightieth birthday with grandson Douglas.

Bishop of Hereford, aged eighty-two.

Plaque in Hereford Cathedral.

Percival Memorial Chapel at Clifton.

Clifton College from the Close, 1997.

other local bodies would fund the necessary bursaries was disappointed and the project was never realised.

Later the same year, in a sermon on undergraduate life preached at Cambridge, he foresaw a struggle between classes and masses, capitalist and labourer, the privileged few and the unprivileged many, which would mean a new order – industrial, economic, political and even religious. Were Cambridge undergraduates prepared for this new order?

The former public school headmaster had no doubt that the public schools were not:

> It must also, I fear, be admitted that our public school education ... is permeated by class influences, and is in many respects a survival which hardly fits us for the true appreciation of the life of the toiling multitudes, and their claim upon us.[16]

How then, he asked, should those educated at public schools and the ancient universities meet this new democracy with its passion for equality and its claim for a fair share of life's blessings? With an open mind (emancipated from class prejudices); with moral thoughtfulness (a soul 'stirred with social pity'); and with the conviction that no man should live for himself ('the life of selfish gain or selfish indulgence is not a true man's life'). Those three represented *the indispensable spirit of the good citizen*.

This homily serves to illustrate Percival's synoptic outlook, embracing education, society, morality and religion in a unity of thought and faith. It concluded resoundingly with a vision of the apocalypse threatened by educational and social divisions, which could be averted only through the operation of the indispensable spirit.

Percival's achievement and lack of achievement in the field of general education must be assessed in the light of the strength of the forces ranged against radical change during a period of intense struggle between reactionaries and reformers.

Educational reform has been judged to be the most necessary of all the reforms of the Victorian age and also the most bitterly contested. The ancient universities did not want to be modernised; the Church did not want secular education; employers did not want an educated work force; ratepayers did not want to pay an education levy.[17]

Percival was prominent among those who made the attempt to overcome these powerful special interests and convince the nation that education was the key to a better life for all, irrespective of class or gender.

CHAPTER 19

President of Trinity

With Percival's departure from Clifton in April 1879 at the age of forty-four his years of triumph came to an end. Yet it was not to be downhill all the way. Intermittent successes leavened years of general frustration and disappointment. In making his mark with grim resolve on a reluctant Oxford, an unhappy Rugby, a resentful Hereford and a hostile House of Lords he enjoyed some notable victories over what he considered the satanic forces of conservatism and inertia. Often thwarted but ever confident that he was acting in accordance with the will of God, he courted unpopularity, thrived on controversy and remained impervious to the slings and arrows of his many critics. As the *Spectator* observed, the persistence of his knight-errantry in good causes was as conspicuous as his scholarship and powers of organisation.[1]

After the strains of a pioneering headmastership, life as the head of an Oxford college was viewed by Percival's anxious family and friends as a sinecure. His own attitude was very different. Certainly he hoped to recover his health under less arduous conditions, but Oxford represented another stern challenge. It was a place crying out for reform.

The university appeared sunk in torpor and, as so often in its long and chequered history, seriously behind the times in all its ways. Out of touch with the modern industrial world, its back firmly turned on women and the poor, it was in urgent need of instruction in its duties and responsibilities to society. Percival saw England's most venerable seat of learning, his own alma mater, as a Sleeping Beauty to be awakened, not with a gentle kiss, but a severe slap. His first objective was to rouse the college which had summoned him to its aid; after that the whole university.

Trinity did not enjoy the eminence of its royally endowed Cambridge namesake, and in the realm of scholarship it lay in the shadow of its immediate neighbour, Balliol. 'Take anything you can get at Balliol. Better at Balliol with nothing than at Trinity with an Exhibition,' Frederick Temple advised his son, William.[2]

Founded on the ruined site of a dissolved Benedictine house during the reign of the Roman Catholic queen, Mary Tudor, Trinity had remained wedded to traditional ways. It strongly supported the royalist cause during the Civil Wars in the seventeenth century and was known for Jacobite sympathies during the early years of Hanoverian rule in the eighteenth. In numbers it was one of the smaller colleges and its endowment income was modest, but it enjoyed a good reputation and could boast of an exceptionally fine chapel and some distinguished alumni, among them two Prime Ministers: Chatham and North.

Friendly and easy-going, the college inspired an intense loyalty among its old members. Once a Trinity man, always a Trinity man. That loyalty, that aversion to change, did not work in the new President's favour. The forward-looking Percival was rightly seen as a disturbing intruder in the comfortable abode of *laudatores temporis acti*.

His election at Trinity was not only as unlikely as his appointment at Clifton, but as fortuitous. President Wayte, the affable outgoing incumbent, had resigned unexpectedly and mysteriously during the Long Vacation of 1878 (and, by an odd coincidence, retired to Clifton). More promising for Percival at that time was a vacancy for the Provostship of Queen's, his own college, where his election would have been wholly appropriate.

Jowett kept a sharp eye on the situation from the Master's Lodgings at Balliol, praying and plotting that one or other position would come the way of a fellow reformer. On 4 October, losing hope over Queen's, he wrote to Mrs Percival:

> From what I can learn I imagine that the Election at Queen's is a foregone conclusion though I have not heard this directly from any of the Fellows: meanwhile there is another Headship vacant in Oxford – Trinity – and a rumour has reached me that there may be a chance of Dr Percival being elected. I have written to those of the Fellows whom I know, to urge them that they could not do a better thing for the College and for the University. Do not be sanguine, but there is a chance.[3]

Jowett was right about Queen's. The Fellows had met the previous day and elected one of their own number, J. R. Magrath, who was to extinguish any rival's hopes for the future by occupying the Provost's Lodgings for the next fifty-two years.

At Trinity the dominant figure among the Fellows in college affairs was R. W. (Bob) Raper, later Bursar and Vice-President, whose caustic wit did not endear him to everyone. (One of his notices as Bursar ran: 'Gentlemen coming from homes where Bread-throwing at the dinner-table is habitual and finding a difficulty in conforming suddenly to the unfamiliar ways of a higher civilisation will be permitted to continue their domestic pastime, on payment of 5/- a throw, during their first year. After that the charge will be doubled.')[4]

A professed agnostic with a penchant for intrigue, Raper was viewed with suspicion by the more pious Fellows, in particular the future Anglo-Catholic bishop, Charles Gore. Either because he lacked the support to win the Presidency for himself or because he preferred to be the power behind the throne, Raper assumed the role of king-maker in the election, and it was he who first proposed Percival.

The leading internal candidate was the then Bursar, H. G. Woods. He was the obvious choice (and was to win the next Presidential election with Raper's support), but some of the younger Fellows believed that the college would benefit from an infusion of new blood. There were only nine electors, and opinion was almost evenly balanced among them. Raper, having floated Percival's name, appeared to have moved over to favouring Woods, and at the conclusion of a meeting in his rooms to thrash out the pros and cons of the rival candidates on the eve of the election, it seemed that Woods was assured of a narrow victory by five votes to four. To the astonishment of the others, however, Raper changed sides overnight, and in the solemn ceremony conducted in due form in the chapel the next morning (22 October) it was Percival who scraped home by the five votes to four.

Professor Robinson Ellis was the Fellow deputed to take the good news from Oxford to Clifton and obtain Percival's accept-ance. Although a Percival supporter, he had become nervous about the consequences of the unexpected election and seems to have been half-hoping for a refusal. 'I do not wonder at your surprise,' he commented on Percival's reaction to the offer, 'but, you see, we had such a very small field.' When Percival mentioned his wife it was the professor's turn to express surprise. 'Oh, but Percival,' he exclaimed, 'one of the recommendations was that you were not married.' Percival noted that he seemed to cheer up on learning that Mrs Percival was in poor health.[5]

Ellis's nervousness was fully justified. News of the election was greeted with outrage among the alumni. Never before, it was said, had Trinity, or indeed any other Oxford college, elected an outsider to be its head. Percival's election had created a precedent for what afterwards became commonplace throughout the university. The alumni appealed to the Visitor, the Bishop of Winchester, to reverse the Fellows' decision, but the bishop refused.

A printed protest was circulated. 'We, the undersigned Graduates of Trinity College,' it began, 'wish formally to express our deep regret that a majority of the Fellows have elected the Rev. John Percival, of Queen's College, to be President of our College.' The protest was, it was explained, not directed against Percival personally; but 'contrary to a wisely cherished tradition, never violated before, a gentleman wholly unconnected with the College has been made its President'.

Continuity had been broken, and the new President (so it was argued) would be an obstacle instead of a link between past and present members. The election was held to imply that no members of the college were fit to hold the office, and this was seen as an unmerited slight. The bestowal of the honour on someone who had done nothing for the college was said to be unfair to those who had devoted the best years of their life to it. It was lamented that widespread dissatisfaction and discord had been introduced into a hitherto united society by a 'mere majority of the electors, a large proportion of whom were very junior members of the University'. The guilty five had committed a 'deeply distasteful act'.[6]

This sensational event at Trinity became the talk of the town. A caricature was published depicting Percival as a cock perched on the wall of the college crowing over the defeated Woods, the one labelled 'DOUBLE FIRST CLASS 1st PRIZE', the other '1st CLASS HIGHLY COMMENDED'.

Displayed in the window of a printshop in Broad Street facing the gates of Trinity, this caught the eye of Percival's wife when she came up from Clifton with one of their sons to inspect the Lodgings. Amused, she went into the shop to buy a copy and was shown another caricature of Percival, which the small boy declared to be not nearly such a good likeness of 'father'. At this the shopkeeper became acutely embarrassed. ('I assure you, madam, I had no idea you were connected with the new President.')[7]

Facing protests was a familiar feature of Percival's life, and the alumni's ran like the merest trickle of water off the broadest of ducks' backs. He was not responsible for his election, was not to be deflected from his purpose, and his supporters rallied round. Charles Gore welcomed his presence as 'very bracing',[8] and others outside the college recognised that Trinity, languishing in a relatively undistinguished phase of its existence, was fortunate in acquiring what a historian of the university was to describe as a 'President of power and distinction'.[9]

Although still headmaster of Clifton until released the following Easter and therefore unable to take up permanent residence, he set to work immediately, coming to Oxford to chair every meeting of the governing body from the date of his election. At a meeting on 19 November it was agreed to prepare for the move of his numerous family and household by annexing rooms above the library to the President's Lodgings.

On 25 March 1879, under his chairmanship, the governing body gave orders for a congratulatory telegram to be sent to Dr Newman on the occasion of his being raised to the rank of Cardinal.[10] John Henry Newman was a Trinity man, and in the eyes of his college that virtue outweighed the sin of apostasy to Rome. Two years earlier he had been elected to the college's very first Honorary Fellowship. Within the Christian communion he and Percival stood poles apart, but Percival was never a bigot. He followed the telegram by commissioning a bust of Newman and making a present of it to the college in a personal gesture of appreciation.

The Cardinal was invited to the next college Gaudy and stayed with the Percivals for several days, when they hosted a party for him which other liberals such as Mark Pattison, the Rector of Lincoln, declined to attend. Later, on a visit to Rome, Percival bought a painting of Newman's cardinalatial church as a gift for him, and this was noticed hanging on the wall at the foot of the Cardinal's bed when he lay dying.

When a freshman at Trinity in 1817 Newman had written proudly to his mother: 'If anyone wishes to study much, I believe that there can be no college that will encourage him more than Trinity. It is wishing to rise in the University and is rising fast ...

In discipline it has become one of the strictest colleges.'[11] That was
the situation which Percival sought to restore. He knew that a fall
in standards over the intervening years was the reason why a
majority of the Fellows had opted for an austere disciplinarian
from outside their own ranks.

Whatever his sphere of activity, Percival remained, unalterably,
a headmaster. At Trinity he achieved instant unpopularity by
treating the Fellows as though they were assistant masters and the
undergraduates as though they were schoolboys. Accustomed to
his word being treated as law, it was hard for him to come to terms
with being *primus inter pares*, unable to issue orders at whim and
without the power to hire and fire teaching staff. With self-assured
undergraduates he never developed the degree of rapport which he
had established with younger pupils whose characters were less
developed and more open to guidance. To win acceptance, he
needed to accommodate himself to different conditions, but neither
by nature nor by conviction was he accommodating.

Division over the election had left 'a very explosive Common
Room', and his dictatorial methods did nothing to defuse hostility.
Soon the draft of a proposed new statute was circulating. Its
purpose was to stamp out autocracy by bringing all college officers
under the complete control of the Fellowship as a body: supremacy
in all matters to lie with the College Meeting, not the President.
The crucial clause was bluntly explicit: 'The President shall in the
performance of his duties be subject to the direction of the College;
and anything done by him may . . . be modified, countermanded,
or reversed by the College.'[12]

This elicited a memorandum from an indignant Percival setting
out the reasons why he felt unable to concur. In it he warned that
constant interference with the President in the exercise of his duties
would in practice prove either inoperative or intolerable. 'I would
submit that every officer should be considered to be free from
interference as to the mere *modus operandi* in the discharge of his
duties,' he wrote and continued:

> My experience hitherto has been that the only certain way of
> combining the conditions of a harmonious life with real vigour
> and efficiency in administration is to define duties with the
> utmost clearness, and then to repose entire confidence in individ-
> uals as to their mode of performing their duties, judging them by
> the results of their work.[13]

In taking this line Percival was speaking for all chief executives, drawing a distinction between policy and execution, demanding trust, and advocating vigorous leadership rather than the weak administration of government by committee. But it may have been the parting shot in his memorandum, hinting at the likelihood of further adverse publicity, which carried the day: 'I may, I trust, be permitted to add as another argument against the adoption of the provision to which I object that I have not seen any such provision in the statutes of any other College.'

Although the opposition had been forced into retreat on this major issue, Percival remained under no illusion about the magnitude of the undertaking facing him without the full support of his colleagues. In commitment to learning and clean living, Oxford was no Clifton. Throughout the university, in senior and junior common rooms alike, hard work was not in fashion. According to one historian, the dons 'were idle; they were dissipated; they reflected those odious class distinctions by which merit is oppressed and insolence fostered; their studies were narrow, their teaching ineffective'.[14]

As for the undergraduates, their routine was set out in some detail in a guide for prospective parents published in the same year as Percival's election. A typical day would start with a breakfast party for 'six or eight congenial spirits', followed by 'the inevitable pipe or cigar, and the perusal and discussion of the daily papers'. Three hours of reading between ten and one might be interrupted by lectures or a visit to a friend or a saunter along the High.

Reading beyond one o'clock was considered inadvisable on medical grounds: it placed too much strain on the brain. The afternoon was therefore devoted to healthy exercise, usually rowing. This left an hour before dinner at six for reading or shopping or billiards or killing time at the Union.

After dinner relaxation was thought to be essential: to begin reading immediately afterwards was not only useless but positively harmful. Some period of study was usual later, between nine and half past ten, but that was liable to be abandoned in favour of a wine club or a smoking party or games of cards or pool: 'It is impossible to imagine the many calls which a man has on his time after dinner.'[15]

Percival could hope for no influence on such habits outside his own college, but within it he had won a relatively free hand over the undergraduates and was armed with one despotic power possessed by the heads of all colleges: the ultimate sanction of rustication. He could send down idle or immoral undergraduates for a term, for a year or for ever.

He at once began to impose the same standards of hard work, discipline, morality and unostentatious living which he had ordained for Cliftonians. Regular attendance at chapel was enforced. Blank forms appeared on a college notice-board for undergraduates to take and fill up with an account of the hours they devoted each day to reading. There were personal interrogations by the President about hours of study and the number of lectures attended. Smoking was frowned upon; and Raper felt obliged to call on the college wine merchant to apologise for a sharp reduction in the level of consumption.

One undergraduate was fined a sovereign for wearing a straw hat in the college garden on a Sunday. Arthur Quiller-Couch, who had come up to Trinity from Clifton, incurred a rebuke for sartorial extravagance. Eyeing what he was wearing one day, the President exclaimed: 'What! *Another* new pair of trarsers, Mr Couch!'[16]

Percival shared with Arnold an inability to focus except on black and white, and the focus was mostly on the black. Percival's 'white' students at Trinity were hard-working, God-fearing, non-smoking, teetotal scholars, but these paragons appeared to him largely outnumbered by lewd and cynical 'blacks' who gambled, hunted and frequented public houses.

In fact, in common with those at other colleges, Trinity's seventy or so undergraduates were predominantly 'grey'. Quiller-Couch, for example, was a brilliant and diligent scholar, but he was also a wine-bibbing member of the exclusive and expensive Trinity Claret Club which dined luxuriously in claret-coloured dinner jackets with brass buttons. Like many others, he fell into debt to Oxford tradesmen, and it was to pay these debts that he first turned to novel-writing.

That was during an Easter reading and climbing party in Cumberland, composed of Trinity undergraduates and dons. Among the former was another writer-to-be, A. E. W. Mason, who watched with fascination while Quiller-Couch wrote *Dead Man's Rock*. Among the latter was Bob Raper, who launched Quiller-Couch's literary career by finding a publisher for the novel. Trinity, wrote 'Q' later, was 'above all things a community of friends'[17] – one feature of the college which Percival, with his belief in the virtues of communal life, must have applauded.

Another Cliftonian became a member of these annual college reading parties. This was Charles Cannan, a young don whom Percival, always on the prowl for talent, persuaded, in 1884, to exchange a Fellowship at Corpus for one at Trinity. Cannan was a classicist praised by Sir Herbert Warren as 'an intellectual force'. He became a pillar of Trinity as well as the university's publisher.

A further connection with Clifton was made when Percival arranged for Herbert Blakiston, the outstanding Trinity scholar of his day, to spend a year at the school as an assistant master. Blakiston then returned to a Fellowship at the college and in due course succeeded Woods in the Presidency.

In Charles Gore's opinion, Percival left a permanent mark on Trinity in being 'largely responsible for its rapid growth and intellectual success'. But Gore also hinted at the ill-feeling which his regime aroused: 'We felt that a strong righteous will was expressing itself amongst us with profound astonishment at our being content to be such fools as we were.'[18]

Archibald Robertson, another Fellow who became a bishop, concurred in the judgment that the whole college was the better for the headship of a man of 'lofty character and ideals', but he too recorded some reservation about Percival's methods.

On a visit to Clifton he took a walk on the downs with a friend who taught at the school (A. M. Worthington, one of the science masters who became a Fellow of the Royal Society), and the conversation turned naturally to Percival. 'Do you like his sermons?' Worthington inquired, adding: 'I can't bear them.' Robertson asked the reason. 'I dislike being kicked' was Worthington's reply; to which Robertson responded: 'No doubt you do, but he's always trying to kick you upstairs and that is something.'[19] Kicking other people upstairs was an apt metaphor for Percival's purpose all through his life.

The most substantial achievement of his nine-year Presidency is still visible today. With the erection of New Buildings (1883–85) and new President's Lodgings (1885–87) the size and face of Trinity were transformed. The number of undergraduate rooms was almost doubled, and the appearance of the college greatly improved. It was a major enterprise, and one which Percival was well qualified to supervise. Trinity was fortunate to have, at a rare moment of opportunity, a President already experienced in the funding and erection of new buildings – a notoriously daunting task in Oxford.

The opportunity arose with the end of a long lease on Kettell
Hall and its garden from Oriel College. Restriction on the development of this property had confined the approach to Trinity to a
narrow strip between high walls, leading to the entrance under the
chapel arch. Negotiations for the purchase of the Kettell freehold
were conducted by the President and the Bursar (Woods) and
approved at a College Meeting in February 1880.

T. G. Jackson, the Fellow of Wadham responsible for the
Examination Schools and a wide variety of other university and
college buildings, was employed as architect. The variety sprang
from his commitment to a policy of 'judicious eclecticism'[20] (named
Anglo-Jackson by John Betjeman). What met with Trinity's
approval was 'a free development of Jacobean'.[21]

Jackson's gabled Victorian version of the Jacobean style at
Trinity may not agree with modern taste, but it compares favour-
ably with the architecture of Balliol's frontage on Broad Street and
New College's on Holywell Street, built during the same period.

His original conception envisaged the demolition of the cottages
which interrupt the view of his New Quadrangle from Broad Street
and their replacement by a 'charming gateway'.[22] But this, the
centrepiece of his design, would have entailed the loss of some
accommodation and was not approved.

The cost of the new buildings was £22,000. Five of the Fellows
subscribed £200 each towards this, the others smaller amounts.
Percival gave £1000 – and lost the use of his house, garden, orchard
and stables during the building work.

Percival's rule while playing the headmaster at Trinity was
certainly 'irksome'.[23] But, as always when he became involved with
an institution, it was, like painful dentistry, all for the good in the
end. Oxford is vastly experienced in resistance to change, and to
what extent his reforms and influence were more than temporary is
debatable. Percival's own assessment, agreeing with Bishop Gore's,
seems correct.

My critics . . . are fond of speaking of my Presidency at Trinity
as a comparative failure, but . . . I sometimes think when I
remember what the life and conditions of the College were in
1878, and what they were in 1887, that I helped in some really
good and successful work.[24]

CHAPTER 20

Frustration at Oxford

Percival was dismayed not only at the idleness but also by the individualism, the lack of discipline, the uncharted freedom, of college and university life at Oxford. He deplored the absence of the moral purpose and sense of social duty which he believed 'the best of our public schools' nurtured. Unlike those worthy institutions, Oxford was flinging young lives into the world without moral instruction or social guidance to protect them from all the dangers he abhorred: the temptations of wealth and materialism, luxury and self-indulgence.

In tackling an undergraduate lifestyle devoted to amusement and 'the glorification of idleness'[1] with no greater authority than the headship of one college he inevitably suffered frustration. But at least he succeeded in doing what he could for the spiritual life of the university.

As at Clifton, the launch-pad of his moral crusade was the pulpit. He inaugurated a course of Sunday evening sermons for undergraduates in St Mary's, the university church, and these became an institution. Although not preaching every week himself, with the vicar's agreement he selected the other preachers and took responsibility for all the arrangements.

His own university and college sermons, like those which he preached in the chapels at Clifton and Trinity, were unadorned, down-to-earth moral exhortations, never touching on the abstractions of dogma. That this style of preaching could sometimes be a stirring performance going straight to the hearts of the impressionable is vouched for in the reminiscences of a former undergraduate at Trinity.

I shall never forget those evenings. The Chapel lighted up in its primitive way by rows of candles fixed on to the pews – the splendid carvings of Grinling Gibbons just catching the gleam here and there – and Percival standing in the President's stall at the west end, his head slightly on one side, his fine, clean-cut features showing up against the candle-light with a strange chiaroscuro effect, his voice retaining still the accent of his northern home as he upheld the sanctities of life and poured vials of scorn on all that was 'low and degraded'.[2]

From outside his own college Percival received little support. 'There was,' wrote Sir Herbert Warren, 'a prejudice at Oxford against schoolmaster Heads of Houses', and Percival's headmasterly eagerness to reform not only Trinity but the whole university was noted with disapproval. 'That's a very ambitious young man,' remarked Dr Bulley, the elderly President of Magdalen, after listening to one of his university sermons.[3] This was not intended as a compliment. Ambition was not considered a virtue in Oxford. Nor was undue activity. 'No one who has a great deal of energy will long be popular in Oxford' was Jowett's warning.[4]

Another charge levelled against Percival was lack of sympathy for scholarship: a criticism which contained an element of truth. He was an educator, not a true academic. Settling '*Hoti*'s business' and the 'enclitic *De*' was all very well,[5] but the purpose of Oxford, as he saw it, was to produce men who would serve the nation. One professor went so far as to pronounce that there were 'no such enemies of learning as the educationalists', and he made no secret of the fact that in saying this he was referring to the schoolmaster who had so mistakenly been elected President of Trinity.[6]

The novelist, Mrs Humphry Ward, who knew Percival well at Oxford, put words into the mouth of her eponymous hero, Robert Elsmere, which could have been taken directly from him: 'To me knowledge has always been valuable first and foremost for its bearing on life.'[7] Elsmere was a nonconforming clergyman who 'felt himself a tool in the Great Workman's hand'.[8]

An educator and a reformer. Those were Percival's twin roles in life, and he threw his considerable weight behind the university reform movement which had been agitating Oxford for half a century and proceeding at a snail's pace in the face of determined opposition. The battle lines were drawn between medievalists and modernists. On the one side stood Tory, High Church traditionalists staunch in defence of the status quo; on the other, the liberals and Latitudinarians among whom Percival numbered himself.

The reformers had won a hard-fought victory with the University Reform Acts of 1854 and 1856. Now, in the 1870s, a new phase had begun with a lengthy investigation by a fact-finding Commission appointed by the government. This resulted in another Act in 1877, which led in turn to the appointment of another Commission, whose brief was to direct teaching and endowments towards meeting current educational needs.

The nub of the problem, as always, was the independence of the colleges and their reluctance either to agree with each other or to divert funds from maintaining the comforts and privileges of college life. The financial hold of the self-perpetuating college oligarchies over university affairs was starkly revealed in the figures uncovered. Land was the main source of income. The colleges owned 184,764 acres; the university 7,683.

The acknowledged leader of the reform party in the university was Percival's friend, Benjamin Jowett, who had narrowly failed to become Master of Balliol in 1854 but succeeded in the next election, held in 1870. He was a bachelor who took no part in politics outside the sphere of education, but in other respects there were significant parallels and connections between him and Percival besides their commitment to reform.

Both were achievers who had raised themselves by intellect and character from relatively humble backgrounds. (Jowett's was doubly shameful: his family was 'in trade' and his father's business as a furrier had ended in bankruptcy.) Both were clerics whose liberalism led to accusations of heresy. Both overstretched themselves and suffered from periodical bouts of ill-health. Both were naturally shy. But Jowett possessed an invaluable asset which Percival lacked – the gift of friendship. The Master gathered disciples who became allies. Percival, despite his charisma and the intense loyalty which he had inspired at Clifton, attracted no personal following. He was too forbidding and remained always a loner, shining by example.

Jowett had connections with Clifton preceding Percival's. He was a visitor at the home of the Symonds family in the year before the school opened,[9] when he doubtless offered some advice to Dr Symonds, who was one of the founding governors (and whose patient he was). Over the years he also paid visits to a cousin who lived in Canynge Square, a few steps from the school, and when there he sometimes dined at the headmaster's table. With their identity of interests, it is not surprising that he became a regular correspondent, viewing the school's progress with approval and keeping Percival abreast of university news. In Bristol the two men collaborated closely over a long period in supervising the conception, birth and infancy of the University College.

They were thus well acquainted when Percival arrived at Trinity after the passage of the 1877 Act. In the continuing fight for reform Jowett, well dug-in and battle-hardened, would inevitably be the commander-in-chief. He was the older man by fifteen years and was soon to become Vice-Chancellor (from 1882 to 1886). But in the push for victory he and his outnumbered forces must have welcomed the reinforcement of a fresh ally at a time when progress continued to be painfully slow and results under the provisions of the Act disappointing because nothing would induce the colleges to part with the income from their endowments.

In 1881 a family tragedy intensified the gloom of Percival's frustration. His youngest, most dearly loved and extremely clever son, Freddie, was killed in a riding accident on Portmeadow while still a schoolboy. It was a hard blow to bear, and Percival wrote a special prayer to comfort the bereaved family: '. . . humbly beseeching Thee so to bless us that remain that we may be enabled to live a pure and dutiful life with quiet minds and thankful hearts'.[10]

Even with God's help he took a long time to recover his spirits, as Jowett's letter of consolation, written the following year, suggests:

I sometimes fear that you are disappointed with Oxford. No wonder that the sky should seem dark and heavy to you after the calamity of last year. I miss the little fellow though I hardly knew his name. He used to touch his cap and come and walk with me as though he thought that I was a friend of his because I was a friend of yours. I do not suppose that I can quite realise the agony which the recollection of him causes to you and his mother. But you must endeavour to get over it, or it will do you great harm, worse than the long overwork of Clifton. You must leave him where he is – with God. If you are depressed it makes you less fit for work in College and in the University. And you are no longer able to take that hopeful view of things which is the soul of success.[11]

Towards the end of that same year (1882) Percival was back on form. Within the university two causes in particular occupied him: the admission of women and the poor. In the battle over the first he was already heavily engaged with the foundation of a women's college. Turning now to the plight of the poor, he conceived the startling notion of resigning the Presidency of Trinity to fill a vacancy as Censor of the Unattached, a post of no standing with a negligible salary.

The unattached were poor students attending the university by means of a faltering, ill-organised non-collegiate system. Many years before, in evidence to a Commission in 1850, Frederick Temple had put forward a plan to reduce the cost of an Oxford education to £65 or £70 a year by building halls which would offer cheap accommodation to undergraduates unable to afford college fees.

The halls had never been built, and Percival now proposed to take the existing scheme by the scruff of the neck. He wished to shame the loafers from the public schools by introducing large numbers of diligent youths from working-class homes. Many of these would be destined for business careers, in which they would serve the nation by creating employment and wealth, not idling away their lives on unearned income. His ultimate objective was to democratise the university.

The proposal that he be appointed Censor was addressed to Jowett as 'My Dear Vice-Chancellor'. Percival wrote that he would never be able to do much good at Trinity, which would get along well enough under Raper if he resigned, and the non-collegiate work would interest him more than anything else in Oxford. But he expressed two reservations: the move might involve his family in financial hardship, and it might be opposed as being eccentric or springing from some ulterior motive (as, with democratisation in his mind, it did indeed).

Jowett was alarmed and wrote back to cool his friend's ardour with some commonsense advice:

I would strongly advise you not to hint to any one an intention or desire to give up the Presidentship. It would be a great error; you would be embarked on a very difficult enterprise without the advantage of a considerable Oxford position. The Vice-Chancellor and Proctors would be too glad to appoint you, but is it quite

certain that you could do as much for the students in the position
of Censor as you might as President of Trinity? . . . I think also
you are mistaken about your success at Trinity. You have surely
got on very well. Does not the College increase in numbers? You
have helped female education; you have gathered a pleasant
society about you and your hospitality is greatly valued . . . If
you leave Trinity at all you should go either to a Bishopric or to
the Deanery of Bristol.[12]

To this Percival responded with the compromise proposal that
no permanent Censor be appointed and the President of Trinity,
being agreeable, should perform the Censor's duties without salary
for eighteen months as an *ad interim* arrangement.

Predictably, this extension of Percival's sphere of influence did
not find favour among the university authorities. His bid to secure
a proper organisation and adequate financing for the non-collegiate
lower class therefore failed, and it fell to Jowett to progress the
opening of the university to the poor on a much less ambitious
scale. This he achieved shortly afterwards (in 1886) by establishing
Balliol Hall for out-college students with remitted fees.

Frustrated within the university itself, Percival used his contacts
and seized opportunities to advance nationwide projects in higher
and adult education. What he had initiated from Clifton could be
better managed from Oxford, not least his scheme for transplanting
Oxford professors to teach in other cities. During his time as
President of Trinity he became known to the world at large for his
efforts to extend university work in the large towns and to facilitate
the entrance into universities of those who would pursue a career
in industry or commerce. Such, at least, was the judgment of *The
Times*, which praised him for a remarkable success in the first of
these enterprises despite a lack of funds.[13]

The movement to extend university teaching had languished at
Oxford until he became its protagonist. In 1885 he took it in hand
with the launch of the Oxford University Extension Movement,
and from that moment 'no one was more energetic and influential
on its behalf'.[14] What drove him was his faith in education as the
means of eradicating poverty and improving the lives of the great
mass of the people. England needed more universities and more
adult education under university supervision to spread enlightenment and bring an end to deprivation, both intellectual and
material.

With the support of Jowett and others, he persuaded the Oxford Delegates of Local Examinations to arrange an ambitious programme of local lectures. Building on these, he then encouraged the organisation of systematic courses and regular classes outside Oxford. In doing so he took a different path from the earlier movement at Cambridge by designing shorter and cheaper courses of lectures to suit the purses of working men and women and the needs of smaller and poorer towns.

Later, when at Rugby, his influence was decisive in the inauguration of Summer Meetings, later known as Summer Schools, at both Oxford and Cambridge. Thereafter the movement gathered pace everywhere. At Oxford his initiative was crowned a century later when the university's successively named Department of Extramural Studies, of Adult Education, of Continuing Education was granted full collegiate status.

Percival's activities in Oxford and the strain of overcoming opposition to them might be thought more than sufficient to occupy his time and exhaust his energies, but it was not in his nature to neglect his cherished creations in Clifton and Bristol. In this he was motivated by a sense of duty, no doubt aggravated by apprehension at the harm which might come to his beloved school and struggling University College if he did not attend governors' meetings regularly and make his voice heard. Others, however well-meaning, could not always be trusted to take what he believed to be the right decisions.

Yet another, and heavier, commitment brought him to Bristol for three months of every year during the Long Vacation, so that he came to spend his summers there as a break from the winters in Oxford. While others took their ease after a not noticeably fatiguing academic year, Percival was hard at work as a Canon of Bristol Cathedral, an office which he held during his last five years at Trinity (1882 to 1887). It was offered to him by Gladstone's Lord Chancellor (Lord Selborne), who knew his man when he wrote (in October 1882):

You would, I feel sure, agree with me that in these days a Canonry in a Cathedral Church ought not to be conferred, or accepted, as a sinecure or mere preferment; and that it is an office, the duties of which ought to be regarded, not as limited to the necessary performance of services in the Cathedral during certain months of residence, but as extending to every kind of salutary influence which may be made to radiate from the Cathedral as from a centre. That you have the gifts and personal qualities, and also the due sense of the high calling of a Christian minister, which are necessary for the exercise of such an influence, I feel sure.[15]

In the cathedral Percival at once made his mark by proposing to introduce a special form of Sunday evening service in the nave. The Dean objected on the grounds that there was no pulpit in the nave and, since no one would come to such a service, the Chapter would not provide one. Percival met this objection by ordering a pulpit from a cabinet-maker, paying for it himself, and having it delivered and installed within a week. The ensuing services mortified the Dean by attracting large congregations and becoming a famous feature in the religious life of the city.

One of his sermons at these services, addressed to members of the YMCA, took as its theme 'A Young Man's Duty to His Neighbours'. It included the injunction that 'no young man should live without a feeling that there is some duty of good service which he owes to the social body, to the community of which he is a part.'[16] Here Percival was seizing the opportunity to deliver to a wider audience the message which he was constantly drumming into the ears of schoolboys and undergraduates.

In 1911 his views on the duty of young men to society were carried to draconian lengths in a good cause when he advocated, in order to attract more into higher education, that any boy under seventeen who had left school and was not in employment be liable to be taken by the police and brought before a magistrate.

In canon's work outside the cathedral Percival encouraged evening schools and patiently attended classes for unruly urchins who were reported to show no respect for him, even when he appeared as an 'august presence, cold, shrouded, awful as an Alpine peak'.[17]

He undertook social work among what others dismissed as the 'wash-outs' and gave wholehearted support to Bristol's workmen and their trade union and co-operative movements. Once he came all the way from Oxford to present plans for a Trades Council's hall and spoke at length without any sign of discouragement or reproach at finding himself addressing an audience numbering less than a dozen.

At times he preached further afield and in a sermon at Plymouth stated his reservation about socialism which was not Christian

socialism: 'Socialism without Christianity has no chance of enduring success. You cannot create a new world except by creating a
new heart and a new purpose in common men.'[18] All the same, this
sermon was heady stuff for an Anglican clergyman in 1886, as the
following passage indicates:

> Competition is neither more nor less than the expression in your
> social activity of individual selfishness . . . it is at bottom nothing
> else but the endeavour to make gain for ourselves out of the
> struggle for individual success. It is, in fact, a sort of strife or
> warfare . . . Competition, then, is antagonistic in its very essence
> to the principles of Christianity, for Christianity is rooted in love
> and sacrifice, in the sense of membership in Christ, and in the
> care for the weak and suffering.[19]

This may have been sound Christian doctrine, but it came
strangely from the lips of one who had trained future leaders to be
winners in class and life, encouraged competitive games and aspired
to educate young businessmen to meet foreign competition in the
market place.

When the period of his canonry came to an end Percival received
an effusive letter from the Archdeacon thanking him for helping to
knit Church and city together and echoing the sentiment expressed
by colleagues in other appointments which he was forced to give
up: 'We miss you much in our counsels.'[20]

Back in Oxford was an enterprise which would continue to
benefit from his counsel even after his departure from the university. After Clifton it was perhaps the dearest of all to him: a college
for women.

CHAPTER 21

Somerville
and Education for Women

Among his many endeavours at good works in Oxford, Percival achieved most success in higher education for women. The time was ripe, and this was a field he had already ploughed while at Clifton.

Until the middle of the century the nation had made little provision for the education of its girls and women. Education for the poor was limited to the elementary teaching of basic literacy at dame schools, charity schools, Sunday schools and the voluntary Church schools. For the affluent it was dominated by social rather than academic considerations, domestic needs and the marriage market being uppermost in mind.

Girls of the upper and middle classes were commonly taught at home by governesses or a member of the family. There were also girls' schools, both day and boarding, in private houses, often with fewer than ten pupils. For the daughters of the very rich there were fashionable academies, or finishing schools, which made few demands on the intellect. One such at Brighton charged fees of £120 a year, which could rise to £500 with extras. Some of the less fortunate might be sent to a grim boarding establishment like the Clergy Daughters' School at Casterton in Percival's home county of Westmorland. Founded in 1823, this was the original of Lowood in Charlotte Bronte's *Jane Eyre*.

Formal higher education may be said to have begun in London with Queen's College, Harley Street, founded in 1848 'to provide advanced education for women', and Bedford College, founded the following year 'to provide for young ladies at a moderate expense a curriculum of general education on the same plan as the public Universities'. Students at Queen's College included two famous future headmistresses: Frances Buss of North London Collegiate School (1850) and Dorothea Beale of Cheltenham Ladies' College (1854).

Secondary education for women then received belated encouragement from the government through the Schools Inquiry Commission of 1864, chaired by Lord Taunton, the Endowed Schools Act of 1869 and the Education Act of 1870 which not only established Board Schools but also led to the foundation of more than ninety grammar schools for girls. In the private sector Miss Buss's school became the model for the girls' high schools founded under the auspices of the Girls' Public Day School Company, established in 1872 by Maria Grey, and for Anglican high schools founded by the Church Schools Company. Miss Beale's was the forerunner of Roedean, Wycombe Abbey and many others. The inaugural meeting of the Association of Headmistresses was held in 1874, convened by Miss Buss and chaired by Miss Beale.

In this area of education Percival was therefore not in the first wave of pioneers nationally, but he could claim that distinction in Bristol, where he made his usual emphatic mark.

The Bristol branch of the Association for the Promotion of the Higher Education of Women which he formed in 1868 with his wife, Louisa, as Secretary was active in arranging lectures and classes to prepare women for the Higher Cambridge Examination, to which they had been formally admitted by the university three years earlier. Doubtless under persuasion from Percival, lecturers came from Oxford to give instruction in history and literature, while masters from the grammar school taught physical science and languages. This was said to have raised the whole intellectual level of polite society in Clifton,[1] and it encouraged Percival to take the decisive lead in starting a girls' secondary school in what was by then a rapidly expanding 'salubrious and sylvan' district[2] appealing to many among Bristol's upper middle class. The growing number of Clifton College's town boys had a growing number of sisters.

Monthly planning meetings were held in the headmaster's quarters in the college's School House during 1877, and Clifton High School for Girls opened in January 1878 with sixty-seven pupils, the first name on the roll being that of his daughter Bessie. As at the University College, Dean Elliot was elected to the honorary office of President. Percival himself became Vice-President and, not formally but in practice, Chairman of the school's Council. In that capacity he attended to the birth-pangs caused by the unexpectedly large number of pupils, and within a year extensive new premises were purchased, allowing for expansion to two hundred and fifty. This number included boarders, and one of the boarding houses was named after him. Percival's eye was always on the future, and once again his far-sightedness was justified. Growth continued and by the 1990s numbers had risen to almost eight hundred.

Bessie Percival had only a short time at the school before the family moved to Oxford and she transferred to the High School there. But later in life she recorded her happiness at her first school: 'My time at Clifton is still to me a dream of delight, and I am sure there is no better school anywhere.'[3]

No sooner was Clifton High seen to be flourishing than a similar school (but for day girls only) was established in the neighbouring suburb of Redland. This was in 1880, when Percival was no longer at Clifton and he was not involved in the actual foundation. He was, however, credited with being one of the moving spirits and became President in 1883. Two years later he was instrumental in doing what he had done at Clifton High: accommodating the school in spacious new premises; on this occasion in Redland Court, a grand Palladian-style mansion. In 1896 he became Chairman of the Council as well as President and maintained his connection with the school for thirty-five years altogether.

Both these schools were fee-paying and therefore catered exclusively for young ladies from 'the best families'. This was a cause of dissatisfaction to him, and in his Prize Day speeches as President of Redland High School he made a point of emphasising the need for secondary schools for girls from poorer homes.[4]

After schools, universities. He had already, in 1876, made a significant contribution to the advancement of tertiary education for women through their admission to the new University College in Bristol. When he arrived in Oxford, the capital of academia, a greater opportunity presented itself.

After a late start the Oxford Association for the Promotion of the Higher Education of Women (the AEW) was doing good work, supported by some of the senior members of the university, together with their sisters and wives (permitted to dons since 1870). Among the most active members of the committee and one of its secretaries was Mary Ward (Mrs Humphry Ward, the novelist), who was soon to become a close colleague of Percival.

At the time of his election to Trinity discussions were taking place about the provision of a Hall to accommodate young ladies coming from outside Oxford to attend AEW lectures. Rival factions, ecclesiastical and secular, were in heated disagreement over the denominational status of such a Hall. Although religious tests had been abolished in the university, the dominant faction of High Churchmen insisted that it be open only to members of the Church of England. The leader of the secularist opposition to this restriction was T. H. Green, Fellow of Balliol and Professor of Moral Philosophy (and a benefactor of University College, Bristol). Neither side being prepared to give way, the outcome was not one Hall but two.

It was typical of Percival that he should throw in his lot with the liberals and non-denominationalists rather than the conservatives of the Church to which he owed allegiance as a minister. Conventional orthodoxy in religion played little part in his practical life.

On 7 February 1879 he attended the first meeting of subscribers to the Hall which he favoured. There a formal resolution was passed: 'That a Hall should be established in which no distinction will be made between students on the grounds of their belonging to different religious denominations'. A Provisional Committee of six was then elected. These included Professor Green and Mrs Ward, but the name heading the list was that of the President of Trinity, who must have come to the meeting from Clifton, where he was still serving out his last term as headmaster.[5]

At a meeting in Balliol three weeks later, with J. R. Magrath, Provost of Queen's, in the chair, Mrs Ward proposed and Percival seconded a motion in favour of the name, Somerville Hall. This was to commemorate Mary Somerville, reputed to be the greatest female scientist of the century, who had died seven years earlier, aged ninety-two. Management of the project was then placed in the hands of a Chairman and committee of fourteen, the committee to consist of 'ladies and gentlemen in equal numbers'. The President of Trinity was elected Chairman 'without opposition'.[6]

The first committee meeting under his chairmanship was held on 5 March, when Mrs Ward was appointed one of two joint secretaries and two sub-committees were formed which were to be crucial to the success of the fledgling enterprise. One was to appoint a Lady Principal (at £100 per annum with board and lodging); the other was to secure suitable premises. Making shrewd appointments and securing suitable premises were two of Percival's areas of proven expertise, and he undertook the chairmanship of both these sub-committees himself. From May, by which time he had moved into residence, all meetings were held in the President's Lodgings at Trinity.

From the list of applicants for the post of Principal three were short-listed and interviewed, but none came up to Percival's high expectations. Faced with this setback, he turned to a likely candidate known to him who had not applied. This was Margaret Elliot, a daughter of the Dean of Bristol with whom he was associated in his educational projects there.

The calibre of Miss Elliot's intellect may be gauged by the impression which she made on the Master of Balliol. Jowett, that inveterate bachelor, had even contemplated matrimony with her. Miss Elliot, however, who may have declined the honour of becoming Mrs Jowett, certainly declined the offer of candidacy for the post of Principal of Somerville Hall, and with such firmness that even Percival was forced to take no for an answer.

Even so, the attempt proved well worth while. Instead of herself, Miss Elliot recommended Madeleine Shaw Lefevre, daughter of the Vice-Chancellor of London University (which had just begun granting degrees to women) and sister of a Liberal Member of Parliament. As usual, Percival lost no time in following a promising lead. Adopting the tactics which he had pursued with such bravado when recruiting masters for Clifton, he descended on the home of this new prospect at short notice one lunch-time.

Miss Shaw Lefevre, aged forty-four, had no intention of moving to Oxford to assume such a responsibility. She was as reluctant as Miss Elliot, but not quite so strong-minded. Percival managed to cajole her into at least coming to Oxford for an interview. She consented only on the understanding that she would be required to bring no testimonials with her, nor, in answering personal questions, to recommend herself in any way at all.[7]

When offered the post after the interview, she was adamant in accepting it for no more than one year, but once in Percival's grasp there was no escape. She stayed for ten years, and her period as founding Principal proved yet another tribute to his doggedness and sure judgment in the recruitment of exceptional talent. Miss Shaw Lefevre's was, in Sir Herbert Warren's words, 'a characteristically bold and unconventional appointment'[8] – and one which assured Somerville's future.

In the scarcely less important search for premises Percival gave serious consideration to Cowley House, later the site of St Hilda's College, before settling on Walton House and buying out the leaseholder. There, on the college's present site, Somerville Hall opened in October 1879 with twelve students, in friendly rivalry with its Anglican sister, Lady Margaret Hall, which opened at the same time with nine.

A leasehold offered no security and Percival spent from January to November 1880 tenaciously negotiating, and eventually succeeding in purchasing, the freehold of the Walton Manor estate from St John's College, which did not readily part with its North Oxford freeholds.

During the same period he was active in exploiting his liberal, Bristol and London connections to raise money for the Hall. He and other members of the committee made fund-raising speeches in London, Birmingham, Reading and elsewhere, urging the need for facilities for women's education. Donations for scholarships were obtained from the Clothworkers' and Fishmongers' Companies. Among individual benefactors Samuel Morley, MP for Bristol, endowed four exhibitions for two years for students committed to a teaching career. Percival's friends, colleagues and acquaintances were expected to contribute unstintingly to his good causes.

In contriving the birth and financial viability of Somerville, Mary Ward was his prized adjutant. Not only was she a prodigiously hard worker like himself, but the fact that she was Thomas Arnold's grand-daughter created a bond between them which was strong enough to withstand the strain whenever she found him too over-powering. It was a heavy loss to him when she had to move to London with her husband in 1881.

In the following year another staunch colleague was lost when T. H. Green died at an early age. In his case, however, there was compensation to come. His burden of work was shouldered to considerable effect by his widow Charlotte, who served as a member of the Somerville Council for thirty-five years, eighteen of them as Vice-President. Charlotte Green also belonged to the Percival network in another connection. She was the daughter of Dr Symonds of Clifton, a sister of John Addington Symonds and a cousin of Mary Symonds, the second Mrs Percival.

In 1881 Percival's title of Chairman of the Committee was redesignated and he became President of the Council, the first holder of that office. On leaving Oxford for Rugby in 1887 he thought it right to resign this post, but his resignation was withdrawn at the earnest request of the other members of the Council. He stayed on as President for a further six years, during which time he returned to Oxford to attend meetings but no longer took the chair except on special occasions.

One of those was the appointment of a successor to Miss Shaw Lefevre. As with the headmasters of Clifton, so with the Principals of Somerville: he was not going to allow an institution which he had set in motion on the right lines to run off the rails through a botched appointment. The awful fate of Rugby when it chose Henry Hayman instead of himself was never to be forgotten. In May 1889 he chaired two Council meetings at which candidates were considered. These culminated in unanimity on the appointment of Miss Agnes Maitland, who was to prove herself another outstandingly successful Principal (although, like Miss Shaw Lefevre, not distinguished academically).

In 1894 Somerville Hall became Somerville College. In 1900, by which date Percival had moved on again, this time from Rugby to Hereford, his successor as President (Henry Pelham, also President of Trinity) proposed an alteration to its Articles of Association to 'connect the Bishop of Hereford permanently with the college'.[9] Three years later the title of Honorary Vice-President was created for him. In 1904, when he was present at the opening of a new library building (to the cost of which he had contributed), he was referred to as 'The Father of the College'.

Among the various problems encountered by the first students at Somerville were strict rules imposed by the AEW to protect their virtue and reputation. These rules could prove a stumbling block for even the most favourably inclined male supporters. When Balliol and Trinity jointly provided the university with a laboratory, for example, the attendance of women at lectures and demonstrations was initially vetoed by Jowett and Percival themselves. In this they were bowing to pressure, not from male colleagues, but from solicitous women.

To overcome the difficulty there was a price to pay, and Percival arranged for it to be paid. The minutes of a Council meeting chaired by him a few years later recorded that 'it was agreed to pay for the present term the Lady who acted as chaperone to Miss Rich in the University Laboratory'. At twenty-five shillings for a single student the cost was not inconsiderable, and the Council decided to plead with the AEW to modify its rules of chaperonage.[10]

Miss Rich – Florence Rich – must have been doubly grateful to Percival, for it was she who recorded an act of personal kindness by the President and his wife. Every Tuesday during term Dr and

Mrs Percival were 'at home' to any Somerville student wishing to take tea at their lodgings in Trinity.[11]

The university authorities were less welcoming. In 1896 Congregation rejected a proposal to award degrees to female students. Cambridge followed suit a year later, and this double rebuff precipitated one of Percival's lengthy letters to *The Times*.[12] If Oxford and Cambridge were so recalcitrant, other arrangements must be made. 1897 was the year of the queen's Diamond Jubilee, and his idea was to mark the occasion by the foundation of a Queen Victoria University for Women as an appropriate, beneficent and enduring monument to the *annus mirabilis*.

In accordance with his usual practice when introducing a controversial scheme, the details were spelt out, the arguments closely reasoned, the objections foreseen and dismissed. The letter, running to nearly two thousand words, had the following passage as its core:

> A women's university has a strong claim upon our support, as among all the various improvements in English life which give lustre to the Queen's reign, few, if any, are more deserving of special record than the progress of women's education, and it would accordingly be very appropriate if the movement could be crowned on this unique occasion by such a memorial, connecting this growth with the Queen's name for all time to come.

Percival went on to envisage this new university growing out of Royal Holloway College, the educational institution for women recently established in a magnificent neo-château building near Windsor by the millionaire proprietor of Holloway's Pills. Here would be located 'the intellectual home and headquarters of at least a prominent group of the best and most cultivated and most influential women of their generation'. He had every confidence that Holloway's governing body – which had not been consulted – would see the advantages of what was proposed in their name. ('Under present conditions the College can never rise above the position of a provincial college or school.')

The new university would thus be established by Royal Charter with Holloway as its first constituent college, and when rich benefactors came forward to found new colleges it would grow as Oxford and Cambridge had done. Its governing council of twelve would be chosen by the sovereign from among the most distinguished women of the Empire, who would be obliged to be in residence for at least two or three months each year. Their appointment would be equivalent to the bestowal of an honour by the Crown: a women's Order of Merit.

After acknowledging the objection that the facilities already on offer at the ancient universities might be superior to any obtainable at a new institution, Percival continued:

> And yet it may reasonably be doubted whether this mixed education under a traditional system formed and intended exclusively for men should be the sole kind of university education accessible to women, and there is much force in the argument that for true progress in this, as in other matters, we need liberty with variety of choice. The provision for women's education is not unnaturally felt to be one-sided and incomplete, until the growing liberty to make such limited use of the men's universities as may be accorded to them is accompanied or supplemented by the establishment of a separate university, in which the higher education of women may develop freely along its own lines . . . If such a university were in existence, there can be little doubt that many parents would prefer it for their daughters, as feeling that it would train and enrich their life under the most satisfactory conditions . . .

In making this proposal Percival had allowed his zeal to outrun his judgment. To his former colleagues at Somerville this was their old President at his most tiresome. He appeared to be suggesting that it would be advisable for existing colleges like Somerville and Newnham to be uprooted and relocated on the Holloway site; otherwise their growth would be stunted as the development of higher education for women became concentrated away from Oxford and Cambridge. Somerville's governing body of academics wondered what qualifications those female OMs would bring with them apart from their distinction 'in life or literature', and where the female tutors and lecturers would be found.

Henry Pelham, Percival's successor as President of both Trinity and Somerville, wrote bluntly in a pained, private letter: 'I cannot believe that such a proposal as yours can do anything but harm.'[13] Agnes Maitland, the Principal, wrote more tactfully, begging Percival to consult women already involved in education before taking hasty action. She called his scheme 'beautiful for the future', but pointed out that, with higher education for women only twenty-five years old, money was needed, not for a new institution, but for Fellowships and research and new buildings and libraries for the existing ones. She accused him of being blinded by kindness and concluded:

> I should very much dread, at present, the founding of a University for Women only, though fifty or a hundred years hence we may be ready for it, if your millionaire will help us with endowment now. We can work on without the degree, which was largely asked for as a help to bread winning, if we can only get endowment for continuance of study.[14]

The splendidly named, but ill-conceived, Queen Victoria University for Women was a non-starter. This was an occasion when Percival's feet were off the ground, his vision no more than a romantic dream.

CHAPTER 22

A New Arnold at Rugby

At Oxford Percival had become frustrated. The university was in need of fundamental reforms which he was powerless to effect. He must have looked back on his time at Clifton as golden years and longed for another such opportunity.

When, in 1884, the headmastership of Eton fell vacant, he allowed his name to be submitted. James Wilson wrote to Eton from Clifton urging his appointment, but Percival himself made no direct application. Conservative Eton and radical Percival were not meant for each other, as he would have realised. The havoc which a zealous reformer was likely to wreak on their cherished institutions would have made the prospect unthinkable to the governing body at Eton. In any event the result of the election was a foregone conclusion. Dr Warre, an assistant master and Old Etonian, was the favoured internal candidate, and he romped home with nine out of the eleven votes cast.[1]

When a similar vacancy occurred at Harrow shortly afterwards, Percival, for whatever reason, refused to stand. Perhaps he was waiting for an invitation and the assurance of a free hand. If so, he did not have long to wait, although it was not Harrow which obliged. Out of the blue in November 1886 came a letter from the Bishop of Worcester, Chairman of the governors at Rugby:

My dear Dr Percival, I have been requested by the Governing Body of Rugby School to invite you to undertake the office of Headmaster of the School on the retirement of Dr Jex-Blake at Easter 1887 ... they feel all confidence that the best interests of the School will be safe in your keeping.[2]

It was third time lucky. After two unsuccessful applications to Rugby Percival was being invited, not to apply for, but to accept the post he coveted above all others. This was clearly no occasion for prevarication, heart-searching, seeking advice, begging time for consideration. 'I gladly and gratefully accept the trust which you have placed in my hands,' he replied by return of post.[3]

The news spread quickly, and his joy was widely shared. To the newspapers this was an event of national importance. *The Times* applauded it in a long leading article the next day: 'The manner of the appointment is unusual; the choice is by no means according to precedent; and yet there can be no doubt that the action of the Governing Body will meet with general approval.'

The article's praise for Percival was glowing. It acknowledged his exceptional ability, judged him to be still in the prime of physical and intellectual vigour (he was fifty-two), and paid tribute to his record: 'Probably Mr Percival's success at Clifton was greater than has ever attended the efforts of any first master of a new school in this country.' Starting life as a miniature Rugby, Clifton had – so *The Times* judged – become the equal of the older school within six or eight years.[4]

Letters of congratulation poured into the President's Lodgings at Trinity. One from Rugby written on the same day as the bishop's implored him to come over to Macedonia and help them:

> We are not heathen, but we are rather slowbellies, and we want the calm firmness and quiet resolution which made Clifton a rival to Rugby now to reverse the operation . . . you are the only man that Rugby will welcome unitedly.[5]

From Clifton the ever faithful Wilson wrote: 'I saw Temple the other day and pressed this upon him. I am truly glad. No one else could so instantly restore public confidence in Rugby.'[6]

Frederick Temple, then Bishop of London, was Deputy Chairman of Rugby's governing body and, most likely, the guiding hand behind a unanimous decision to take the exceptional step of making this offer without opening the vacancy to competition. As an ex-headmaster of the school he would have been fulfilling the same influential role in the appointment of a successor as Percival was still undertaking at Clifton. Largely responsible for the young Percival's appointment to Clifton twenty-four years earlier, he would now have been performing a second, similar service for the protégé he so much admired.

From Clifton, too, came ecstatic congratulations from Graham Dakyns:

> As a friend I am well pleased that you should have a new sphere of action open to you, and that an ancient and laudable ambition to sit in the seat of Arnold should be satisfied. As a schoolmaster and Englishman I applaud the wisdom of the selection. As a Rugby man I dance about and am mad ... And I do devoutly hope and expect and believe that another Rugby will ere long arise, and that you will not only have created one school at a time of life when some thought you too young, but at an age when some, judging by their own inertness and senilities, may look upon you as too old, you will recreate another.[7]

From the nearby Woodstock Road in Oxford another Rugby man, Professor Arthur Sidgwick, wrote to reminisce about 'that day when I was in bed with malaria in Perugia (19 Feb. 1874), being an exile from Hayman, and had the telegram that Jex was appointed at Rugby – and how I turned my face to the wall that it was not you.'[8]

As with Percival's election to Trinity, the appointment was without precedent. Then it had been the election of someone who was not a Trinity man. Now it was the move from the one post to the other. According to *The Times*: 'There is no previous case of the Head of a House exchanging that position for the more arduous and, as some would think, lower position of a Head Master of a school.' But the newspaper was not surprised that a man of Percival's temperament should prefer school work to what it characterised as Oxford's perpetual motion without progress: 'Activity, not stagnation, is now the disease of Oxford. Perpetual Committees ... occupy the Day.'[9]

At Rugby the era of strife between governors and headmaster was over. Order had been restored by Jex-Blake, who had pulled the school back from the brink into its old groove after the disaster of Hayman and his law suits. Professor Sidgwick subscribed to the prevailing view that Rugby was a good school again but could no longer claim the supremacy it had enjoyed in the epic days of Arnold and Temple. All that was needed now, he believed, was 'spirit and a leader'.

Percival himself was less sanguine. In the eyes of a perfectionist what was once the very best of schools had not regained the status of even a moderately good one. What Jex-Blake had contrived was quiescence after a period of turbulence: an achievement not to be under-rated, but far from good enough. He had bequeathed a low moral tone (Percival's pet aversion) and disappointing intellectual standards. The new headmaster found it all too apparent why the governing body had sent for him. Faced with the same situation as he had encountered on arrival at Trinity, he descended on Rugby like a wrathful Jehovah on the erring children of Israel. Here he did indeed have the free hand denied him in Oxford.

The most perceptive observer of his stormy reign at Rugby was G. F. Bradby, a lifetime Rugbeian. It was he who afterwards supplied William Temple with a first-hand account for his *Life of Bishop Percival*, and he was the author of the entry on Percival in *The Dictionary of National Biography*. The son of a headmaster of Haileybury, Bradby had been educated at Rugby and then at Balliol before returning to the school as a master (1888–1920) and housemaster (1908–1920). During those years he wrote a revealing novel, not about the young Toms and Erics of public school life, but about the masters.

The Lanchester Tradition, first published in 1914, is a witty and stylish fictional account of the arrival of a reforming headmaster at a public school and his battle with a conservative housemaster resolved to preserve the traditions of the revered Dr Lanchester, who had re-founded the ancient grammar school of Chiltern as a public school.

Characters, physical appearances and circumstances were altered, but it does not require much discernment to identify Chiltern with Rugby, the great Dr Lanchester with the great Dr Arnold, the feckless retiring headmaster, Dr Gussy, who had allowed the school to go to pot, with a joint portrait of Hayman and Jex-Blake, and the reforming Mr Flaggon with the reforming Dr Percival.

There is much which is familiar about Mr Flaggon, 'who, with the principles of a democrat, combined all the instincts of a despot'. Moreover:

To a childhood spent among the Cumbrian Fells he owed a robust constitution and a toughness of fibre that defied fatigue; perhaps, too, a certain gravity and reticence which seem to come naturally to those who are bred among mountains.[10]

All ends happily at Chiltern with the defeat of Mr Chowdler, the traditionalist housemaster, and his faction, followed by the triumphant discovery of letters revealing that Dr Lanchester, the conservatives' idol, had been in his day as radical a reformer as Mr Flaggon.

In the masters' common room in the real-life Rugby, too, there were differing views about the new headmaster. And the boys in the school who knew of his reputation as a scourge must have greeted his arrival not with joy but justifiable apprehension.

Arnold in one of his best-known dicta had declared that the first, second and third duty of a schoolmaster was to get rid of unpromising pupils, and this duty he had performed unflinchingly. Mass expulsions had been his answer to rebelliousness during the Troubles of 1839.

Percival's attitude towards the unsatisfactory boy seems to have been poised between this and the contrary dictum of the more enlightened Edward Thring of Uppingham: that the first, second and third thought of a teacher must be for those he has to teach. 'What he teaches is not his subject,' Thring argued. 'His subject is the immature human mind.'[11] Resort to expulsion was therefore a confession of failure.

But Percival's expulsions were for moral, not academic reasons. During his first term at Rugby he expelled five boys instantly for what was condemned as 'vice', striking their names off the school list in a public gesture calculated to intimidate and deter others. At the end of the term a number of other undesirables were ordered not to return. Jex-Blake had been too mild a man to flog or expel. Discipline under Percival was a full return to Arnold's 'abhorrence of evil'.

Bradby has described the 'white-hot scorn and disgust' with which he opened his relentless campaign against vice and how he held the moral cowardice of the majority responsible:

Nobody who was present at that gathering in New Big School will ever forget it. One could feel the School wincing and writhing – the tall stern figure on the platform (he seemed about forty feet high), the white face lit up with intense but controlled moral indignation – the pause, and then the word or phrase that fell like a lash. And behind it all the feeling of power and righteousness and judgment to come. The School went out smarting, some of them angry, all of them frightened. Like Lady Macbeth, they had suddenly realised in the face of another the horror of their own deeds.[12]

The sixth-form boys were particularly blamed, however innocent their own conduct. In another incident Percival pinned responsibility on them for failing to impose moral discipline by checking bad language. He told them, as reported: 'An auld Rugbeian came down to this school; he proposed to send his boy to his auld house; and he was met with such a flood of filthy language that he said, I shall not send my boy to that house.'[13]

Percival was reputed to have an unerring eye for the unwholesome boy, even when only momentarily glimpsed in assembly or on the playing field. During house prayers in School House one day his sharp look detected a moving bulge in a young boy's cheek, indicating that something succulent was being rolled round the mouth. The culprit was ordered to step forward and, sure enough, the bulge was revealed to be a large sweet. The headmaster's rebuke delivered from a towering height was another of his explosions of wrath which stuck in the memory of those who witnessed it: 'How dare you or any boy come gorging and guzzling into the presence of his Maker!'[14]

Yet Bradby for one came to realise that, although he turned to terror when his implacable devotion to duty demanded, the despot was not at heart a hard man. Beneath the shell of the stern disciplinarian the kernel of the real Percival was full of compassion. He was a lonely man, and his loneliness was self-imposed. Concealed by an iron will was a hunger for friendship; a wish to be spoken to without fear by master or boy, man to man; a longing to give free rein to an innate kindness which surfaced in patience and sympathy towards those who tried and failed through no fault of their own – although no indulgence was extended to those who had their chances and would not take them.[15]

Restoring Rugby's faded academic brilliance was a harder task than raising the moral tone by punishing delinquents. One move was to increase the number and value of scholarships. In his letter to Old Cliftonians in 1908 soliciting funds for additional scholarships at Clifton, Percival referred to his experience at Rugby:

When I went as Head Master there was hardly any first-class ability in the school, and to remedy this defect I established a system of scholarships equal in attractiveness (though less exten-

sive) to those at Winchester, and the result is that Rugby is filling
the public service with men of ability, and is more successful at
Oxford and Cambridge than any other school.[16]

But it was a long haul back to scholastic pre-eminence, and much
of Percival's endeavour to this end came to fruition under his
successor, when the scholarships became fully effective in attracting
exceptional talent. Meanwhile in raising standards throughout the
school the calibre of the teaching staff was all-important, and here
Percival had the advantage of an inheritance second to none. In the
words of an exuberant doggerel delivered by E. V. Knox at an Old
Rugbeian dinner in 1921:

> Of famous Rugbeians the list never closes,
> And Dr Jex-Blake said the first one was Moses,
> And deep though your search into history dug be,
> You'll not find a school that's had masters like Rugby.[17]

One may doubt the seriousness of Dr Jex-Blake's claim to Moses,
allegedly implied in the course of a sermon, but it would not be
easy to dispute the accuracy of the second couplet. Although he
himself towered above them intellectually as well as physically,
Percival inherited an experienced team of well-qualified teachers,
lacking leadership. If they had a collective fault it lay in hardened
arteries, and when filling the dozen vacancies which arose during
his headmastership Percival seized the opportunity to introduce a
healthy infusion of younger blood and men whom he could shape
in his own ways.

As formerly at Clifton, his practice was to seek sound advice and
trust to this and his own judgment in assessing quality, sometimes
on grounds of promise alone. On the strength of a recommendation
from the college dean, for example, he offered a post to a young
scholar of Balliol a year before he had sat his Finals. This was
Frank Fletcher, who duly came to Rugby after taking his degree
and spending two terms as a Balliol tutor.

Fletcher was to prove another triumphant example of the success
of Percival's recruitment policy. His subsequent career included
headmasterships at Marlborough and Charterhouse; and he was by
no means the only Rugby master at this time to reach the top of his
profession. Like Arnold and Temple before him, Percival ran a
school for headmasters as well as boys. Dulwich, Cheltenham and

Manchester Grammar School were other schools to draw from his pool of talent. So also were the two dearest to him. A. A. David, whom he lured from Oxford and a Fellowship at Queen's, was destined to follow twice in his footsteps as headmaster: first at Clifton (1905–10) and then at Rugby itself (1910–1921).

It cannot be claimed that familiarity, the passage of time, the experience of working together and the raising of morale through strong leadership made Percival any more popular with his staff. They respected him, but found him to be high-handed in the extreme, uncompromising in the demands which he made on them. 'Under Percival,' wrote Bradby, echoing T. E. Brown's plaintive cry from Clifton, 'we were always moving towards noble ends along a sure road; but he sometimes forced the pace to such an extent that we almost dropped from fatigue.'[18]

At one masters' meeting, for example, deeply felt grievances were aired about the amount of extra work expected of them. When told that the health of some of them was being impaired, the headmaster displayed no feeling of sympathy. He responded instead with one of his deceptive smiles which signalled anger. These were described by Fletcher as slow and dangerous; by William Temple as cold and steely. On this occasion he made one of his grim little quips, promising to review the matter the following year 'if we're alive'.[19]

Percival took steps to raise masters' pensions but not (as he had at Clifton) their salaries. They thought him a tight-fisted northerner, while he saw himself as exercising necessary prudence on behalf of a governing body which was short of funds and could not even finance the new scholarships and other grants which were his priorities. For those he was forced to look outside the school to Old Rugbeians and other benefactors.

The loyalty of the masters was particularly sorely tried one Prize Day when the headmaster publicly thanked them for their generous contribution to grants for remission of the fees of boys whose parents could no longer afford to keep them at the school. In fact, the generosity was involuntary. He had arbitrarily docked their salaries without their consent.

Bradby and Fletcher both used the phrase, 'a great man', in writing about Percival, but the tributes they paid to him made no attempt to disguise his unpopularity. According to Fletcher's memoirs:

His work at Rugby did not end when he left; his ideas and ideals lived on, kept alive by masters who had worked under him, and by them passed on as an inspiration to others who came afterwards. But by no means all his staff liked him while he was with us. A few never acknowledged his greatness; others, after he had left, built the sepulchre of the prophet they had stoned. He *was* something of a prophet – stern, puritanical, lacking in humour, like Arnold to whom he looked back as his ideal, but in his best moments inspired.[20]

With boys Percival had an instinctive understanding. He knew them from the inside and read their individual characters uncannily. He was straightforward and they knew where they stood with him, but the experience was usually unnerving. No amount of understanding could endear him to his pupils at Rugby after a tyrannical opening term and every indication that he intended to go on as he had begun. The enduring impression which he made on them was very far from that of an enlightened and approachable liberal. Where they were concerned, he was first and foremost a puritan disciplinarian. His much proclaimed liberalism came a poor second.

He was ready to trust absolutely an individual boy who had not forfeited his confidence; but in the boys as a whole he put little or no trust. He feared liberty; with all his liberalism, he feared liberty.[21]

That was the verdict of William Temple, another not uncritical admirer, who vividly recalled the headmaster's address to new boys in a dramatic scene in New Big School:

There the names were 'called over' by the Headmaster, and as each boy answered, the keen, searching eyes were fixed on him for some seconds. After this came an allocution. On the occasion when I was one of the new boys, I remember that he spoke for some time in a genial and kindly manner about the opportunities and even the delights of life at a Public School. Then the tone abruptly changed, and the north-country accent became more pronounced. 'There are many bad boys here; there is a lot of evil in the place.' ... At the end came a ray of comfort in the assurance that it was good for us to have temptations to face, and that if we did our part we should have strengthened our characters in addition to serving the School. Then came a pause; a concentrated glare; a rapid turn, and he was at the door. But he was not gone; he had passed the door, and it was nearly closed; then it swung open again, the magnificent white head reappeared, and the voice, a good deal raised, cut the silence like a knife: 'Eh, I shall be watching you every day of your lives.' The door banged, and this time he was gone.[22]

Another picture of him at this time comes from the diary of an eighteen-year-old girl, Mabel Scott, who accompanied her mother on visits to her brothers at the school and attended chapel services to hear the headmaster's 'discourses':

He looks very sublime in a long surplice & scarlet & white silk hood. He hangs his head, as though he were the meekest & the mildest of men & gives out his text in a subdued murmur. The north country twang was very noticeable: 'Saul' and 'all' both rhymed with 'snarl'. We hear the Dr is not liked by the generality of the boys, which is very sad considering he is such an exemplary head master.[23]

Clifton had been his own creation, but at Rugby Percival had to grapple not only with a fall from grace but also with traditions not of his own making or to his liking. Perhaps it was because of his conviction that in these circumstances exceptionally harsh measures were called for that he chose to govern with a severity not experienced by his pupils and colleagues at Clifton. There he had been implacably stern, but won popularity in the end nonetheless. That was certainly not the case at Rugby.

Frederick Temple, when headmaster, had not been much liked, but his natural kindness was apparent. When he flogged, it was with tears pouring down his cheeks. One of his pupils dubbed him 'a beast, but a just beast'. By contrast, Percival was thought an unjust beast. His dreaded punishments seemed pitiless: 'His discipline was absolutely firm, and to evildoers he was a terror.'[24]

One boy was flogged for the crime of a bad half-term report; two others were sentenced to a birching for missing Sunday lunch to go birds'-nesting – a time-honoured Rugby pastime. The terrors of the rod were enhanced by scathing remarks addressed to the sufferer between strokes. Those most commonly reported were the standard 'It'll hurt ye, but it's for your good' and the more menacing 'I mean ye to remember it every day of your life'.[25]

Written test questions at the beginning of every lesson were a hated innovation. Sometimes, too, the headmaster would appear in a class-room, subject the form to an impromptu oral examination and express dissatisfaction when no one could answer a question which he must have been aware was beyond their knowledge. In one instance a class in eighteenth-century English history incurred grave displeasure when unable to tell him in which order the American colonies revolted.

Most resented of all was his disapproval of the esteem in which organised games had come to be held. He condemned the privileges of hero-worshipped athletic 'swells' as unmerited, and his abolition of the right to distinctive gold braid on caps honouring prowess at the game which had made the name of Rugby famous throughout the world was not to be forgotten or forgiven.

Yet he took as keen an interest in cricket as he had at Clifton. Shortly after his arrival he received a letter from some distinguished Old Rugbeian athletes, who:

> observed with regret that for some few years past the national games of Cricket and Football have not received the same attention or been practised and played with the same zest and spirit that in previous years had combined to win for Rugby a leading place among the Public Schools of England.[26]

More than intellectual standards had slipped, and Percival had already made cricket compulsory. His response to the letter was to receive a deputation, agree to the permanent appointment of a first-class cricket professional and pay for an additional coach for the younger boys out of his own pocket.

The professional employed was a Yorkshireman named Tom Emmett, with whom the headmaster established a close rapport. Their respective Cumbrian and Yorkshire accents could sometimes be overheard debating the finer points of batsmanship in the headmaster's study.[27] But this concern did not extend to any wavering of insistence on work. 'Dreaming of Emmett or soom sooch stooff' became a rebuke to the inattentive in class.[28]

What steps Percival took to improve the standard of Rugby football is not recorded. His interest in that game is known only for a ruling on the length of the shorts to be worn.

On that subject his puritanism was revealed at its most bizarre. Fearful that the sight of too much bare thigh might inflame other boys with impure thoughts, he ordered shorts to be lengthened to cover the knees. Hanging so low, they flapped loosely. Those who were forced to wear them therefore tucked them up, again exposing the temptation of naked flesh too near the groin for the head-master's peace of mind. He countered this defiance by ordaining elastic attachments which fastened the bottom of the shorts to the tops of stockings.

The boys' satirical magazine, *Sybil*, entertained its readers by publicising the affair. It printed a photograph of the controversial below-the-knees shorts for all to judge, and it reported, in the style of *Punch*, an imaginary exchange between a chaperone and 'a lively young lady' watching a football match in the Close: 'It is quite disgraceful, my dear. Just look how short those knickerbockers are. Why, you can see the knees of some of them.' The lively young lady, however, thinks 'it's rather nice'.[29] In a hitherto rare lapse of judgment the headmaster had made himself a laughing-stock. As soon as he left, the length of Rugby's football shorts reverted to the *status quo ante*.

This was not the only incident of its kind which suggested that Percival was losing his sureness of touch with advancing age – and, perhaps, a growing consciousness that he had less and less time left to put the world to rights. In School House one day he memorably denounced the hot cross bun as 'a relic of paganism and an excuse for guzzling'.[30]

In 1895, towards the end of his reign, a humiliating incident revealed the full depth of his unpopularity. In a ceremony known as 'house cheering' it was customary for the boy who was head of a house to call for three cheers to welcome visiting guests on some special occasion. In the garden of one house, where the boys were assembled to welcome the headmaster and his wife, the call of 'Hip-hip-hurrah for Dr and Mrs Percival' was met with total silence. The mortified head of the house muttered an excuse to the effect that the boys must all have lost their voices, only to be further embarrassed when the names of the housemaster and his wife were called and greeted with deafening cheers.[31]

More a slave-driver than a headmaster was the boys' verdict on him, and they nicknamed him Rameses the Second of Clifton after the pharaoh who had persecuted the Israelites. Under his lash Rugby became a worthier but not a happy school. He was approached with awe out of fear not respect, and his very presence spread an aura of gloom. One head of the school recorded sadly:

He is very often desponding. He does nothing but work; work all the day long . . . I don't think he is by nature gloomy, but he seemed to think that, after all, this is rather a poor world to be in . . . Perhaps this may account for the prevailing melancholy.[32]

The headmaster did not make himself popular with parents either. Although numbers in the school rose, they were not sufficient to fill a newly built house. The trouble lay not so much in his commitment to liberalism – radical views were, after all, in the Rugbeian tradition of Arnold and Temple – as in his aggressive manner of expressing it. Some prospective parents thought this offensive and found him morally arrogant.[33] As a young man making his way in the world at Clifton he had exercised some discretion and taken pains to win the support of conservative parents. Now, in successful middle age, he could afford to be forthright and preach his principles to adults.

So, under Percival's intensive care, an ailing Rugby was subjected to a regime of even more violent purgatives than Trinity had been forced to swallow. But, however distasteful and resented, this cure was surely just what Dr Arnold would have prescribed. In raising the moral tone and intellectual standards Percival's treatment worked wonders. The patient made a rapid recovery and became its former relatively moral and exceptionally industrious self again. In the teeth of discontent, the school was force-fed with its reforming headmaster's ideals of Godliness, clean living and hard labour.

CHAPTER 23

Rugby's Two Reformers

At Oxford and Hereford, where Percival's ability to steer a new course was restricted, his influence was limited. But at Rugby, as at Clifton, where he was armed with dictatorial powers, it endured. Clifton had been his own, unopposed creation. Rugby, with strong roots in the past, proved less malleable. Only someone of Percival's dominant personality and strength of will could have forced lasting changes on a tradition-bound institution of Rugby's eminence.

Some reforms he was able to accomplish with confidence by introducing what had proved successful at Clifton. The most notable of these were a Modern Side with a Military wing, expansion in the teaching of science, and a Town House. Another project pioneered at Clifton, and one very dear to his heart, was the involvement of a public school in social work. A Rugby Home Mission was established in 1889 with boys' clubs in London and Birmingham.

Day boys at Rugby were still looked down upon, as they had been in Arnold's day. If their homes were within five miles of the school they were entitled to admittance as 'foundationers'. Paying no fees, they were allotted no premises, nowhere even to hang their clothes. They had no tutor of their own and were forbidden to play games in the Close. In 1878 the separate school on the same foundation sought by Arnold for these charity boys had at last been established. It was named Lawrence Sheriff School after Rugby's founder, and a master from Clifton with experience of day boys was appointed first headmaster.

Under Percival the remaining boys in the 'Town' became fully integrated. They participated in house matches and enjoyed equal status with boarders. On Speech Day in 1891 Percival announced that he was particularly anxious to see the day-boy element developed, because he had a great belief in that kind of education. There was, he bluntly informed the assembled company at this famous boarding school, no education to compare with membership of a great public school when combined with living in a good and cultured home.[1]

Physical changes in Percival's time were few, partly because funds for capital expenditure were lacking. A drawing school was built in 1888, and in 1895 forty-three acres were added to the playing fields, thanks to a bequest from an Old Rugbeian. Unlike the infant Clifton, Rugby was adequately provided with buildings and real estate, and these had recently been modernised and extended by Jex-Blake. Percival was therefore free to concentrate on minds and souls.

At Clifton his influence had radiated most strongly from the chapel pulpit in the widely observed tradition established by Arnold. According to James Wilson: 'His words somehow rang true in the ears of the not naturally religious boy and enlisted him on the side of right, of public spirit, of purity, of large-heartedness and courage.'[2]

At Rugby according to Frank Fletcher: 'His sermons were well worth listening to for the earnestness of purpose that lay behind them, but except on special occasions they were not arresting; they were too dry and unadorned to hold the attention of most boys, who are attracted by rhetoric and a forceful delivery.'[3] At least one boy at Rugby found the headmaster's informal talks to school or house on moral questions much more interesting and helpful.[4]

Percival's sermons, whether at Clifton or Rugby, were the usual headmasterly exhortations. The text most pertinent to what he perceived as his Herculean task of cleansing Rugby's Augean stable was Job xiv 4: 'Who can bring a clean thing out of an unclean?' On this he preached, much as he had at Clifton, that the character of societies are fixed by prevailing influences. The common life emerges from the individual life: the tone of the life of a school is the sum of individual influences. Thus every boy has a responsibility for it and has to ask himself: What influence do I bring to the common life?

More controversial was Mark vii 13: 'Making the word of God of none effect through your tradition.' Those were the words of Jesus to the Pharisees, and Percival used them to challenge the school's conservative element. Good traditions were a great help and support, he conceded, but others could be pernicious. He saw a possible conflict between traditional custom and personal inspiration: 'If the spirit of traditional usage and influence holds the citadel of a man's life, the spirit of Christian progress cannot gain an entrance.'[5]

Dedication to Christian progress and impatience at the obstacles which lay in its path were at the heart of Percival's beliefs and motivation. They governed all his actions and principles, religious and educational, social and political, and he did not mince his words from the pulpit on that theme.

> If you are living here simply according to traditional rules, doing this or that because, as you may be told, everybody does it; accepting standards of conduct and rules of practice because, as you understand, or, as someone undertakes to persuade you, they have always been so accepted, why, then, you are growing up to be one of that never-ending succession of men who are the Pharisees, the opponents of Christ, in every generation, who live with a tame conscience in any sort of company, and perpetuate the bad traditions of the world. But if you listen to the call of Christ . . . you will rise superior to the influence of any tradition or custom, no matter what its authority may seem to be.[6]

This passage must have enraged some of the senior members of the congregation. Was the headmaster really telling the boys to reject any tradition or custom which contradicted what they took to be 'the call of Christ'? Was he really denouncing right-minded housemasters and other respected guardians of Rugby's precious past as Pharisees and inciting those in their charge to flout their authority? Rugby's reputation as the shrine and breeding ground of liberals was cherished, but this must have been seen as flirting with subversion.

After eight years' hard labour, battling for change in attitudes and morals, teaching and curricula, Percival's health once more began to fail. When in January 1895 the Prime Minister (Lord Rosebery) wrote to offer him the see of Hereford he therefore accepted. The mission he had been called upon to undertake at Rugby had been accomplished, and it was probably as well both for himself and for the school that he did not stay longer. Rugby had had as much of a shake-up as it could take. 'We want rest,' T. E. Brown had sighed at Clifton. At Rugby G. F. Bradby noted that 'the sense of loss at his departure was tinged with a feeling akin to relief. He had strung us up to such a pitch that the tension was sometimes unbearable.'[7]

The school then settled more comfortably into the safe hands of the Rev. H. A. James, who came from Cheltenham, already an experienced headmaster. William Temple's assertion that Rugby then became aware that it not only revered and trusted the departing despot but genuinely loved him sounds like the wishful thinking of a loyal godson.[8] Even allowing for the indulgence evoked by most departures, it seems wide of the mark. Like Arnold, Percival had a devoted following among favoured sixth-formers and sentimental Old Boys, but except within his own family circle he was not a lovable man.

Yet *The Meteor*, the school magazine edited by the boys, published a polite but evidently genuine expression of its own regret at his leaving and reported 'we are sure, universal regret'.[9] Some years had passed since the 'house cheering' incident, and it was perhaps a measure of Percival's success that familiarity had bred at least acceptance.

'I am sure that he was a great Headmaster, and that Rugby owes him a deep debt of gratitude' was James's tribute to his predecessor.[10] The new headmaster's policy was to modify Percival's methods but not his ideals, whose inspiration – the invaluable gift he brought with him wherever he went – thus survived and blossomed. During James's reign the rise in numbers, scholarship and reputation accelerated, mainly as the result of Percival's reforms. An epigram by Frank Fletcher provided a neat summary: 'Rugby under Percival deserved success; under James it achieved it.'[11]

Yet in marked contrast to the remembrance of him at Clifton, Rugby today appears to have little awareness of the rescue operation which Percival performed and the importance of the revival which he instigated. Instead of standing second to Arnold and alongside Temple in esteem, he has become just one in a long line of forgotten headmasters.

A plaque to him in the chapel bears the apt, but in the event ironical, injunction: 'Remember those that had rule over you which spake unto you the word of God...' The testimonial portrait painted by Hubert von Herkomer for New Big School Gallery hangs skied in semi-darkness. It is in the town that he is most fittingly commemorated: by an adult education centre bearing his name.

How then do the characters, careers and reputations of Percival and Arnold compare and contrast? Both were extreme and fearless radicals whose loudly proclaimed views made them immensely unpopular. Both were intensely concerned about matters of Church and State and the condition and education of the poor. They would have made effective statesmen, but both ranked education above politics and placed a higher value on training a new generation in leadership and spiritual values.

Arnold's school reforms were more concerned with morals than intellect. Percival's were more strictly educational and practical. In moral terms his perspective was much the wider. To him imperialism meant the spread of morality, and he preached to his pupils the gospel of Britain's moral leadership of the world. Fear of loss of that leadership to nations better equipped in science and technology was one impulse behind his radical overhaul of the school curriculum.

Arnold's stint at Rugby was almost twice as long as Percival's, and his contribution to the school correspondingly greater. In his case it was nearly fourteen years of trial and tribulation which wore him out.

During that period the activities of the Chartists in the 1830s shifted his politics to the Right, and he came to detest some fellow radicals as heartily as he detested Tories. Whatever his sympathy with the aims of the Chartists, he was alienated by their methods because he regarded it as the first duty of every citizen to protect society and obey its laws.

Percival, too, was no revolutionary, but age did not mellow his radicalism and towards the end of the century he welcomed the rise of the Labour Party without fearing proletarian militancy. Despite his air of melancholy, he remained an optimist by conviction, whereas Arnold was always deeply pessimistic about the world around him, even declaring that he rejoiced in the death of loved ones because they were happily removed from it.

Religion was the dominant force in both men's lives and, although they gave serious offence to the orthodox, each might have made a lifetime's career in the Church.

Percival once said that schoolmastering was not his deliberate choice.[12] It was only the accident of the offer from Clifton that made him an educationist and delayed his working for the Church full-time. Arnold would probably have become Archbishop of Dublin after only three years at Rugby if the Prime Minister (Grey) had accepted the recommendation of his Lord Chancellor (Brougham) in 1831. Melbourne, the next Whig Prime Minister, offered him no higher preferment than the deanery of Manchester, which he refused. He shared Percival's love of Cumbria, where he built himself a home, but the urban north country, where Percival longed to work in order to improve the lot of the slum-dweller, did not hold the same attraction for Arnold in the earlier years of the Industrial Revolution.

Neither man could have expected favours from a Tory government. Melbourne was again urged to do something for Arnold in the dying days of his ministry, when it was about to fall to Peel, but he declined to make him a bishop because of the furore which this would have precipitated. Rosebery was more robust when confronted with opposition to Percival's appointment. Yet Melbourne's grounds for refusal – that Arnold had 'impaired his own utility' by publishing indiscreet opinions – applied no less to Percival.

Arnold's consolation prize was appointment as Regius Professor of Modern History at Oxford in 1841 – being thought unfit to occupy a Chair of Divinity. There he gave lectures during three weeks in the year while retaining his headmastership at Rugby. In June of the following year, he died suddenly of angina pectoris in the headmaster's house on the eve of his forty-seventh birthday. Percival, by contrast, left Rugby at the age of sixty with more than twenty years of active life ahead of him.

Arnold's early death did more for his reputation than Percival's long career did for his. It denied him the opportunities which came to Percival in later life, but focus on a single achievement over a relatively short period produces a sharper and more vivid picture than the bringing together of a wide range of disparate achievements spread across several decades.

Arnold was, in the words of a classical obituarist, *felix opportunitate mortis*: fortunate in the occasion of his death. Dying at the peak and seat of his achievement, he became the perfect subject for myth-making among the faithful, and no time was lost in inflating his reputation. Percival, by contrast, was heading for further valuable work in affairs of church and state, but those were also the years of his long diminuendo, which ended with an octogenarian clinging to office despite failing powers, the days of glory long past.

A. P. Stanley's *The Life and Correspondence of Thomas Arnold D.D.* in two stout volumes was published in 1844, only two years after his subject's death. The author had been one of the great man's brightest and most admiring pupils. His purpose in writing the biography was to overcome the odium in which his old headmaster's name was held everywhere except at Rugby. This he achieved in spectacular fashion with a hagiography from which anything reflecting unfavourably on his hero – the flogging scandal, for example – was omitted.

Arthur Stanley's credentials were impeccable: he later held the Chair of Ecclesiastical History at Oxford and finished his career as Dean of Westminster. The judgment of such a man was not to be questioned, and his success in rehabilitating Arnold's good name was total. He remains today the chief architect of Arnold's reputation: 'the founder of the legend'.[13]

A second devoted apostle and influential contributor to the legend was Thomas Hughes. His semi-autobiographical *Tom Brown's Schooldays*, in which Arnold is also portrayed in a heroic light, was published in 1857 and has been a bestseller ever since. By the time Percival left Rugby it had run through more than fifty editions. When it first appeared, Stanley professed himself astonished at the account of all the bullying, violence and vice which had gone on under the saintly headmaster's nose, not an inkling of which had been conveyed to his own readers.

Arnold's sudden death in office was a sensation, but Percival's exit from Rugby was not without its drama too. On 24 March 1895, as he was waiting in his study to take the train to London for his consecration as bishop, a gale blew to the ground seventeen elms which had stood in the Close for generations. Their uprooting provided a symbolic farewell to one responsible for a salutary but stormy interlude in the school's history.

CHAPTER 24

Welsh Disestablishment

However demanding his duties at Clifton, Percival had found time to address wider issues. At Rugby it was the same. His conscience required him to speak out against injustice wherever it was to be found and whatever the consequences to his own career. In the national arena he extended his campaigning from involvement in education to knight-errantry in matters political and ecclesiastical. As ever, his prime motivation was social concern. He seemed intent on demonstrating that a public school headmaster could be the enemy of privilege and a champion of the underdog.

In 1894 the issue of the day was the disestablishment of the Welsh Church. The Liberal government's Bill to effect this was furiously opposed by Tory politicians and all the bishops of the Established Church, to which Percival owed allegiance. At their head was Archbishop Benson, a former Rugby master.

To Percival's way of thinking, loyalty in a bad cause was no virtue. In one of his hard-hitting letters to *The Times*, headlined 'Welsh Disestablishment – An Appeal to the English Bishops', he trod heavily on the toes of the great and not so good.[1] His opening salvo referred to the bishops' opposition to an earlier piece of Liberal legislation, a Local Government Bill:

It is felt by a large number of churchmen that our Bishops are incurring a grave responsibility and doing serious injury to the prospects of the Church by their tone and attitude in regard to the legislative measures of the present Liberal Government, and yet hardly any one inside the Church ventures publicly to express in plain language the deep disappointment so widely felt at their lack of wise statesmanship and foresight.

A liberal clergyman's Address to the Archbishop protesting about his opposition to that Bill and the social benefits which it would bring had been too mealy-mouthed for Percival's taste and ought, he now wrote, to have run as follows:

Your Grace and your colleagues have caused much pain and disappointment to all liberal churchmen by your failure to show any earnest sympathy with the undoubtedly beneficial purpose of the Bill, and by acquiescing in the cynical and selfish tone of the House of Lords in dealing with it. It is probable that your example may have a mischievous effect on the minds and attitude of many clergymen, while it may be taken as certain that it has tended to rouse suspicion and bitterness in the minds of many of the poorer class, and we therefore venture most respectfully to urge your Grace to do what you can to make amends for your mistake.

The whole bench of bishops was thus 'most respectfully' subjected to a public wigging by the headmaster of Rugby. Their uncompromising hostility to the Welsh Disestablishment Bill he went on to denounce as 'another mistake which can hardly fail to be disastrous in its consequences'.

The Anglican Church in Wales was the Church of a minority, and the majority view of the Welsh people and their Members of Parliament at Westminster was against the continuance of its privileged position in establishment and endowments. In his letter Percival argued, in the name of democracy, that a people should be free to make its own choice and, on practical grounds, that disestablishment would, by removing hostility, increase rather than diminish the spiritual influence and power of the Church in Wales.

As for the dispute over what would happen to the endowments, they should, he insisted, continue to be devoted to spiritual and philanthropic causes, not seized and squandered by the state. Although he refrained from throwing further fuel on the fire by saying so on this occasion, he wanted them fairly distributed among all the Churches in Wales.

His letter, cogently argued and intemperately phrased, fell on the nation's breakfast tables like a bombshell – as he had intended. Conventional opinion was deeply shocked. Old Rugbeians, in particular, were incensed. A number of parents who had entered sons for the school withdrew their names, and a similar fall-out affected Clifton. A fellow liberal churchman wrote to Percival to say how extremely glad he had been to see the letter, but how extremely surprised that Percival had been so incautious as to write it, doing possible injury to Rugby and certain injury to his own chances of promotion in the Church, 'which you deserve and were certain to get'.[2]

The injury to both was real. In Percival's case, it was his ambition to return to the north and work among the urban poor. In August 1894 he had written to the Bishop of Ripon: 'As some of my friends have been writing to me about the Deanery of Durham, which it appears is soon to be vacant, I feel moved to tell you that there is no post I should like so much.'[3] The deanery would have brought with it the wardenship of the university and a stipend of £3000 a year, but it was not to be his.

Yet his conscience could not be silenced. After alienating the Conservatives he proceeded for good measure to launch a public attack on the Liberal Prime Minister. In the course of denouncing the sin of gambling during a sermon in Westminster Abbey he deplored racing and the example set by Lord Rosebery, one of whose horses had recently, and regrettably, won the Derby.

Rosebery's offer of bishopric a few months later was both forgiving and clever. It was something which Percival might no longer have expected. On the other hand, the see on offer was a rural backwater where a notorious firebrand could do little harm, and the terms of Rosebery's letter made it hard for him to refuse an appointment which was not at all what he would have wished.

Reverend and Dear Sir, [the Prime Minister wrote] I am extremely anxious that you should fill the vacant See of Hereford. It is not merely that your standing, experience, and ability give you a claim to a Bishopric; but the circumstances of Hereford make it of the highest importance that it should be presided over at this juncture by one who entertains large and liberal views as to the true nature and function of Church Establishments.[4]

The diocese included thirteen parishes in Wales, and Percival was seen as the ideal person to minimise friction over these. After pointing this out, Rosebery added an inducement very similar to that employed by his friends to persuade Percival to leave Clifton for Trinity:

One word more. I was concerned some time since to learn that your health required change and some degree of repose. I am very far from insensible to the heavy work that devolves on Anglican Bishops in these days. But Hereford is not one of the heavier Sees, and I trust that you will not be deterred from undertaking it by fear of undue pressure.

Lack of pressure was no attraction to a man of boundless vigour, but Rosebery was well briefed. On doctor's orders Percival had just obtained leave of absence for two months from Rugby. Return tickets to the Second Cataract had already been purchased for a recuperative journey up the Nile for himself and his invalid wife.

Should he accept or not? Was it intended as a real job or nothing more than a sinecure? Was he perhaps being tempted into exile? The see of Hereford dated from the seventh century, and in the nineteenth its boundaries had altered little since the age of the Heptarchy. The Lord Marcher bishops had experienced turbulence in Norman times; Hereford had not been isolated from the civil wars which had erupted in England since then; but all had been quiet for the previous three centuries, through which Hereford appeared to have slumbered serenely. Known as the Dead See, it seemed even further behind the times than the University of Oxford. Should he, could he, stir it into life?

Ten days before receiving the Prime Minister's letter he had confided in Oakeley, one of his housemasters at Clifton, that he hoped he would not be invited to fill the vacancy as he would not care to say 'no thank you'. He was well aware that Hereford would not welcome a bishop with radical views or present him with the opportunities for good works which he would find in an industrial area.

Full of misgiving, he at first replied to Rosebery with a stalling letter, begging for two or three days to weigh the matter and consult with his wife. His decision to accept, made after this initial hesitation, may have been influenced by the hope of translation in due course to a more suitable see. But if so, he was to be disappointed.

He was not the only person to show reluctance. The Prime Minister had encountered exceptional difficulty in persuading the monarch to accept his nomination. When writing to Queen Victoria, Lord Rosebery had mentioned the Rev. Dr Percival's posts at

Clifton, Trinity and Rugby and added by way of an additional recommendation: 'He bears a high reputation for administrative capacity, and is well known in the causes of University extension.'[5]

But the Queen read *The Times* and knew less pleasing things about the Rev. Dr Percival. Mindful of her Coronation oath to maintain the Established Church, she instructed her secretary to consult her ecclesiastical adviser, the Bishop of Rochester (Randall Davidson, formerly Queen's Chaplain and Dean of Windsor and later Archbishop of Canterbury). She wanted to find out from him '*how* she can refuse Dr Percival, as she will on no account appoint a Disestablisher'.

Bishop Davidson cautiously advised that Rosebery's nomination was unfortunate 'solely and only on account of the Disestablishment question'. He continued:

> On almost every other ground Dr Percival is admirably suited for such a See as Hereford. Nor is he, in general politics, an advanced Liberal or Radical (or at least so I believe). But certainly to place on the borders of Wales, in a See such as Hereford, almost if not quite the only prominent clergyman in England who has declared himself in favour of Welsh Disestablishment, is to run a grave risk.[6]

However – so the bishop advised – the risk would be the Prime Minister's, not the Queen's, and 'considering the high qualities and merits of Dr Percival, I certainly see great difficulty in the Queen giving an absolute refusal, on the single ground of his opinions upon the political question of the hour'. Since Percival was 'an honourable and kindly man', he added hopefully, he might see Welsh Disestablishment in a different light when faced with the problem in practice.

This was not what the Queen wanted to hear, and she was neither mollified nor convinced by the unwelcome response. From her seat on the throne she probably had a rather different view on whether or not Percival was an advanced Liberal or Radical. She persisted in her objection, and an acrimonious correspondence ensued between her secretary and Rosebery's.

Rosebery assured her that he would never have submitted Percival's name if Percival were in favour of the disestablishment of the Church of England. He and Percival held the same view that 'Church Establishments are apt to be injurious to national religion when carried on against the national will'. In England it had the approval of the nation, but in Wales the Church of England 'has lost its hold on the mass of the people, and so acts as an offence and a stumbling block'. He was confident that Percival's appointment would strengthen the Church Establishment in England and the real interests of the Church in Wales.[7]

Percival himself made the same point to a correspondent at a later date:

Establishment to my mind is a question of expediency and it must depend on circumstances whether it is desirable or not; and as regards Wales I hold that the Welsh people and not the English people should decide, just as I hold that the English people should decide the question for England, and not the Welsh, Irish and Scotch.[8]

'This is the most extraordinary answer, in fact no answer and very objectionable,' the Queen wrote to her secretary on receiving Rosebery's letter, and the services of the Bishop of Rochester were once more enlisted as adviser.

He agreed that the Prime Minister had not met the Queen's real objection, which was to the appointment of a Disestablisher, and reiterated his opinion that she could not constitutionally decline to accept the nomination of a man as eminent as Percival for the sole reason that he was in agreement with government policy. But he did suggest another line of argument: Would Percival, if appointed, be acceptable to the clergy and laity in the diocese? He wrote to the Queen's secretary as follows:

What would certainly happen would be that he would be placed in grave difficulties with his own clergy, and this I think the Queen might ... point out to Lord Rosebery, and ask him for some reassurance – (which he will find it difficult to give in any cogent form).[9]

This objection was evidently not thought strong enough to be pursued and the Queen was forced to give way; which she did with a bad grace. The dispute between the palace and Downing Street rumbled on, each side reproving the other for political partisanship. The Queen accused the Prime Minister of playing party politics with his nominations for ecclesiastical preferment. The Prime

Minister accused the Queen of criticising Liberal government appointments but not Conservative ones, which, he alleged, were just as party-political. At this the Queen expressed herself as 'not a little pained' and proceeded to win the argument by naming four Liberal bishops appointed under the previous Conservative administration.[10]

A few months later, in a confidential letter to Percival, Rosebery wrote: 'It is a great satisfaction to me to have been the means of placing your lordship on the bench, and I look forward with eagerness to the opportunity of meeting you face to face.'[11]

As a footnote it may be added that nearly twenty more years passed, and Queen Victoria was long dead, before the contentious issue of the status of the Welsh Church was settled in the Liberals' favour. It was in 1914 that the Welsh Disestablishment Act finally reached the statute book, and even then, owing to wartime, its provisions did not take effect until 1920 (when some of the Welsh parishes concerned opted to stay within the Hereford diocese). Thereafter Rosebery and Percival were proved right. Once disestablished, the Church in Wales gained in strength and public support.

Meanwhile, presented by Frederick Temple, then Bishop of London, and the historian Mandell Creighton, Bishop of Peterborough, Percival was consecrated in Westminster Abbey by the Archbishop of Canterbury (the insulted Benson) on 25 March 1895. The archbishop recorded the event in his diary with the comment: 'I do not think he will be well received, but I doubt if his disestablishment views are so fierce as his Diocese believes. And living between the Cathedral and the Wye must soothe him.'[12]

Benson was right about Percival's reception at Hereford, but over-optimistic about the soothing effect of residence in the bishop's palace, whose peaceful grounds enjoyed a fine view of the cathedral tower and an extensive river frontage. Percival returned from his consecration to spend the remainder of the Easter term at Rugby and make his preparations for the resurrection of the Dead See.

CHAPTER 25

Bishop of Hereford

Percival's misgiving about Hereford proved fully justified. Despite what the Bishop of Rochester imagined, it would have been hard to name a see for which he was less suited or one which offered less scope for his talents. The bishop's palace became an island of liberalism surrounded by Tory squires and a staunchly conservative agricultural community. He was an outspoken advocate of continuing free trade; their livelihood was severely threatened by a collapse in the price of wheat and lack of protection from the competition of American prairie farming.

He was, too, an extreme Protestant imposed on a stronghold of High Churchmanship. On a whole range of subjects, political and social as well as ecclesiastical, he and his clergy stood poles apart, and neither silence nor compromise came naturally to him. He lectured them as he had been accustomed to lecture his pupils and became known as the Schoolmaster Bishop. Having no appreciation of his opponents' point of view or doubts about his own, he was never one for the give and take of intellectual argument. He could admire Anglo-Catholics for their devotion but was dismissive of their beliefs. So he failed to build bridges or make converts.

It was also a drawback that, because his powers of patronage were unusually small, he was unable to introduce a liberal element among the clergy. The result was a stalemate. When after some years he sought to alleviate his isolation by appointing canons who shared his own advanced views, this created a rift between those inside and those outside the precincts of the cathedral. It remained the clergy, not the bishop and his canons, who were in tune with the local church-going population.

These divisions did not deflect Percival from the main task. The practical affairs of the diocese were tackled with his usual efficiency and determination. Prebendary Archibald Wynne Willson, his domestic chaplain and secretary, summarised the situation in these words:

> His hindrances were heavy. He was a radical amongst bigoted conservatives, a liberal churchman and reformer amid a population whose soft relaxing climate caused them to dislike effort, and whose remoteness made them suspicious of new thought. He was a keen temperance reformer amongst a cider-making, hop-growing community. He was not always served loyally by men whom he himself appointed to positions of importance. But there is no doubt that his power of organisation, and to still greater extent his power of awakening a sense of duty, achieved the main purpose of a bishop's life, that of getting his diocese to work.[1]

Another verdict was pronounced after his death in the columns of *The Church Times*, a High Church organ characterised by Percival as 'thoroughly unchristian'.[2] Its obituary of him, however, although sharp, was charitable:

> Few bishops have lived lonelier lives. Yet for Dr Percival as a man the diocese had no unkind feeling. It is a rare experience for a bishop to find himself in so small a minority, and the diocese had a certain admiration for one who had the courage of his opinions. He could exhibit considerable charm of manner, and his private charities were understood to be large. That he was summoned from work which he did well to work for which he was wholly unfitted, was a consequence of the existing relations between Church and State, and his episcopate offers a very strong practical argument for their immediate modification.[3]

A man of principle will always command respect, and chief among the qualities for which Bishop Percival was respected personally despite his detested opinions were, indeed, sincerity, generosity and (almost) unfailing courtesy.

According to one Anglo-Catholic layman in the diocese: 'His was a delightful personality, and it was to me quite wonderful that so many of us were so attached to him when our views in matters of Church and State were so far removed from his.'[4] 'Delightful personality' is not a phrase which would readily have sprung to the lips of his pupils at Clifton and Rugby or those of the undergraduates of Trinity.

Dedication to pastoral care was one reason for the extent of his personal popularity at Hereford. This exceeded all normal bounds, as two small incidents will serve to illustrate.

During the interregnum between the death of the previous incumbent and Percival's enthronement some confusion arose over a date for confirmations by a visiting prelate. This was brought forward without due notice, with the result that some candidates missed the occasion. The vicar of one parish was so upset about the six disappointed candidates whom he had prepared for what he impressed on them was one of the most important steps in their lives that he wrote an indignant letter to the bishop-designate, who was still at Rugby.

The parish was Criggon in Montgomeryshire, one of the most remote in the whole diocese. The population numbered a hundred and fifty seven, and the nearest railway station was thirteen miles away. There had been no visit from its bishop for more than twenty years. But now a prompt reply from Rugby was followed by the arrival of Percival, accompanied by his wife, to spend the Easter weekend in Criggon in order to confirm the six young peasants.

On Easter Sunday he celebrated the eucharist and preached the sermon at matins and evensong. Ironically, the parish was one of those due for disestablishment, and the vicar had found it hard to persuade his churchwarden to read the customary address of welcome. But when the bishop was seen to be so genial and earnest, so humble and unpretentious, a triumphal arch was hurriedly erected over the church gate in his honour.

'I cannot say,' wrote the vicar afterwards, 'how grateful I felt to Dr Percival for this great act of sympathy with out-of-the-way, forgotten folk, who rejoice and take fresh courage on finding that some one does care.'[5]

Mrs Percival, too, won the hearts of parishioners. She had made the journey to be at her husband's side in spite of poor health and insomnia, but so far from complaining she left with a smile, praising Criggon as the only place where she had been able to get a good night's sleep for a long time.

In a second incident at a later date the bishop's secretary received a telegram from the vicar of Donnington, near Ledbury, on a Friday urgently requesting a locum because he had been taken ill.

On the Sunday the bishop answered the call in person, driving out from Hereford in his carriage, taking the prescribed services at eleven o'clock and half-past three and driving back the same day. Knowing the living to be a poor one, he brought sandwiches with him to save the vicar's family the expense of entertaining him to lunch.

His generosity manifested itself in anonymous gifts, generally of the order of ten pounds, to the poorer of his clergy at Christmas time. One year, to guard the secret of the source of these presents and put the recipients off the scent, he employed as his almoner a clergyman with whom he was frequently at loggerheads at diocesan conferences. It was, too, a firm principle with him to spend the whole of his income as bishop within the diocese, never on his own holidays or personal needs.

His loneliness while at Hereford was initially diocesan only, not domestic. At the bishop's palace the Percivals began by leading a full social life, entertaining hospitably on a large scale, as they had always done. A very different picture from that of the solemn, aloof figure, the enemy of pleasure in gloomy isolation, was painted by Wynne Willson:

> He has been called a puritan, but those who knew him at home surrounded by young people saw his power of enjoyment, his delight in merriment. He was no foe of sport or games; it was the debasement of them by gambling that he fought against. In those days he rode regularly, played golf in his holidays, and played 'drawing room' games with the greatest zest.[6]

This happiness was not to last. Louisa Percival – 'my dear Loo', as her husband called her – fell ill. The doctor forbade guests, and all entertainment ceased. To aid recovery, she was moved to a farm-house in the neighbouring countryside, but died there on 13 June 1896, little more than a year after their coming to Hereford. The date was the anniversary of the day, fifteen years earlier, when her precious young son Freddie had been killed in a riding accident. Unable to bear the thought of being parted from him for ever, she had clung to the hope that he would be waiting for her, and her expiry on that date seemed no accident.

No headmaster or bishop could have hoped for a better wife. Louisa's vitality and high spirits, her affectionate nature and wholehearted sympathy for others were irresistibly endearing. At

Oxford and Rugby and Hereford, as at Clifton, those who found Percival hard going were often reconciled to him through her. Her contribution to his achievements was the unobtrusive management of the infrastructure of his life, which she undertook with cheerfulness, intelligence and tact. While he was on the bridge, she was always in the engine room. Shy and reserved with others, Percival relied heavily on the closeness and support of his family, his dear Loo above all.

The cure for loneliness was work and, although out of his element on the rustic border between England and Wales, he had set about fulfilling every episcopal duty with his customary conscientiousness: all the more assiduously, perhaps, because doubt had been cast on his ability to perform them adequately by reason of his lack of parochial experience.

Hereford was a diocese with a population of two hundred thousand souls scattered across three hundred and seventy-seven parishes, most of them inaccessible by rail. Percival therefore spent much of his time travelling, which, as a countryman, he enjoyed. The impressive figure of the tall bishop in his tall hat on horseback or in horse-drawn carriage became a familiar sight on the roads around Hereford. He was the last Bishop of Hereford confined to those modes of transport. An episcopal motor car arrived with his successor in 1917 (and frequently broke down).

Percival was also constantly on the move outside the diocese, when he went by rail. Meetings in London, Bristol and Oxford and confirmations at Rugby and Clifton made regular calls on his time. In London he had bases at the Athenaeum Club, of which he was a member from 1888 until his death, and in the Lollards Tower of Lambeth Palace. Yet his devotion to the primary duty of nourishing the moral and spiritual life of his flock was never stinted.

In 1900, in response to an inquiry about the respective work loads at Rugby and Hereford, he replied: 'No bishop, I believe, has such an arduous position as headmaster at Rugby. During the eight years I was there I was at work from half-past six in the morning till ten at night.'[7] At Hereford, nevertheless, he quickly acquired the reputation of being rather more than a glutton for work. 'An ogre for work' was the term applied by members of his staff. One of his chaplains complained that the bishop's pace was too hot for him even though he was already accustomed to working fourteen hours a day.

Restless and peripatetic, Percival left the comfort of his palace

for the rough roads of his diocese with enthusiasm. It was his
ambition to become personally acquainted with every one of his
clergymen and church workers, and everywhere he went he issued
a stream of invitations to formal conferences and informal get-
togethers at parish halls and garden parties.

Because Hereford was close to the southern extremity of the see
he made a point of travelling north every summer and spending six
to eight weeks preaching and holding meetings in the archdeaconry
of Shropshire, whose case for becoming a separate see he supported.
To keep in touch with remote rural parishes, he instituted Diocesan
Missions and launched a monthly magazine, the *Diocesan Messen-
ger*, whose initial heavy losses he met out of his own pocket.
Church Army vans manned by lay evangelists toured the diocese.
A special mission ministered to the spiritual needs of the host of
hop-pickers who made an annual invasion from towns in the
Midlands.

The most formal of the bishop's lines of communication were his
triennial Charges: the first in 1898, the last in 1916. These reports
were a mixture of general principles and practical detail in the well-
established Percivalian manner: factual, uplifting and admonitory.
The first part of each was parochial and contained a review of
returns by clergy and churchwardens. The second provided an
opportunity for the bishop to air his personal opinions on Church
doctrine and general conduct. The Charge published in May 1904,
for example, was entitled *The Church and National Life*.

Recurrent topics covered in these Charges identify Percival's
particular concerns. They were: forms of public worship (in which
he deprecated ritual as 'the sacramental superstition of the darker
ages', appealing to the 'wealthier or materialised classes');[8] teaching
in church schools (which the clergy were earnestly enjoined not to
leave to others); intemperance (drunkenness); impurity (resulting in
illegitimacy); and the housing of the poor.

Extracts from *Church Work & Church Reform, A Charge
delivered to the Clergy & Churchwardens of the Diocese of
Hereford 1901* will serve to convey the flavour of all:

The work of *Temperance Reform* – more urgently needed for the
good of our people in town and country than almost any other
single work that could be named – is, I think, felt to be making
some real progress amongst us, in spite of the torpor or timidity
of the Government, and the growing wealth, organisation, and

influence of the distillers, brewers and publicans. The benefits
that have accrued from the Sunday Closing Act, wherever
adopted, are beginning to impress the public mind.[9]

A passage on church schools well illustrates what had been
demanded of teaching staff at Clifton and Rugby. The duty of a
schoolmaster in any grade of school is, Percival wrote, 'to instruct,
to train, to impress, to inspire [his pupils], to fix their purpose, and
to mould their tastes and character, and for this he has to be at his
post hour after hour by the clock'. When pressed by a Royal
Commission on Ecclesiastical Discipline in May 1905 to explain
why so many parishes in his diocese failed to hold daily services, he
made no secret of his priorities in stating that his clergy were often
too busy in their schools at his instigation.[10]

Next in the 1901 Charge came a reference to 'my scheme of
Circulating Book Boxes for the use of country parishes'. This was
to stimulate the habit of reading. Where a parish met the cost of
two such boxes, the bishop would donate a third. The importance
of literacy to the poor was never far from his mind.

Nor were the overcrowded and insanitary conditions of their
homes. Under the heading, *Dwellings of the Poor*, he posed the
question:

How long shall we be content to live our conventional Christian
lives, while suffering these things to continue in our midst, eating
like a cancer into the moral life of both the present and future
generation?

Under *Impurity* he noted with a modicum of satisfaction that
between the 1850s and 1890 illegitimacy in the diocese had fallen
from 11 per cent of all births to 7.6 per cent. But in his next Charge
three years later it was said to be still a 'prevailing evil'.

Under *Church Reform* he argued the case for a movement at the
grass roots through the establishment of a Church Council in every
parish. At the other end of the intellectual scale he mounted a
defence of the Higher Biblical Criticism.

Finally came some trenchant comments on affairs of state. 'We
do not begin the new century well,' he wrote. The fighting in South
Africa was 'a desolating war ... in which the Church has given
little guidance'. There were 'heavy burdens of taxation and debt'
and 'much needed social reforms indefinitely postponed in conse-

quence'. A 'materialistic spirit and the greed of wealth' were 'very strong'. He believed that the prosperity of the English during the queen's reign had infected them with hubris, and warned that the 'inevitable attendant of the insolence of pride' was nemesis.

Religious education was the subject of most concern to him and one in which his influence was exceptionally strong because Hereford was a diocese where most primary education was still the responsibility of church schools.

Inheriting a well organised Bible and Prayer Book Prize Examination Scheme, he increased the number of the 'Bishop's Special Prizes' and after Louisa's death endowed twelve further annual prizes in her memory. Nearly every year he held a prize-giving ceremony with tea at the palace for all the prize-winning children, their parents, their head teachers and the clergy from their parishes: several hundreds in all.

But hard work could not eliminate dissension. A diocese is crucially dependent on harmonious relations between bishop and clergy, and in striving for this Percival's best endeavours continued to be handicapped by the obstinacy of his radical opinions. His calls for reform fell on deaf ears. The important issues of Welsh Disestablishment, modern thinking and ecumenicalism were deeply divisive, and his personal popularity was not universal. In William Temple's words:

Percival was not an easy man to know. He was deeply sympathetic, except on the intellectual side, but he did not easily show his sympathy. Those who took the first step found that he welcomed approaches, but it is not easy for the ordinary country clergyman to take the first step towards intimacy with his Bishop. Consequently there were to the end many who knew him only as an official and as a controversialist on what was in their judgment the wrong side. And it cannot be denied that, when known only in this way, he seemed both formidable and chilling . . .

Only those who could penetrate his reserve ever knew his greatness of spirit or his tenderness of heart. To others he seemed austere, remote, and even rather contemptuous. Just as at Rugby he would trust individual boys, while putting little trust in the School as a whole, so at Hereford he honoured his clergy taken singly for their devotion and ungrudging labours, but he had no high opinion of the clergy as a whole, whether in his diocese or out of it.[11]

In private and public life alike the warm-hearted, outward-going, ice-breaking Louisa was an irreparable loss. Mary Georgina, his new bride when he married again in January 1899 at the age of sixty-four, was the second daughter of Dr Frederick Symonds, the Oxford physician who had attended him when his health broke down as an undergraduate, and a cousin of John Addington Symonds. The wedding took place in Westminster Abbey with the bridegroom hurrying from a meeting at Church House to arrive just on time.

The second Mrs Percival did not win the praises heaped on the first. She was said to give herself airs and graces as the bishop's wife. Her step-children did not take to her, and there was trouble with the servants, who found her 'difficult'. It became necessary for Percival to tell James Bateman, his highly prized butler, that he must come to him if the new mistress of the house dismissed him. Percival himself, however, appears to have been comforted by her companionship after a period of domestic solitude.

The unimportance of Hereford in the life of the nation must have preyed on his mind. His vision stretched far beyond the boundaries of his diocese, and after eleven years in office he was tempted by the prospect of elevation to the Archbishopric of York.

York was in the north where his roots were and where the coveted deanery of Durham had already eluded him. The north was one of those areas where the rising Labour movement which excited his sympathy was burgeoning. Social conditions in the great industrial towns were crying out for drastic improvement. The new northern universities were in need of guidance and funds. While his talents were being under-used in the west, Percival's public utterances were making his name and reputation well known and respected in the north. Whenever he visited the region to preach or address meetings, the churches and halls were packed. The province of York would offer ideal opportunities for a crowning achievement to his career.

In 1905 the Unionist government fell and a Liberal administration took office under Sir Henry Campbell-Bannerman. At York Archbishop Maclagan celebrated his eightieth birthday the following year. It was then understood between the Prime Minister and

Percival that he would be nominated when the imminent vacancy occurred.

But Maclagan lived on and by the time he resigned in the autumn of 1908 it was Campbell-Bannerman who had died and the new Prime Minister had different ideas about the archbishopric. He chose to nominate the 44-year-old Bishop of Stepney (Cosmo Gordon Lang) instead of the 74-year-old Bishop of Hereford. Percival, he thought, was too old for such an arduous post, and he wrote to tell him so.

His hopes crushed, the plans he had been making aborted, Percival was desolate. The promised prize had been snatched from him. He was not, after all, to be the spiritual Headmaster of the North. It was the bitterest disappointment of his life. 'Asquith has sent me my obituary notice,' he wrote plaintively to the Dean of Bristol. Yet even his closest friends and colleagues found it hard to quarrel with the view that he would have been physically unable to bear such a heavy load, however undimmed his spirit.[12]

Hereford, though, was still not beyond his powers. Four years later he curtly dismissed rumours that he was about to resign, expressing himself as determined to 'plough my allotted field until my work be done'.[13] Retirement while still fit to work would have seemed a dereliction of duty, akin to 'loafing'.

CHAPTER 26

A Divided Church

The Victorians were ardent believers and regular worshippers. Indeed, in the judgment of one historian, among highly civilised countries Victorian England was one of the most religious the world has known.[1] The correct forms of Christian doctrine and observance were hotly debated and disputed. Even the minutiae of religion were matters of general concern and argument. Towards the end of the Queen's reign and in the years that followed, Percival was in the thick of this fray.

From the beginning of the reign, with the recently emancipated Church of Rome (the Old Faith) threatening on one flank and Wesleyan dissenters, Quakers and other Nonconformists flourishing on the other, the established Church, which should have been holding the majority of the nation together, was itself split into warring factions. As an institution born of compromise, the Anglican Church 'required conformity, but left some doubt about the doctrines' to which the faithful were expected to conform.[2]

The Queen herself stood staunchly by her oath to 'maintain the Protestant Reformed Religion established by law'. In this she enjoyed the support of the conservative consensus among Anglican clergy. But the word 'Protestant' was scarcely applicable to the Anglo-Catholic wing of the Church whose ranks were swelling among the clergy from the middle of the century. Inspired by the Oxford Tractarians, they believed in the primacy of the eucharist and in the Real Presence – that the body and blood of Christ were present in the bread and wine of the Holy Communion. Their services were solemnised by elaborate ritual, featuring ceremonial robes and processions.

Liberals and conservatives alike condemned these popish practices. Denial of the doctrine of transubstantiation lay almost
as close to the heart of Protestantism as rejection of papal supremacy. Accused of bringing back the mass, Anglo-Catholics were
thought to be heading for Rome. But, although what was dubbed
Newmania became widespread, they preferred Anglican tolerance
to papal authoritarianism and few followed their leader all the
way.

To men like Percival ritual was an abhorrent symptom of a
materialist society. Its appeal was to the eye and ear, not to the
heart; to the senses and emotions, not to the spirit. It tended to blur
and destroy the line of demarcation between Rome and Canterbury.
As bishop, he on two occasions flouted the law by refusing to
endorse the nomination of 'ritualistic' clergymen to parishes in his
diocese. 'I risked, of course, prosecution, but no steps were taken,'
he told the Royal Commission on Ecclesiastical Discipline.[3] In each
case he avoided legal action by persuading the patron of the living
to nominate a different incumbent.

In other evidence to the same commission in 1905 he spoke of
his belief in simplicity of worship and his opposition to the Roman
Church because it was 'essentially sacerdotal, essentially obscuran-
tist, essentially intolerant'. He had voiced a similar sentiment to his
clergy in 1898:

> With all her aggressive claims, all her deep-seated antagonism to
> educational and intellectual enlightenment, and to individual
> freedom of conscience; with all her mediaeval superstitions, and
> her modern decrees, her Mariolatry, her image-worship, her
> Jesuitry; with all these at our gates to tempt and to mislead the
> weak or the unwary, it is, to say the least, extremely unwise to
> dally with her doctrinal ritual and observances.[4]

The principle of the Reformation as Percival saw it was 'to lay
stress on freedom of conscience and personal responsibility'. To his
way of thinking, rigid dogma was a straitjacket and the Church of
England ought to interfere as little as possible with individual
freedom and give as liberal an interpretation as possible to set
forms.[5]

He and the liberal wing of the Church to which he belonged
wanted, not the *semper eadem* of Rome, but a Progressive Church,
one that looked to the present and the future, not the past; one

which would concentrate on improving social conditions and not be distracted by the niceties of ritual.

In wrestling with the problem of reconciling Christian belief with the new revelations of science, churchmen experienced much heart-searching over the truth of the Bible. It had to be conceded that the world was somewhat older than the six thousand years calculated by Archbishop Ussher on the basis of the generations of Adam as recorded in the Bible, but the Old Testament as well as the New was the word of God and every good Anglican remained under some obligation to cling to this fundamental tenet of Christian faith. If too openly doubted by anyone in holy orders, a charge of heresy might be brought.

Those within the Church of England who clung to biblical truth most tenaciously and took it as the sole and sufficient guide to Christian conduct were the Evangelicals. The strength of their movement reached a peak in the middle of the century when it is said to have attracted the loyalty of more than a quarter of Anglican clergy. But it attracted also the scorn of the Anglo-Catholic High Churchmen, who looked down on such puritan piety as naive and such clergymen as ignoramuses.[6]

Men who thought like Percival were naturally in sympathy with a Low Church movement, but they too found Evangelicalism unacceptably low intellectually. 'Our faith,' Percival acknowledged in his Charge to his clergy in 1901, is 'founded on the rock of Holy Scripture', but 'newer study of the Bible in what we may call a scientific spirit ... deserves to be welcomed both for its truth-seeking aim and because it brings new interest and reality into the religion of the more educated classes'. He believed that a reformulation of faith to meet the challenge of science was the only hope 'of keeping Christianity really influential in the life of a scientifically educated community'. 'Consequently,' he continued:

> whenever I hear devout and good men inveighing against the Higher Criticism, I have to confess that I listen with regret. They sometimes remind me of the picture in the history-books of our childhood, representing King Knut with his courtiers seated on the sands, and flinging his futile prohibition at the advancing ocean tide ... Advancing knowledge must necessarily affect and modify many traditional conceptions ... the advancing tide of that progressive revelation which is bearing us gradually onwards to a fuller and clearer apprehension of Divine Truth.[7]

The Broad Church, which attracted the allegiance of liberal churchmen with advanced views, was Percival's spiritual home. Its adherents believed that neither scientific truth about the age of the world nor Darwin's theory of evolution was in serious conflict with biblical truth. They laid emphasis on the general spirit of Christianity rather than any one brand of dogma. While the central tenets of Anglo-Catholic belief were the authority of the Church and the importance of the priesthood, Broad Churchmen believed in an unfettered exercise of individual reasoning and judgment.

Some were thought to carry rationalism too far by denying miracles and the authenticity of some of the books in the Bible and preaching morals at the expense of faith. Archbishop Tait (the former headmaster of Rugby) expressed his criticism of Broad Churchmen (and their opponents) in these words: 'What is wanted is a deeply religious liberal party ... the great evil is that the liberals are deficient in religion, and the religious are deficient in liberality.'[8]

In 1860 Frederick Temple and Benjamin Jowett, Percival's friends and fellow Broad Churchmen, narrowly escaped disgrace in a great storm over *Essays and Reviews*, a publication in which other contributors had appeared to cast doubt on biblical truth. The stated purpose of the volume was a provocative challenge to High Churchmen. It was 'to show the advantage which religion might derive from the free handling of certain great subjects too often conventionally treated'.

At Oxford Jowett, already denounced by Puseyites as 'the arch-heretic' and denied the university pulpit, eventually suffered nothing worse than a disciplinary appearance before the Vice-Chancellor. Temple, then headmaster of Rugby, was rescued by Gladstone who, in the teeth of vehement protest, nominated him to the see of Exeter, thus opening for him the road to London and Canterbury. When the matter was brought before the Privy Council, it ruled that the Holy Scripture contained the Word of God but was not in itself the Word of God: a nice judgment which preserved liberty of interpretation.

Religious differences in mid-nineteenth-century Oxford and their relevance or irrelevance to current conditions were forcefully pinpointed by Percival's friend, Mrs Humphry Ward, in words which he himself could not have bettered:

But how little the leading ideas of that seething time of social and industrial reform, from the appearance of *Sybil* in 1843 to the Education Bill of 1870, mattered either to Pusey or to Liddon [a Puseyite canon of Christ Church], compared to the date of the book of Daniel or the retention of the Athanasian Creed! Newman, at a time when national drunkenness was an over-shadowing terror in the minds of all reformers, confesses with a pathetic frankness that he had never considered 'whether there were too many public-houses in England or no'.[9]

At Hereford from the day of his enthronement in 1895 Percival set about putting into practice the ideals which he had shared for many years with Temple and Jowett. Assiduousness in promoting them led him inevitably into controversy and conflict, both local and national.

In April 1899 his reputation as the leading liberal Anglican cleric was recognised when he was invited to take the chair at a Conference of Churchmen at the Royal United Services Institution in Whitehall. This was announced as being 'convened in conse-quence of the gravity of the present Church crisis'. At its conclusion it was resolved that:

We who are assembled at this Meeting of Churchmen, being distressed and anxious on account of the dangers that so seriously threaten the continued welfare of our reformed branch of the Catholic Church, do hereby pledge ourselves to co-operate in maintaining by all lawful and Godly means its Protestant and comprehensive character.[10]

The resolution continued with a condemnation of Romish prac-tices within the Church of England, such as regular confessions. It stated emphatically that the Real Presence of Our Lord in the Sacrament of His Body and Blood was a purely spiritual presence.

This declaration of liberal faith attracted more than five hundred signatures from among the clerics and laymen attending the meeting and two thousand more when it was circulated afterwards. Outside his own see Percival enjoyed a sizeable following.

Christian unity was an aim of Broad Churchmen, even if certainly not with Anglican popery or Rome on Rome's terms. They believed that the Church of England must embrace a greater majority of the population in order to justify its privileged position as the national Church. A census conducted on one Sunday in 1851 had found that only 51% of those attending church or chapel went to the Anglican services; 44% to the Nonconformist. The greater piety of Nonconformists made it a likely estimate that they represented some 30% of the total population, while 60% thought of themselves as Church of England. Roman Catholics numbered no more than 5%.[11] Percival's move towards unity was therefore to cultivate exceptionally fraternal relations with the third of the population who were chapel-goers.

When in Bristol he had come to like and respect that city's many Nonconformists, who included the Symonds family. Now, in the interests of Christian unity, he wanted to absorb them. The backward current towards medievalism and Romanisation had to be resisted, but the demarcation line between Anglicanism and Nonconformity he regarded as 'elastic'. While, as he put it, a policy of drifting towards Rome would mean drifting towards Niagara, only good could come of winning back dissenters in order to form a genuinely national Church.[12]

In an early display of ecumenicalism he became a prominent supporter of the Christian Conference, a national organisation open to members of all denominations. At one of its meetings, in 1899, he delivered a fighting speech in favour of reunion, asserting his right to participate in that mixed assembly whatever the contrary views of other bishops.

In 1908 he took the initiative in celebrating the tercentenary of the birth of the Puritan poet, John Milton, with 'a neighbourly gathering of Christians of different denominations for common worship and conference in honour of his great name' in Hereford's cathedral library.[13] This was succeeded by a Christian Ministers' Club with a membership of canons from the cathedral, local clergy and Nonconformist ministers meeting monthly for prayer and study of the Scriptures. Three years later, on the occasion of George V's coronation, he went so far as to invite Nonconformist ministers into the cathedral itself for a United Service of Holy Communion.

That was a step too far and, as he himself noted, 'the hot water boiled over'. Members of the cathedral chapter, headed by the Archdeacon of Hereford, remonstrated at 'an indiscriminate invitation to persons unconfirmed and possibly even unbaptised to Communicate in the Cathedral'. In Convocation Percival was censured by the Bishop of Winchester, with the concurrence of the Archbishop of Canterbury.[14]

As always, he was unrepentant. Attack being the best form of defence, his response to the archdeacon was a lofty rebuke. 'I have looked at your protest,' he wrote, 'and it certainly does little credit to its composer . . . or to the men who signed and presented it. Its tone is contemptuous, in an insolent way, to Nonconformist bodies, and offensive to the Bishop.' He concluded by accusing the signatories not only of prejudice but also, for good measure, of warped minds and feelings.[15]

The remonstrance, as phrased, justified none of this. A more seemly reaction might have been a soothing attempt to restore harmony. Instead it was a reversion to type: the headmaster confronting an insubordinate common room. Absolute monarchy came naturally to him, constitutional restraints did not, and life for his colleagues in the close could never have been easy. On this occasion he had deliberately provoked them, knowing their views and then ignoring them. That their objections were valid and they had the archbishop on their side evidently made him all the more imperious and headmasterly.

There was, too, an angry exchange of letters with the archbishop (Randall Davidson), whom Percival accused of siding with 'sacerdotalists and medievalists' and an 'aggressive and insolent faction' of High Churchmen. Davidson counter-attacked with a lengthy reprimand, accusing Percival of driving those who were working hard for a better spirit of unity *within* the Church, (including 'one friend after another of most moderate opinions') almost to despair.[16]

Another divisive incident concerned the Athanasian Creed with its promise of the direst of punishments for anyone who doubted the unity of the Trinity. Eternal damnation was not a concept endorsed by Broad Churchmen, and after one Easter Day service Percival remarked to one of his canons: 'How terrible it sounded – those innocent choir boys repeating those awful words, "without doubt he shall perish everlastingly." '[17]

Use of the Athanasian Creed was thereupon abandoned in cathedral services. This time, although in the wrong again, he had the support of the chapter. It was the minor canons who objected that this was a violation both of the cathedral statutes and of the declaration signed by all priests on their ordination, and was therefore illegal.

In a compromise which met the requirement of the law the creed was restored at eight o'clock matins but not at the eleven o'clock service. When the minor canons maintained their protest by boycotting the latter, Percival recorded his satisfaction: 'We had a beautiful service at 11 A.M. without either Athanasian Creed or Minor Canons.'[18]

His policy when making appointments to canonries during his later years was another cause of dissension. He was at pains to select only 'leading members of the Liberal Progressive Broad Church of Theology, that school to which, as it happens, I myself more or less belong'.[19] Earlier he had shown unwonted tolerance and even appointed an Anglo-Catholic.

Opposition to his later practice erupted with the appointment in 1915 of the Rev. B. H. Streeter, Fellow and Dean of Percival's undergraduate college at Oxford: Queen's. Streeter was among the most distinguished of academic theologians, but the views which he held and published were among the most advanced. With perhaps the single exception of Percival himself, no one could have been less welcome on doctrinal grounds among Hereford's conservative clergy.

Once more Percival was unrepentant. In his defence he pointed out that when, in a goodwill gesture to the chapter, he had appointed High Churchmen to cathedral stalls during his first ten years there had been no complaints. Yet now:

> when I have looked on for twenty years and seen Liberal Churchmen, however distinguished, relentlessly boycotted and passed over with depreciation and detraction almost everywhere, and have thought it necessary in the interest of the Church to do something to prevent this freezing out of Broad Churchmen and the narrowing of our National Church into a sect, there is raised this outcry.[20]

The outcry was not confined within the diocese. Over the years Percival's struggle to resuscitate the Dead See had attracted national attention and comment. By some it was seen as magnificent; by others as entirely fruitless – both with some degree of truth. Enthusiastically praised by journals such as *The Times* and the *Spectator*, it was severely criticised in the church press by traditionalists.

One dignitary, the Bishop of Zanzibar, became so incensed by Streeter's appointment that he took the remarkable step of issuing, through the church press, a lengthy indictment of what he considered to be Percival's errors of patronage, ending with a formal sentence of excommunication. The bishop was a missionary priest and High Church polemicist named Frank Weston who had been an undergraduate at Trinity shortly after Percival's presidency. This was his solemn climax:

> Therefore do We, Frank, Lord Bishop of Zanzibar, hereby declare and pronounce that, so long as the ground of our complaint set forth above remains, there can be, and from this day forward there is, no Communion in Sacred Things between Ourselves and the Right Reverend John, Lord Bishop of Hereford, nor between Ourselves and any priest within his jurisdiction who shall make known his approval of the false doctrines now officially authorised within the Diocese of Hereford; and We do further warn and charge all Our faithful people that, pending the meeting of Our Sacred Synod, they duly observe this Our Declaration and Sentence.[21]

What 'all Our faithful people' off the coast of East Africa made of this can only be imagined, but on this occasion Percival stood well within his rights. Canon Streeter held a licence from the Bishop of Oxford and had not been arraigned before, let alone condemned by, any ecclesiastical court or synod. Hereford's response to Zanzibar was a freezing put-down thinly cloaked in Christian courtesy:

> I regret the pain it must have caused you to adopt the course you have felt it your duty to adopt. I freely acknowledge the excellence of your motives, and this leads me to regret all the more your lack of Christian sympathy, your apparent inability even to understand the position of those from whom you differ, and your misguided conception of your own position and of your duty. For one bishop to take upon himself to excommunicate another bishop on his sole authority because of an alleged misuse of the patronage in his diocese is a proceeding which it is not easy to justify and which certainly does not tend to edification. And I must confess to some surprise that your modesty did not suggest to you that if public action was called for it should have been left to the proper authority . . . Thus I may venture to say, as an old man to a younger, that although acting no doubt

in all sincerity and from the highest motives, you have been led to take too much upon you . . .[22]

'Gentle though the whole reply is,' wrote one of Percival's admirers, 'it is not without suggestion of the iron gauntlet beneath the velvet glove – a favourite metaphor of T. E. Brown's, in talking over the methods of his Chief.'[23]

CHAPTER 27

Political Causes

On 10 May 1900, watched by members of his family, the Lord Bishop of Hereford took his seat in the House of Lords, filling a vacancy created by the retirement of the Bishop of Liverpool. There was, noticeably, no welcome. The chamber was almost empty.

'This won't greatly affect the British Empire or your father either,' he wrote to his son Arthur in South Africa,[1] but then spared no effort to belie those words. Hitherto he had had to rely on the goodwill of *The Times*; now he had a second platform from which to broadcast his views, promote his causes and influence events. This opportunity he seized, usually to the irritation and often to the fury of his fellow peers, few of whom shared his fervent aspirations for educational, ecclesiastical and social reform.

These strenuous endeavours in the political field made little impact on legislation. As a lone radical too resolutely independent to follow a Liberal Party line, he had no forces at his command and few allies, even on the bench of bishops. In 1895 he had written prophetically in a private letter to Lord Rosebery: 'I fear that during my working years [as a bishop] I shall remain a somewhat solitary and ineffective member of the Episcopal body.'[2] In 1901 after his initial experience of the Lords he wrote, also to Rosebery: 'I have, as a rule, to plough a somewhat lonely furrow; and doubts will sometimes arise as to whether the schoolmaster's field might not have produced a more abundant crop of things worth producing.'[3]

Nevertheless, as what might nowadays be termed a loose cannon, he achieved some success in publicising evils and injustices, shaming those responsible, and rousing the national conscience. By proposing extreme measures which had no prospect of passing into law he sometimes led his critics into conceding the case for a measure of moderate reform. In all things it was fundamental to his thinking:

> to give effect to the principle of devolution in politics based on trust in the people, which is I feel sure destined to become more and more the guiding principle of the highest statesmanship as the mass of the people become better educated and more intelligent.[4]

In any public controversy which embraced religion, politics or education Percival was sure to become embroiled. One which started before his entry into the House of Lords lasted intermittently for twelve years from 1895, when he entered the fray in a tussle over the financing and control of church schools. Here, as over the disestablishment of the Welsh Church, he once again set himself at odds with virtually every other senior member of the Anglican establishment, driven by the conviction that he was the only one in step with Christ's teachings.

The Education Act of 1870 had introduced elementary education for all. In the new schools, administered by lay school boards, religious instruction was strictly non-denominational. Faced with subsidised competition, the denominational church schools, hitherto the sole providers of elementary education, found themselves increasingly at a financial disadvantage. While the board schools enjoyed full government funding, the denominational (or voluntary) schools received minimal state aid and had to rely largely on their own resources to pay teachers, maintain buildings and purchase equipment.

In November 1895 the two archbishops led a delegation of bishops, other senior clerics and distinguished laymen to present a 'memorial' to the Prime Minister (Lord Salisbury) appealing for help for the church schools. This provoked a thunderous letter of dissent in *The Times* from 'J. Hereford'.[5]

When he was, as so often, swimming against the tide and arguing a dissenting case, *The Times* was pleased to allow Percival ample space and he had no need to economise on words. The gist of his prolixity on this occasion was that government grants in aid of denominational teaching should be made only on certain conditions. The most crucial concerned control, which the church leaders did not visualise relinquishing. But Percival maintained that 'in all schools that are largely supported by public money the local public ... ought in common justice to have some share in the management'.

Warming to his attack, he went so far as to charge the right reverend and other distinguished petitioners with insincerity in suggesting that they were acting in support of the right of parents to decide on the character of their children's religious education. This he held to be untrue: 'The real object of the present struggle is to secure larger grants from the State, and yet hold on to the exclusive denominational management of schools and the exclusive denominational appointment of teachers.'

Denominationalism ran counter to the Church unity for which Percival strove. It discriminated against his friends, the Nonconformists (who were content with the religious teaching at the board schools). The abolition of discrimination against these devout Christians constituted his second condition: 'I submit that no Voluntary School ought to receive larger grants from the public purse so long as its managers are prohibited by its trust deeds from employing any teacher who is a Nonconformist.'

Even his admiring successor at Clifton, J. M. Wilson (now Archdeacon, later Canon), felt obliged to take issue with him publicly over the language of this letter. Wilson was one of the liberal signatories of the petition, whose laudable objective was to preserve Church of England schools threatened with closure for want of adequate funds.

The dispute rumbled on until 1902, when Balfour succeeded Salisbury in Downing Street and an Education Bill was drafted which met some, but not all, of Percival's objections. Ever a pragmatist, he then switched from outright opposition to compromise, while still arguing vigorously for the principles of fair dealing between citizens of different denominations and of rates and taxes being administered by a management responsible to those who paid them.

These views were reiterated at length at a Church Congress, in Convocation and in the House of Lords, where he derided other provisions of the Bill for their timidity in moving education forward. At the committee stage in the Lords he moved several amendments, one of which would have allowed local authorities (subject to the approval of the Board of Education) to make attendance at continuation classes compulsory for those under seventeen no longer at school.

Meanwhile, as a practical step towards extending educational opportunities in his own diocese, he launched a Vacation School, following an initiative by Mrs Humphry Ward. This was hailed by the *Hereford Journal* as 'novel Experiment under the Auspices of the Bishop of Hereford'[6] and publicised by himself in a letter to *The Times*, where he claimed an average attendance of more than three hundred boys and girls.[7]

The passage of the 1902 Bill did not put an end to the argument over church schools, and in 1906, when the Liberals had succeeded to office, the new administration attempted to satisfy objectors and settle the matter in another Bill. Some of its terms failed to satisfy Percival, but he supported its principles against the continuing opposition of the hierarchy, the only bishop so to do. In another of his letters to *The Times* he complained of 'the unwarranted assumption, unblushingly reiterated in certain quarters, that the Church of England is united against the Bill'.

> Many High Anglican denominationalists, both clerical and lay – some of them more Roman than Anglican – have acquired the habit of posing on platforms and in the Press as the Church *par excellence*. We speak, they say, on behalf of the Church; we represent the Church; even bishops sometimes try our patience by countenancing this assumption; and what I feel it my duty to submit is that statesmen will make a mistake if they are influenced by this baseless assumption of a small but aggressive minority, which happens to be prominent in Parliamentary circles out of all proportion to its numbers, because of social connections and advantages, and because it is so largely clerical. Its voice is not really the voice of the people at large.[8]

To Percival's chagrin, Unionist opposition in the House of Lords proved strong enough to force the government to drop the Bill altogether. But, undeterred, he continued to air his own vision of the future of education in whatever forum was available to him: locally in his episcopal Charge and a Presidential Address to his diocesan conference the following year (1907) and nationally in a spate of further letters to *The Times*: on 'A System of National Schools', 'The State and Secondary Education' and 'The State and the Training Colleges'.

Over the years the debate had widened from the original issue of funding church schools to these more general aspects of the involvement of Church and State in education. But in his final letter

Percival returned to what was for him the central issue so far as the Church was concerned:

The separatist, sectarian, denominationalist tendency to segregate our children into rival pens for all religious instruction may produce Pharisees, but hardly Christians. Indeed, this denominationalist spirit, which has taken such a strong hold on some sections of our clergy and a few laymen, is doing much harm to the national Church and the national life. It is quite foreign to the spirit of an enlightened evangelical Christianity; and we should keep it as far as may be out of all our educational system.[9]

Members of the House of Lords in those years enjoyed real power over legislation. Indeed in the cut and thrust of debate between 1900 and 1902 the solitary, humbly born bishop was in face-to-face confrontation with the most powerful and highly born ministers of the Crown – the Marquess of Salisbury, Prime Minister; the Marquess of Lansdowne, Secretary of State for Foreign Affairs; and the Marquess of Londonderry, Lord President of the Council and President of the Board of Education. There were icy exchanges too with the Earl of Durham and other blue-blooded eminences of whose conservative views and entrenched positions Percival so heartily disapproved.

Only two months after his introduction he was voicing numerous objections to another Education Bill, designed to re-organise the secondary education system. This, he complained, largely ignored the 'excellent' report of a Royal Commission and made no provision for more money for schools in rural districts, which could not afford qualified teachers.[10]

During the following years his voice was heard in the Lords on other aspects of education, always on behalf of the children. In speaking extensively on the two parties' rival Education (England and Wales) Bills in 1902 and 1906 he received more support from outside the House than within. His speeches in December 1902 elicited many letters of congratulation. A 'sincere admirer' sent 'most heartfelt thanks for your outspoken opposition to what is beyond all doubt an iniquity'. 'May God Bless you in defending the Right,' wrote another correspondent.[11]

In 1905 he introduced his own Continuation Schools Bill, arguing that truncating education at twelve or thirteen was responsible for ignorance, inefficiency, low taste, drunkenness and lust.

He had, he said, been pleading for thirty years for compulsory evening classes up to the age of sixteen or seventeen. Recently, in 1903, he had presided over a Conference on The Working Class and Higher Education; and at another in 1904 he had spoken on the need for Evening Schools.

As in 1902, his plea for these went unheeded, not only in 1905 but again in a debate in 1910, when he pointed out that the great mass of children 'drift away from all the higher influences of life at the very time when your Lordships are sending your sons to Eton or some other public school for the best part of their education'.[12] His persistence was to be rewarded, but not until an enactment in 1918.

In 1907, in supporting an unsuccessful motion proposing a new inquiry into university affairs at Oxford and Cambridge, he could not resist quoting the comment made by a foreigner a few years before he himself had come up to the university in 1854:

> Oxford cannot be considered a place of research. We cannot look upon it as a home of scientific education. It is not even distinguished as a home of liberal education, but it has one remarkable and unique distinction – it is a training place for gentlemen, especially Tory gentlemen.[13]

Percival acknowledged the improvements which had taken place during the sixty years since then, but he was still far from satisfied. Amongst other changes he wanted the passman eliminated: a proposal which the conservative Bishop of Oxford heard, as he said, 'with a shudder'.[14] Here again Percival's thinking was ahead of his times. The passman made a gradual disappearance, and Percival's special bête noire, compulsory Greek, was abolished in 1919.

Temperance was another subject on which he could not remain silent. In March 1901 he spoke in favour of an Intoxicating Liquor (Sale to Travellers) Bill which was strongly opposed by the Salisbury government. He urged the Conservatives to drop their laissez faire policy over traffic in drink and temperance reform, 'one of the most pressing matters of the time'. 'It is our duty, a duty involving no interference with devotion to the principle of individual freedom, to take measures to regulate a dangerous trade,' he told the Prime Minister, but Salisbury was unmoved.[15]

The temperance cause made little headway. During the second

reading of the Unionist government's 1904 Licensing Bill he vainly denounced those whom he identified as its real authors:

> Who assisted at the birth of the Bill? The brewers! Who have been the most earnest promoters of the Bill in the other House? The brewers! By whose critical votes in one division after another have the provisions of this Bill been sent up to this House? Again, by the brewers! And who are the most whole-hearted supporters – indeed I might almost say the only whole-hearted supporters – of the Bill in the country? Again I have to say, the brewers![16]

That Bill became law; whereas the Liberal government's Licensing Bill in 1908, which provided for tighter control over the liquor trade and measures to reduce excessive drinking, was defeated by the Tory majority in the House of Lords.

Disappointed, Percival came to believe that a take-over by the state would be the best means of controlling the liquor trade. But his temperance principles were not offended by a Hops Bill the following year. This was to prohibit the use of hops substitutes in brewing and he supported it on the grounds that it would materially benefit the farmers in his diocese. But he was careful to add that he would not be sorry to see a large number of acres in Herefordshire and Worcestershire changed from growing hops to breeding Hereford cattle.[17]

As was to be expected, Percival was himself a life-long teetotaller, but in the privacy of his home his liberalism and liberality forbade him to impose temperance on his less puritan guests. They were hospitably served with fine wines.

Gambling, that 'blemish in our national life', was another target, and here he enjoyed marginally more success. In 1901, because he saw no hope for the passage of a Bill, he moved in the Lords for the appointment of a Select Committee to inquire into an increase in public betting. The outcome, three years later, was an Act regulating street betting – which he condemned as inadequate, pointing out that at Clifton, for example, where the downs were intersected by roads and paths, 'a bookmaker need only stand on the grass by the side of the road to be free to carry on his calling'.[18] That year, in addressing a Church Congress in Liverpool on the Ethics of Commerce, he referred to 'two noxious parasites – the professional betting man and the sporting journalist'.

When he tried again in 1912 with a Bill to restrict gambling

advertisements, he was not surprised that it failed. By then in his
late seventies, he was becoming resigned to failure. 'I should have
hesitated to introduce this Bill because I am conscious that I have
no influence with your Lordships, and I am an old man and
increasingly disinclined to take any part in public controversy,' he
told the House.[19]

His leading adversary was the Earl of Durham, a member of the
Jockey Club and the man who had chaired the Select Committee
ten years earlier. The earl described Percival's Bill as 'tyrannical
and preposterous', 'foolish' and 'absurd'. Its purpose was to ban
tipsters' advertisements in the press and circulars through the post,
and Percival claimed that it was aimed simply at the betting trade
'to purify and cleanse our English sport'. Durham argued, however,
that it would make racing columns in newspapers illegal, no one
would know when meetings were taking place, and that would
mean the end of horse-racing. Moreover, he added pointedly, the
proposed restrictions on lotteries and competitions would prevent
advertisements for entrance scholarships to public schools unless
authorised by the Home Secretary or Board of Trade.[20]

The motion was withdrawn, but Percival returned to the subject
later in the year, proposing amendments to a more modest, but
also ill-fated, Betting Inducements Bill. This provoked angry disagreement in committee over the publication of starting prices. 'It
is my misfortune,' said Lord Durham, 'always to be in antagonism
to the right reverend Prelate.'[21]

Gambling was also in the prelate's mind when, as a champion of
all oppressed creatures, he took up the cause of animal welfare. In
1902 he had moved the second reading of a Prevention of Cruelty
to Wild Animals Bill. The Lords were hostile and it was withdrawn, but a year later he was enthusiastically promoting a
substitute, The Spurious Sports Bill, and explaining its *raison d'être*
in *The Times*:

> As the law now stands it is penal to maltreat a wild animal in
> captivity. This Bill simply extends that law so as to make it
> equally penal to do the same wild animal to death when let out
> of its trap or box or bag or hamper for the purposes of sport . . .
> Men and boys may still gather in scores or thousands to see the
> helpless rabbits dragged from their hamper, shaken in front of
> the dogs, and then torn in pieces, while they yell around them in
> wild excitement over their bets.[22]

In his address to the Church Congress held that year in Nor-
thampton, he denounced 'the working-man's rabbit coursing' as
the lowest of all forms of sport.

That Bill too failed, and in 1909 he made a third unsuccessful
attempt. His Cruelty to Animals Bill was 'virtually the same Bill
which I introduced seven years ago'.[23] It proposed to prohibit three
'highly objectionable' forms of sport: the hunting, coursing and
shooting of animals which had been kept in confinement. These
included pigeons let out of traps, deer crated to a starting point and
the rabbits shaken out of crates. Percival believed that these
activities were more of an offence to the public conscience than
the hunting of wild animals, although he was also horrified
by the 'barbarities perpetrated in order to procure Fashionable
Furs'.[24]

For Percival politics and morals were inseparable. Free Trade
versus Protectionism was one of the most hotly disputed political
issues of that time, and he saw this as a moral question, not one of
economic expediency. As a passionate Free Trader he was tempted
to intervene on behalf of the Free Trade candidate in a by-election
at Ludlow in 1904. By reason of his membership of the House of
Lords, this would have been a serious breach of privilege and he
managed to restrain himself until the election was over.

He then let fly by publishing a letter which complained that his
diocese had been subjected to 'Protectionist propaganda, manufac-
tured in Birmingham', with Ludlow being 'flooded by an invasion
of political bagmen from Birmingham with their heterodox and
misleading speeches and tracts, perverting our simple folk'. Their
motive was, he declared, self-interest, because a system of tariffs
and preferences would increase their profits. These were men with
no consideration for the poor, who would suffer hardship from
higher prices:

> Every Bishop has solemnly promised to be merciful for Christ's
> sake to poor and needy people; but this Birmingham Gospel is
> all in the interest of the rich, and is without mercy for the
> poor and needy. Therefore ... it is my bounden duty to oppose
> it.[25]

As regards our Ludlow election the rumour reaches me that
many of our clergy supported the Protectionist candidate. I am
very sorry to hear this, but I indulge the hope that it may be

incorrect; for of this I feel assured, that every bishop or priest
or other minister of the Gospel who may be led to give
any countenance or support to any Protectionist candidate for
Parliament will fall into the very serious error of aiding the rich
at the expense of the poor, and the strong at the expense of the
weak.[26]

This letter provoked a furious reaction from laymen and clergy
alike and added greatly to Percival's unpopularity. As members of
an agricultural community the 'simple folk' of Herefordshire not
only wanted cheap bread but also needed protection from cheap
imports, and the local press was inundated with letters denouncing
the bishop and all his perversely radical opinions. Who was he,
living in the comfort of his palace, to side with foreign competitors
against his own hard-working flock struggling to earn a decent
living from the soil?

To Percival Birmingham was a birth-place of evil. In 1901 he
had written about the defection of the Liberal Unionists:

It almost looks as if our smaller politicians, who call themselves
liberals, were drifting away from that trust in the people without
which progressive liberalism has no chance against the vulgar
commercial imperialism – hard and soulless, and without any
high ideals – which has been made in Birmingham.[27]

The personification of Percival's hatred for Birmingham was the
local Member of Parliament, Joseph Chamberlain, the radical who
had opposed Gladstone over Home Rule for Ireland and, as the
leader of the Liberal Unionists, joined the Conservative government
in 1895 to become Secretary of State for the Colonies during the
period of the Boer War. The result was 'the mischievous moral
results of the Tory-Radical (Salisbury-Chamberlain) alliance, with
all its cynical hollowness and hypocrisy'. In Percival's view, nothing
but evil could come of this 'unnatural alliance'.[28]

Busy as he was in his diocese and with the affairs of the nation,
his Christian compassion embraced the world. Oppressed peoples
everywhere attracted his vociferous support, none more so than the
Christian subjects of the Turkish Empire.

In 1887 a sermon preached in the chapel at Clifton was published
under the title *Political Sympathies Astray* with the sub-title: 'Is
Sympathy with Turkish Rule and Warfare natural to a Christian

Gentleman?' In 1895 and 1896 he was positively Gladstonian in his outspoken outrage over the Turkish massacres of Armenians. This atrocity was the subject of his sermon at his enthronement at Hereford in April 1895. In December Gladstone wrote to him in appreciation: 'The case of Armenia is indeed terrible beyond words, and we are all sadly impotent . . . Would God there were more utterances like yours from the Episcopal Bench.'[29]

But was Britain really impotent? That was something Percival would not accept, although Lord Salisbury's remarks on the subject were 'enough to make one despair'.[30] In 1897, when William Watson published a collection of poems on the massacres entitled *The Year of Shame*, he contributed a trenchant Introduction protesting at 'ignoble acquiescence' in Turkish barbarities and lamenting that Britain's inheritance of honour and duty had been supplanted by 'the pinchbeck patriotism of the commercial jingo'. 'The Pharaohs of modern Christendom harden their hearts against the bitter cry of those perishing in misery and want in Armenia.'

When the spotlight switched to Macedonia in 1903 he returned to the same theme even more passionately and insistently. In the House of Lords, addressing the Foreign Secretary directly, he attributed responsibility to the Great Powers of Europe and subsequently wrote in similar vein to his speech:

> The published accounts of Macedonian horrors and miseries are so shocking that men are asking on every side, 'How long will our Government remain silent and do nothing but look on in apparent acquiescence?' . . . What a mockery it is for the Great Powers of Europe to call themselves Christian Powers . . . The stain of an indelible personal discredit will rest upon every monarch and upon every statesman in Christian Europe who, from whatever motive, can be held to have been in any sense primarily responsible for the continuance of such atrocities . . .[31]

Percival wanted action, even if it meant the use of force. In a significant aside in a debate on another topic in the House of Lords he had expressed admiration for Oliver Cromwell, 'that great Englishman' who believed in a combination of prayer and the sword in a righteous cause.[32]

Beyond Europe Percival's conscience was stirred by sufferings in Africa. In January 1902 he clashed with Salisbury over the policy

of public executions during the war in South Africa and conditions
in the concentration camps, where he claimed that between ten and
twelve thousand children had died. He begged the Prime Minister
to turn South Africa into another Canada, not another Ireland.[33]

In 1904 he was drawing attention to the ill-treatment of natives
in the Congo Free State and further iniquities in South Africa,
where Chinese coolies had been employed to meet a shortage of
labour when the war ended. These imported labourers came under
a system of indentures which he and fellow liberals equated with
serfdom. They were allowed to bring no women with them and the
physical and moral conditions in the compounds to which they
were confined were deplorable.

In the House of Lords in March he accused the government of
authorising a recrudescence of slavery in listening to the voice of
Lord Milner and the mine-owning interests in the Transvaal. In
May of the following year he fulminated against Lord Salisbury's
'unblushing cynicism' over the conditions to which these 'alien
serfs' were subjected.[34] In 1906 he joined in calls to the new,
Liberal government for their immediate repatriation, 'so that we
may be able to say that whenever a man sets foot in the British
Empire he is a free man'.[35]

In home affairs the most quixotic of Percival's proposals in the
Lords was an amendment to a Housing Bill in 1909 which would
have required the name of the owner or leaseholder to be conspic-
uously displayed on every dwelling house. Its purpose was to shame
the owners of working-class cottages in disrepair. Not surprisingly,
it was withdrawn for lack of support.[36] In November 1909 he was
one of the few to speak in support of Lloyd George's 'People's
Budget', which he welcomed as a measure of social welfare based
on sound finance.

His final campaign was fought between 1912 and 1914 with
lengthy speeches in support of the Established Church (Wales) Bill,
which was to achieve at last the goal of Welsh Disestablishment.
Although supported on this occasion by the Bishops of Lincoln and
Oxford (his old Trinity colleague, Charles Gore), he was once more
in fierce conflict with most of his brethren on the bishops' bench as
well as the Tory peers and complained of all the 'vituperation and
obloquy' which he suffered. 'I am an old man and very weary of
ecclesiastical divisions and disputes,' he told their lordships; but he
was a stubborn old man who would not give up until the Bill had
become law.[37]

Percival's contribution to a Lords' debate made in July 1914, a few months before his eightieth birthday, was his last. The years since 1900 had been another period of frustration: the frustration of not being headmaster of the nation.

CHAPTER 28

War and Peace

Percival was not pro-Boer, but he was tarred with that brush, and at Hereford on Mafeking night (1900) a band of revellers marched on the bishop's palace to give vent to their patriotic feelings by smashing the windows. Fortunately for all concerned, the bishop's coachman got wind of it in time and the premises were secured. The mob had to be content with hammering on the barred gatehouse while Percival sat inside the palace undisturbed and unaware. Had he known, he might well have emerged to deliver one of his homilies on jingoism – or perhaps intemperance – and been stoned himself.

Before the outbreak of hostilities in South Africa he had been openly critical of British policy, which he considered inept. When, in 1899, the fighting began he blamed the government, not the Boers, for a war which was, in his view, both unnecessary and unjustifiable. In October the two archbishops circulated to all dioceses a prayer which they considered suitable for the occasion. Its opening sentence ran:

> Most Merciful Father, we humbly beseech Thee, let Thy protecting care be over those who have now gone forth to fight the battles of their country for the deliverance of the oppressed and for the maintenance of justice and equity between man and man.

In the copy surviving among Percival's papers all the words after 'country' have been crossed out.[1]

Throughout the war he pressed for a negotiated settlement, urging the government to offer reasonable terms instead of demanding unconditional surrender, which made the Boers all the more determined to fight on. But when it came to the fighting he rejoiced in the British victories. How could he be pro-Boer with one of his own sons a serving officer in South Africa? When Arthur Percival won the DSO for bravery in a skirmish beside the Modder River, his father was immensely proud.

How, too, could he be pro-Boer when so many regular officers trained for military service at Clifton and Rugby were risking their lives for their country, and when these were joined by other Cliftonians and Rugbeians who abandoned civilian jobs and volunteered for armed service, inspired by the patriotism instilled in them at school?

One such volunteer was C. W. Boyle, Clifton's idolised demon bowler and rugger international. At the age of nearly fifty he left his London office in the City to answer the call to arms and became the first yeomanry officer to be killed in action. He was commemorated in a Newboltesque poem by Sir Herbert Warren, published in the *Spectator*, in which he was said to have been 'captaining men as once he captained boys'. His name, with others, was to be commemorated too on a South African War Memorial overlooking the Close which had been the scene of his schoolboy triumphs.

At Clifton the relief of Mafeking was celebrated more soberly than at Hereford. The whole school assembled in the quadrangle between the chapel and Big School to sing the national anthem.

Patriotic self-sacrifice had the blessing of their former headmaster, but he was angered by the general outbursts of jingoism which greeted even the most trifling military success and saddened by what seemed to him to amount almost to national hysteria at the news of any setback. 'It looks too much as if we were losing grit,' he wrote to Arthur. 'Over every little victory we shout ... and at every check we are all in a tremor as if the Boers were going to eat us up. That is your jingo Briton at home. In camp, thank God, you are of different stuff.'[2]

The cost in human lives was his principal concern as the war dragged on; but, as a practical man, he counted the cost in money too. In another letter to his son, written in April 1901, he reported on a 'gloomy' Budget: a deficit of £53 million; an £11 million increase in taxation, including a rise of twopence in income tax; and borrowing powers for a further £60 million – millions which could have been so much better spent alleviating the lot of the poor.[3]

In December of that year he wrote in his private correspondence with Lord Rosebery:

As regards this unhappy war which I believe we owe to this alliance [the government of Tories and Liberal Unionists led by Lord Salisbury and Joseph Chamberlain] I hardly dare to say anything except that if the influential members of this coalition cabinet had been men accustomed to give due weight to moral considerations in politics and to the great inheritance of our moral prestige they could not have treated the Jameson Raid and its chief concocters as they did and they could never have made the dismal mistakes of the farm burnings and spectacular executions and the concentration camps – mistakes of this kind surely come from that moral purblindness which leads both men and nations to their ruin.

He then 'ventured to add' this criticism of two of Rosebery's successors among the Liberal leadership:

Having a great respect for both Mr Asquith and Sir Edward Grey and expecting much from them I must confess that, like a good many other people, I have been greatly disappointed by their *tone* about the war, and in particular by the lack of moral fervour, the moral flatness which both of them have lately exhibited in dealing with it.

It seems to me as if their voices had lost that note of moral elevation or earnestness or nobility which is surely the true note of liberalism, and is, I verily believe, the only note that can touch and hold and uplift the heart of the people.[4]

Even before the war Percival had assumed a leading role in the peace movement, and this activity intensified when the fighting ended. The achievement of world peace became another cause which he pursued with all the formidable vigour still at his command. He travelled long distances to address congresses and conferences in different parts of Britain and in Holland and Germany and even the United States. At these meetings he frequently took the chair or was the main speaker. At Bristol in 1905, for example, he presided over a National Peace Congress. In London in 1908 he chaired the annual meeting of the Christian Conference on Peace.

The most ambitious of his excursions in this cause was his attendance at the Boston Peace Conference in the autumn of 1904. For this, his first and only visit to America, he sailed to Boston from Liverpool on the S.S.*Republic*, accompanied by James Bateman, his butler and mace-bearer, who acted on this expedition as minder and gentleman's gentleman.

On 27 September Percival celebrated his seventieth birthday in mid-ocean and wrote to his wife in buoyant spirits: 'Three-score-years-and-ten today . . . I ought to be thankful that at such an age I am strong enough to be careering across the Atlantic as I am doing.'[5]

On arrival, as the guest of the Principal of the Episcopal Theological College at Cambridge, he was hospitably and flatteringly entertained. On the following Sunday he was robust enough to preach at both morning and afternoon services before the ordeal of delivering the key speech in Symphony Hall in the evening. His message, his plea, to the world was taken from the text of his morning sermon, the well-known pacifist passage from the book of Micah: 'They shall beat their swords into ploughshares and their spears into pruning hooks; nation shall not lift up sword against nation, neither shall they learn war any more.'[6]

At the evening assembly he was the star speaker and at his most imposing and charismatic in addressing an audience of four thousand. His reputation had preceded him and when he rose to speak it was several minutes before wave after wave of cheering died down and he could begin. When he had finished, the crowd pressing to shake his hand was so great that he had difficulty in getting away. 'The people were pleased with my little address,' he reported modestly on this triumph to his wife.[7]

The speech was well tailored to appeal to his American audience. He praised the United States for its dedication to freedom and peace and embraced those present as fellow followers of Jesus, the Prince of Peace. He attacked the national greed and pride which was debasing life in England and denounced jingoism as a bastard form of patriotism very different from true, Christian patriotism, which dwelt on righteousness, peace and good will. He contrasted the paeans to peace and order and humanity sung by the Massachusetts poets – Emerson, Whittier, Longfellow – with the barrack-room voice of Kipling which dwelt on violence and the baser elements in human life. He warned against the evils of what he called 'commercial militarism', which he saw spreading across Europe like an epidemic.

His peroration was an exhortation to the United States to be mindful of the purity of its Christian heritage and take the lead in establishing a world-wide reign of peace and concord. 'Thank you warmly for your stirring call to my countrymen to perform their great and obvious duty to mankind,' wrote the editor of a local newspaper the next day.[8]

In the after-glow of such appreciation Percival moved briefly on to New York. There he was again the main speaker at a peace meeting and afterwards joined the Archbishop of Canterbury in attendance at the opening of the American Church Convention.

After two hectic weeks, during which he had glimpsed a New World and made new friends, he sailed for home on 13 October on the S.S. *Cymric*. The archbishop (Randall Davidson) sailed the following day, irritated by the perverse pleasure which Percival had expressed at the prospect of the bad weather forecast for both of them in the Atlantic. Refreshed and rejuvenated, the radical controversialist was in his element sailing through stormy seas. The conservative archbishop was not. In a letter of thanks to his host in New York, written as his ship neared Liverpool, he wrote with evident satisfaction: 'We hear the Cymric had a fearsome time on the ocean, and Hereford must have had his powers tested.'[9]

In contrast to his success in Boston, a clerical peace delegation in which Percival took part in 1914 proved a disillusioning experience. With it he travelled to Berlin only a few months before the outbreak of the First World War, and as his address to a subsequent Peace Congress in Cardiff makes all too clear, he was the victim of self-deluding optimism and a cynical deception.

> Fresh as I am from the visit of the ministers of religion to Germany, I feel more strongly than before that the cause of peace is making real progress in spite of all signs to the contrary. It is impossible to doubt the sincerity of the welcome with which we were everywhere received or of the desire for peaceful and friendly relations with England expressed by the Kaiser and his Chancellor, by the burgomasters and councillors of every city we visited, and by private citizens in every rank of life, and we were assured that the masses of the working men were solid for peace.[10]

The sentiments expressed by the ordinary citizens are likely to have been genuine enough – and throughout the war Percival was

insistent that England had no quarrel with the German people –
but the real intentions of the German government were soon
apparent. 1914 was to be Percival's *annus horribilis*. Not only did
Europe become engulfed in the bloodiest war in history, which all
his efforts had failed to avert, but during the year he lost two of his
three remaining sons – one in peace, the other in war.

He fought for a peaceful settlement to the very end, exploring all
channels, spiritual and political. On 1 August, three days before
the declaration of war, he wrote to every incumbent in his diocese
underlining the need for more and more prayers for peace and
urging them to call a meeting of parishioners for the purpose of
sending a resolution to the Prime Minister in support of a policy of
neutrality and continuing efforts for peace. By this means he hoped
to counter what he called 'the mischievous utterances of our jingo
Press' with what he was convinced to be the true voice of the
people.[11]

But when Germany launched the war by breaking its word and
violating Belgian neutrality Percival at once changed his tune. There
was no inconsistency in this, as he insisted. His attitude towards
warfare, based on unshakeable moral principles, never wavered.
This is William Temple's assessment of it:

> He was no 'Pacifist', though he was a lover of Peace. He believed
> there was a place for the use of force in Christian statesmanship.
> On behalf of oppressed peoples he perpetually urged the employ-
> ment of force. But he would have used it, not for aggrandisement
> nor chiefly for self-defence, but for the protection of the
> oppressed. When he demanded armed intervention on behalf of
> Armenia or Macedonia and statesmen replied that it might cause
> a European conflagration, he was not impressed. His one concern
> was to be brave in succouring the weak; the issue he was prepared
> to leave in the hands of God, whose bidding he sought to obey.[12]

To a man of peace who did not flinch from the prospect of a
European conflagration in a righteous cause, the First World War
presented fewer moral dilemmas than had the war in South Africa.
Here was an armed conflict which Percival believed that a Christian
could – and should – support unreservedly. Lest anyone were to be
left with the wrong impression, he hastened to explain his thinking
and announce his conversion in a letter to *The Times*, which was
published on 12 August.

His first aim in this was to defend himself against the slur that in labouring for peace and advocating neutrality he had been unpatriotic. In its attempts to avoid entanglement in the intrigues of the rival military powers in Europe, he argued, the Liberal government under Asquith and Grey had adopted a similar policy. Now, however, the cynicism and duplicity of the unprovoked German attack on Belgium allowed Britain no choice but to take up the sword in the cause of honourable dealing. The evils of maleficent and unscrupulous military despotism were greater than the horrors and miseries of war. The price would be heavy, but when duty called it must be paid.

The heavy price paid by Percival himself was the death of a son. There were no children from his second marriage, but Louisa had borne him what had seemed an ample enough supply of sons, seven in all. Yet three had predeceased her, and Robert, the eldest, a chronic invalid, had died in 1908 in a house which his father bought him in the country near Hereford.

In January 1914 Guthrie, the second son, an educational publisher, returned from a visit to Mexico. He had embarked in good health, but caught a chill on the voyage and died within a few days of reaching London. Percival met this further blow with Christian resignation. 'One can only say God's will be done,' he wrote to Launcelot, then one of the only two sons to survive.[13]

The other was Arthur, the soldier. Before winning his medal in South Africa he had been on the march up the Nile with Kitchener's army in 1898 and seen action at Omdurman, where he emerged from the battle unscathed, only to be severely wounded afterwards in the explosion of a Dervish mine.

In October 1914, fully recovered, he was a lieutenant-colonel on General Haig's staff. His services during the retreat after the battle at Mons were rewarded by the French with the Legion of Honour. He was about to be promoted to the command of a brigade when, on the last day of the month, he was killed in action at Ypres in the desperate campaign to prevent the German army from outflanking the Allied line and overrunning France.

That was the cruellest blow of all. To an old man the loss of a son or daughter is irreparable. Percival confessed that it had taken all the strength and feeling out of his life. Two years later he wrote to Arthur's widow that his thoughts were still with him every single day and he kept wondering what he might have achieved as a general. She was still young enough to recover from the sense of loss and enjoy new interests in life; he was not. He had reached his eightieth birthday a month before Arthur's death and celebrated it by sending gifts of money to the members of his clergy with the poorest livings.

His generosity in commemorating his son's valour was also in character. He had loved Arthur and he loved Clifton, where he was still Chairman of the Council. He gave the school money to found an annual scholarship, 'open to the sons of British officers in His Majesty's service, in memory of Lieutenant-Colonel Arthur Jex-Blake Percival, Fifth Fusiliers, DSO and Officer of the Legion of Honour'. Arthur Percival scholars were to perpetuate his son's name at the school.

In 1914 Cliftonians once more flocked to the colours. More than three thousand served in the armed forces during the war, and nearly six hundred of them lost their lives.

Sporting heroes were again prominent among the casualties. Of the cricket XI of 1914 five were killed, one died on active service and four were wounded. Among the very first of Old Cliftonians to be killed was Lieutenant Arthur Collins, better known to cricket-lovers as A. E. J. Collins. In a Preparatory School house match played in the Close in 1899 he had made, at the age of thirteen, what still remains the highest recorded individual score at cricket: 628 not out.

Arthur Collins died eleven days after Arthur Percival in the same fiercely fought campaign, which succeeded in averting the disaster of a defeat similar to that suffered in 1940 during the Second World War.

As his own death approached, Percival could only console himself that the sacrifice of so many Cliftonian lives had not been in vain, that they had been laid down in what he believed to be a just cause, and that no man had striven harder than he had to put an end to such warfare.

CHAPTER 29

Letting Go

It was the habit of Victorian schoolmasters to take refreshing holidays, often on walking tours through romantic landscapes or exploring classical sites. In this Percival was no exception, ogre though he was for work. The precarious state of his health demanded periods of rest, and these may well have served to prolong into old age a life despaired of sixty years earlier. Doubtless, too, he put those periods of relaxation to purposeful use, reading and thinking and writing letters to further one or other of his causes and campaigns.

In England the Lake District, which had inspired the much admired Wordsworth, was the schoolmasters' favourite holiday resort. Thomas Arnold regularly retreated there from Rugby. To men like Percival and T. E. Brown, who walked and talked together among the peaks and lakes of Cumbria, there was the added attraction that they were revisiting their homeland.

Mostly, though, it was a drier mountainous or sunny climate abroad which Percival's health demanded. He and Louisa had first met as invalids recuperating at Pau in the Pyrenees during the winter of 1858–59, and he was there again with Mary, his second wife, in January 1912. In the years between, he had taken holidays in other parts of southern France. In 1894 he spent his sixty-sixth birthday at the Hotel Britannique in Aix-les-Bains, 'doing battle with an obstinate attack of rheumatism'. He was nearing the end of his time at Rugby then and, as he wrote to a correspondent, 'my doctors are beginning to warn me that I have had nearly enough of schoolmastering with its incessant nervous strain'.[1]

Switzerland, Italy and Egypt were among other holiday destinations. A characteristic incident during a visit to Switzerland was an altercation with a dishonest waiter over an exorbitant bill. The culprit was soundly tongue-lashed and experienced the full force of headmasterly displeasure. Spending money freely in a good cause was one thing; being overcharged quite another.

At Hereford, as Percival grew older and had done all he could with the diocese, the breaks lengthened and he was frequently absent on other business or vacation. In 1905, a year after the trip to America to attend the Boston Peace Congress, he made the most adventurous of his expeditions overseas. Arthur Percival, then Colonel of the Camel Corps in the Sudan, had written to invite his father to pay him a visit and take a camel ride across the desert.

To Percival, then in his seventies, the prospect of ten days on the back of a camel was not daunting; on the contrary, he found the invitation too tempting to refuse. Taking the invalid Robert with him for the first part of the journey, he sailed to Port Said and made what was for him a second visit to the sights in Luxor and Karnak and the cataracts at Aswan.

Public school Old Boys could be found in positions of power in many parts of the world in those days. One of Percival's former pupils, an Old Rugbeian from School House, was in charge of the railway between Luxor and Aswan, so Percival and his son were made comfortable for the journey in a reserved carriage to themselves. On arrival in Khartoum they were the guests of two Old Cliftonians. One, Edgar (later Sir Edgar) Bonham-Carter, was Legal Secretary to the Sudan government; the other was head of the government Land Department.

With their influence there proved no problem over borrowing the Sirdar's launch to make an excursion to the battlefield at Omdurman, where Arthur had fought; and on the Sunday Percival was granted the use of the ballroom at the Sirdar's palace for a service, when he had the satisfaction of preaching to a large congregation.

The 360-mile camel trek from Um Duem to El Obeid and back was a great excitement, and he sent a full account of it to his wife at home. Every day Arthur shot an animal for dinner: a meal which was eaten at night under the stars. Percival was no vegetarian. He enthused over gazelle chops, which he thought as tasty as veal. Water from the wells was unsafe, so he was provided with Apollinaris and lime juice while Arthur drank whisky. His personal needs were looked after by one of Arthur's orderlies, assisted by a boy named Koko whom Arthur had rescued from slavery. On his return to Hereford life must have seemed humdrum after such a romantic interlude.

Old age eventually forced him to take life more easily even when on duty. During the later years of his episcopacy he mellowed and gave the (sometimes deceptive) appearance of a benign old gentleman. He was still reserved and aloof and courteous, as always, but gentler.

His sympathy for the poverty-stricken and sufferers from ill-health remained inexhaustible. No appeal on behalf of the poor or the sick went unanswered. Word that anyone was in need had him instantly reaching for his wallet or cheque book. Support for the underdog too was an enduring principle. Whenever there was trouble between an incumbent and his curate he invariably took the curate's side.

His life-long work on behalf of the poor earned him the admiration of the Salvation Army, among whom his reputation was elevated almost to sainthood. On a visit to Hereford, General Booth himself fell on his knees before the bishop and begged to be blessed – much to the bishop's embarrassment.[2]

Yet within the benign and saintly figure the fire still flickered. Percival's severity never wholly deserted him. Those guilty of conduct which he judged less than straightforward or honourable continued to receive very short shrift, and a spark of controversy re-ignited in his last years when he saw his Protestant Church once again drifting perilously close to Rome by not standing firm against the practice of the adoration of the Blessed Sacrament. Too frail to attend a meeting of bishops in person, he sent an appeal urging resistance to this new threat from what he described as 'the Romanising section' of the Church.

Percival's intense puritanism also remained with him to the end. Tennis-players on his lawn were reported to experience some difficulty in scoring because they were forbidden to use the word 'deuce'.

His kindliness was most overt towards children, and his natural sympathy won their hearts. Three of his sons, Robert, Guthrie and Arthur, had married but died childless. His only and much loved daughter Bessie also had no children. But Launcelot's wife produced grandchildren for him to dote upon. Visits from the young Douglas and Roger Percival enlivened the palace, and he enjoyed himself giving them lessons in reading and Latin.

For young visitors he kept a special small-sized chair. An infant son of his chaplain, Prebendary Wynn Willson, was so taken with this during a visit with his father that the bishop gave it to him to take home. The boy had been christened John Percival after him, and more than eighty years later he was still gratefully remembering his namesake's spontaneous act of generosity and displaying the chair in a place of honour in his home near Clifton.[3]

Prebendary H. E. H. Probyn, another of the bishop's chaplains (from 1909 to 1913), recalled how his children used to be invited to the palace for games. On one occasion, when they were playing hide and seek, a missing daughter was eventually discovered sitting happily on the bishop's knee in his study.

Percival had a way with animals too. Towards the end of his life he had a dog to which he was never heard to say anything but a disciplinary 'Down, Toby, down!' – or so it was reported by the Probyn family. Yet the bond between dog and master was so strong that when Percival died Toby lay down and died too.[4]

With birds Percival followed the example of St Francis. He kept a flock of white fantail pigeons as pets and fed them almost every morning from the palace porch, 'the birds evincing the most affectionate confidence in their benefactor' (according to a visiting journalist). Some perched on the episcopal shoulders, while others 'fluttered around his head in circles and semi-circles that seemed to express delight'.[5]

When the flock grew too large and numbers had to be reduced, the bishop made it known that a pigeon would be given to any boy or girl who applied and assured him that it would have a good home and be kindly treated. There were sixty lucky applicants and Percival kept the remaining twenty birds.

During his last two years in office he was physically incapable of performing all his duties, but while his will remained strong and his memory good he saw no reason to resign and 'loaf' on mere grounds of old age or bodily disability.

In the end, though, his mind and spirit weakened too. In 1916, on medical advice, he had to beg to be excused from his usual practice of preaching in the cathedral on Christmas Day: 'My powers of thinking and of utterance are both going from me, and there is nothing more to be said,' he wrote to one of the canons.[6]

Even so, he hung on until the following summer, resigning only a few months before his eighty-third birthday, and even then he went down fighting. On his last Sunday in Hereford he summoned sufficient strength to defy doctor's orders and make his way to the cathedral for a final Eucharist.

The next bishop was critical of his predecessor's clinging to office when no longer capable of doing the work. He also noted what was generally agreed to have been 'the deep and general unpopularity of Bishop Percival's regime at Hereford'. 'In Hereford,' he wrote, 'I followed a Bishop who certainly was neither incompetent, nor scandalous nor personally disliked, but who was decidedly unpopular.'[7]

The newcomer was Herbert Hensley Henson, another controversial churchman, whose unorthodox views on the Creed and other central tenets of the Christian faith led to protests at his consecration and events in 1917 and 1918 which achieved national notoriety as 'The Hereford Scandal'. Nominated by a radical Prime Minister (Lloyd George), he had quickly demonstrated that in more modern times there were further reaches of radicalism than those represented by the Victorian Bishop Percival.

Henson condemned as a failure Percival's attempt to raise the intellectual quality of the diocesan clergy and make the cathedral 'a centre of sacred learning', and there can be no disputing that verdict. Except for the obligatory three months' residence each year, the academics appointed to canonries had shunned this rural area remote from scholarship, where their presence was resented, and continued to keep their homes and Fellowships in Oxford.

Henson acknowledged that Percival had been caring, hardworking, sympathetic and generous, but identified in him the defects as well as the merits of a headmaster, the greatest defect being the autocratic manner which made him seem cold and uninterested. Percival, he also thought, was 'too great for the diocese'. 'His interest and his influence were national rather than diocesan, educational rather than ecclesiastical.'[8]

Those, again, seem indisputable judgments. Percival was, first and last, a headmaster. When a bishop he remained incorrigibly authoritarian, and he was more effective in educational and social reform on a nationwide scale than in local diocesan business, where his talents were sadly under-employed.

He retired, not to Clifton, but to a leased house in Oxford, his wife's home town and his own university city. He had completed his life's work and did not live beyond the end of the following year. During his last weeks he was unable to speak, but survived just long enough to learn that peace had been restored to Europe. It was the end of an era for the world and for him.

On 3 December 1918, from 64 Banbury Road in north Oxford, he went to meet his Maker.

CHAPTER 30

Conclusion

On resigning his see Percival refused to claim the pension to which he was entitled, saying that he had enough to satisfy his wants without becoming a burden on the Church or his successor at Hereford. Victorian headmasters and bishops were well paid and, even after his many gifts and benefactions, he died a wealthy man. His estate was valued at £40,437 11s 4d, a not inconsiderable sum in 1918: equivalent to more than a million in the depreciated money values of the 1990s.

Disposing of it to family and deserving causes had been arranged with his usual care and attention to detail. His will, drawn up in January 1912, ran to more than eight closely typed pages, and it was subsequently amended by four codicils, the first in December of the same year and the last towards the end of 1917 after the final move to Oxford.

The varying terms of will and codicils suggest that he experienced difficulty in striking the right balance between his children and their stepmother. Initially, each surviving son or daughter was to have £4000 and a share in the residuary estate. This was in addition to 'certain portions of my property' which they had received when he remarried. In one of the codicils the £4000 was raised to £5000.

To his widow Percival at first bequeathed £300 and the interest on £12,500 at four per cent, giving her an annual income of £500. The capital was to remain in the hands of trustees during her lifetime. In codicils this sum was reduced to £10,000 plus a share in the residuary estate, and finally to £7,500 plus the leasehold of 64 Banbury Road, the gaunt pile to which they had retired.

In addition to her other legacies his artist daughter Bessie (Elizabeth Anne Johnson) was bequeathed the Watts portrait of her father as well as other paintings, including her own, except for the pictures of previous bishops of Hereford which he had commissioned from her. These copies of earlier portraits in other collections were to remain in the palace and become the property of his successors.

A valuable additional bequest to his only surviving son, the Rev. Launcelot Percival, was The Hermitage, the house at Burghill near Hereford where his brother Robert had lived and died. This was a farm-house bought for Robert after he had returned from a similar open-air life on a farm in the United States. It was a freehold property standing in grounds of a hundred and thirty-five acres.

Launcelot (always Lance to his father) was one of two executors and trustees. The other was John Alexander Neale, a London barrister and one of Percival's Cliftonian disciples. He had been head of the school when Percival was headmaster and won an exhibition to Queen's, the college at Oxford which had started Percival on his career. When Neale himself died (in 1930) he left landed property in Wiltshire to the college to endow scholarships and exhibitions for persons of the 'name and kindred' of Neale and, failing them, for boys from Clifton. Through this bequest the connection between school and college which began with Percival was intended to be perpetuated.[1]

Percival's own bequests to the institutions with which he had been associated were to be made when the death or remarriage of his widow freed the capital held by his trustees. He left £2000 to Clifton College, to be invested and the income used for the benefit of deserving scholars in need of pecuniary assistance, and £1000 each to Appleby Grammar School, Queen's College, Oxford and Trinity College, Oxford for the same purpose. The Bishop of Hereford, too, received £1000, the income from which was to be used for the education of boys or girls of meritorious character and good ability who were the children of clergy in need of assistance.

Retainers and other members of the family too were remembered with smaller monetary bequests. The relatives were his half-sisters Jane and Anne, his sister-in-law Ada Morris (the widow of his brother William, who may therefore have been adopted under the surname of Morris) and the children of his late half-sister Elizabeth.

The news of Bishop Percival's death released a flood of obituaries and tributes which recognised his pre-eminence as a leader of educational reform and Anglican liberalism. Some were fulsome, others guarded or barbed. *The Times* remarked that at Rugby 'he certainly represented the sturdy and even aggressive Liberalism which men had learnt to associate with the heads of that school' and that 'Rugby, therefore, prospered under him'. It described him as 'the one bishop who could be relied upon to take a radical view on any given question of national or ecclesiastical interest'.[2] The *Morning Post* similarly noted that as a bishop he 'represented a type somewhat rare on the bench – broad Evangelical and democratic'.[3] The *Church Times* could not forgive him for that broad liberalism in Church affairs.

The *Oxford Chronicle* listed his battle honours, describing him as a stout opponent of the Education Act 1902, a fearless critic of government policy which led to the South African War, a strenuous advocate of Church reform, a supporter of settlement of international disputes by arbitration, and outspoken in denunciation of the liquor trade and betting and gambling. In championing those causes, so the *Oxford Chronicle* reported, he 'frequently appeared a lonely man and few if any of his brother ecclesiastics desired to toe the line with him'; but nevertheless he 'endeared himself to thousands outside the Church of England'.[4]

'Sturdy', 'aggressive', 'stout', 'fearless', 'strenuous' and 'outspoken' were epithets well earned. 'Rare' and 'lonely' too were precise.

Among individuals paying tribute was Cosmo Gordon Lang, the usurper of the promised throne of York. He wrote to the widow acknowledging the dead man's 'Christian chivalry' and the veneration in which he had been held, while stressing that this was all the more remarkable in view of the unpopularity of his convictions, from which the archbishop was at pains to distance himself. His letter concluded:

> I am sure that he will still have a high place in the spiritual army which watches over the course of truth, justice and freedom. I often differed from his opinions but I never failed to see and to reverence the nobility of his spirit.[5]

The most perceptive of the tributes came from his successors as headmaster, Canon Wilson and Dr David, and from his godson and former pupil at Rugby, William Temple. In David's words:

> On all he did was the mark of greatness . . . We feared him, and we knew the fear was good for us. He exacted, he insisted, he

was not afraid to repeat again and again in his gentle and rather melancholy voice, often in the same words, his appeals for corporate life, for high tone, for unworldly purpose, for scorn of feebleness, for determined leadership. All this we accepted because we knew that what he demanded of us he gave himself, at cost. And we were aware that there glowed behind it a great passion for righteousness.[6]

Wilson, in a sermon at a memorial service in the chapel at Clifton, dwelt on Percival's detachment. He had the ability to look at anything from the outside – a school, a city, a Church, a country, even a planet; and he 'possessed one characteristic quality in a very unusual degree. He was exceptionally uninfluenced by his time and by the people around him. He took no colour from his surroundings. He had no party.' And 'in his early years at least' he was 'incorrigibly hopeful'.

Wilson also referred to the immense demands which Percival had made on both masters and boys, and how sparing he was with praise: 'One of his boys said to me: "I would have done anything, *anything*, to win a word of praise from Percival, and the word never came".' He spoke of the 'glow of white heat' below the quiet, flat, seemingly cold delivery of his sermons and found evidence of their effectiveness in the comment of the head of an Oxford college, who told him that Cliftonians who came up to the university retained and widened their faith while many from other public schools 'scattered like a covey of last year's partridges'. Percival's creative moral force, said Wilson, marked him out even more than his intellectual force.[7]

In an address at another memorial service William Temple went to the heart of the apparent paradox in Percival's character:

This is a democratic age, and Bishop Percival was a believer in democracy. Yet there has never been a more thorough believer in authority nor a man more expert in the exercise of it . . . The great democrat was a stern disciplinarian. And the two found their reconciliation in his own obedience to conscience and reverence to God . . . I remember my father saying to me one day after he had visited us at Lambeth: 'Merely to be in his presence is to be drawn nearer to God.' Experience proved that this was true. There was in him something of the Puritan and a great deal of the Stoic. His faith was founded on the rock of solid intellectual conviction and absolute dedication of will.[8]

Yet it was this overpowering certainty and confidence in proximity to God manifested by Percival and his admirers that so riled those who were dismayed by the views he expressed and the causes he advanced with such single-mindedness. 'Completely arbitrary,' 'intellectually aloof' and 'brooking no opposition' were the well-founded accusations of his critics.

The hostility he aroused rendered his career as a churchman of little permanent account. Too full of indignation and direct in his approach to get his way by tact, he was a gadfly who stung the orthodox but left no lasting mark. It may be that he achieved most success through his influence on the younger Temple, who followed Percival's political path to its logical conclusion by embracing socialism. Successively Archbishop of York and Canterbury and known as 'the people's archbishop', William Temple denounced capitalism as organised selfishness and inspired the Welfare State, whose name was his invention.

The future archbishop's much fuller tribute to his godfather was his *Life of Bishop Percival*, published in 1921, little more than two years after Percival's death. This was not a hagiography like Stanley's life of Arnold, as might have been expected, but an unvarnished picture of the whole truth. Consisting mostly of letters and personal reminiscences from those who knew the great man, it forms an invaluable record of Percival's life, especially his life as a churchman.

As a bishop himself (he was Bishop of Manchester at the time of writing), Temple's interest was primarily ecclesiastical. The focus of his book, as the title indicates, is on national and diocesan Church affairs, but it is not for his work as a bishop that Percival most deserves to be remembered.

A critique of Temple's *Life*, making these points, is contained in a letter from the Rugby schoolmaster, G. F. Bradby. It was written to a former pupil after a first reading of the book.

John Percival was so great a man that he did not need to be washed and brushed before being presented to the public, and Temple has not washed and brushed him . . . He [Percival] would have done better in the North, but I don't believe that any bishopric would have suited him entirely. It was as a headmaster that he really left his mark on his generation, and Clifton was his greatest achievement. There is too little about Clifton, and what there is is not very enlightening.

It always seems to me astonishing that in his brief (and not particularly successful) apprenticeship here [at Rugby] under [Frederick] Temple he should have grasped so surely what are the things that really matter. He didn't have to learn anything at Clifton. He had the principles already clear in his head and just applied them. Astounding, too, that at 28 he should so completely have dominated the parents as well as the boys . . . He stamped his personality on the institutions at Clifton and here; and it has endured. His real life was as headmaster, not as bishop.[9]

The essence of Percival's genius, like that of Arnold, was far-sightedness. Both were men ahead of their times, resolutely forward-looking in challenging orthodoxies of their time and urging reform. A generation separated them: Percival was still a child when Arnold died. Together their lives spanned the nineteenth century. What made them the two great schoolmasters of that age of unprecedented growth in education was their vision and the influence it engendered. Both were liberal in principle and, in order to achieve their ends, despotic in practice. They were propagators of moral and spiritual values, and their forceful impact on education, intertwined with religion, proved irresistible.

But within the Church their reforming zeal encountered well-entrenched resistance. They were premature ecumenicalists and the hierarchy was too powerful for them. The widely read volumes of Arnold's sermons were influential mainly among the laity – even being recommended to the young Queen Victoria by her Prime Minister, Lord Melbourne. But the same could not be said of Percival's. The copy of his *Collected Sermons* deposited in the Bodleian Library in Oxford had remained on the shelves for more than a century before the present author made so bold as to cut the pages.

Percival's undeserved neglect by succeeding generations who have benefited from the educational reforms which he initiated may be attributed partly to Clifton's distance from metropolitan life and partly to the diminishing effectiveness of his over-long career. Had he died at the height of his powers, as Arnold did; had he been eulogised at length by Herbert Warren (to whom he was 'Jupiter Olympius'), as Arnold was by Arthur Stanley; had Henry Newbolt's *Twymans* enjoyed the success of Thomas Hughes's *Tom Brown* – then his contribution might have been no less universally recognised.

As it is, he is commemorated by portraits in the school at Rugby, in Trinity and Somerville Colleges at Oxford (the latter painted by his daughter) and at Hereford in the Bishop's Palace, but none is easy to find and view. There are plaques in Rugby chapel and Hereford Cathedral, the latter prominently displayed in the crossing. Rugby has its Percival Guildhouse, and Hereford its Percival Hall, opened as a YWCA hostel by Mrs Percival in 1901. At Appleby Grammar School the brilliant schoolboy is remembered by a portrait in the library, by the Percival Bequest and by a headmaster's carved chair and lectern still in daily use.

In the university at Bristol Percival's contribution to its existence is acknowledged by the display of two Percival coats of arms in the Old Council Chamber – one as headmaster of Clifton at the beginning of his involvement, the other as Bishop of Hereford at the end – and by another, since 1953, in the Founders' Window which looks down on the Wills Memorial Hall, the main entrance to the university.

Otherwise John Percival has all but disappeared from public view and awareness, his name unkown, except at Clifton, where he will never be forgotten.

His body was brought from Oxford to lie there in the vault which he had prepared for himself. A memorial service was held in the cathedral at Hereford, attended by the bishop, the dean and the mayor and corporation; another in the chapel at Trinity, conducted by President Blakiston (then also Vice-Chancellor) and attended by other heads of houses; and a third in London at St James's, Piccadilly, attended by Launcelot and other members of the family, where William Temple gave his address. But the funeral took place at the school which was his creation and in the chapel which had been reconstructed on his initiative and to his plan.

The mourners there were headed by the Bishop of Bristol, the Lord Mayor and Sheriff, the Vice-Chancellor of the university, the President of Magdalen representing Oxford University, and all the four headmasters of Clifton who had succeeded the creator. The rest of the congregation was composed of masters, boys, friends and Old Cliftonians, some of whom had been the dead man's pupils. Others, unable to attend, expressed their feelings by telegram. General Birdwood wired his 'sincerest sympathy in the great loss which the school and all of us have sustained in the death of our old and great headmaster'. Sir Francis Younghusband greatly regretted that influenza prevented him from paying his last respects to his 'Revered Headmaster'.[10]

In a well prepared service the lesson was taken from 1 Corinthians 15: 'Ye are saved if ye keep in memory what I have preached unto you.' 'Know ye not that there is a prince and a great man fallen this day in Israel?' (2 Samuel 3 38) was the text of Canon Wilson's sermon. The hymn was one of the school's favourites: 'For all the saints who from their labours rest'. Its most moving lines were sung by the trebles of the choir unaccompanied:

> The golden evening brightens in the west;
> Soon, soon to faithful warriors cometh rest.

Then:

> The hymn ended, the service moved to its close and the coffin was carried out of the Chapel while the choir sang the *Nunc Dimittis*. Clifton boys had formed up in a double line that wound from the west door of the Chapel down the steps alongside the Close and on towards the entrance of the crypt: through the silent ranks the coffin moved on a bier wheeled by past and present members of the teaching staff and some of the oldest surviving Old Cliftonians. The Bishop of Bristol spoke the words of the committal prayer and Percival's long and venturesome journey ended where it had begun so unexpectedly over half a century before.[11]

Three and a half years later, at Commemoration in 1922, the vault was ceremonially consecrated as the Percival Memorial Chapel. A large white cross extends over the top of the black marble tomb. There is no inscription, not even the name of the person whose body lies within. In place of words, the story of his life is told in the coats of arms of the schools, colleges and dioceses with which he was associated. These are carved in stone and provide the only touch of colour on the otherwise bare walls surrounding the tomb. Impressively austere, without embellishment or boast, John Percival's last resting place truly reflects the character of the Christian ascetic.

His creation, if not his name, has endured. Eighty years after his death Clifton College is a co-educational school with a roll of nearly twelve hundred boys and girls. The youth of Bristol, for whom it was founded, still have first call on its services, but Percival's ethos, cherished by his successors, has spread ever more widely as new pupils enter the school not only from different parts of Britain but also from a growing number of other countries throughout the world.

> Let the sound of those he wrought for,
> And the feet of those he fought for,
> Echo round his bones for ever more.[12]

Acknowledgments

At Clifton the help of Tom Gover and Richard Bland has been invaluable, and I am grateful for the encouragement of Hugh Monro, the headmaster, and Andrew Thornhill, Chairman of Council. At Rugby my thanks are due to Jenny Macrory, D. S. R. MacLean and Ian Barlow; at Trinity College, Oxford to Clare Hopkins, Matthew Steggle, Bryan Ward-Perkins and the research of John Fraser; at Hereford to the bishop, the Rt Rev. John Oliver, and Tom Oliver; and, among the Percival family, to Catherine Barne and Lance Percival.

Others who have kindly provided information or comment include Martin Scott and Derek Winterbottom (former Heads of History at Clifton); Jack Wynne Willson and Margery Probyn (respectively the son and daughter-in law of Percival's chaplains at Hereford); the headmasters of Appleby Grammar School, Cheltenham College and the Perse School, Cambridge; Sara Stewart-Feilding of the Headmasters' Conference; Diana Barnard of Clifton High School; Ernest Polack; Canon Arthur Johnson; Sarah Hargreaves; and Tracey Mathias Potter.

I am grateful, too, to the archivists who have found material for me or responded to my inquiries at Cumbria Record Office, Kendal; Durham University; Eton College; Hereford Cathedral Library; Hereford Record Office; Lambeth Palace Library; National Library of Scotland; The Queen's College, Oxford; St Andrews University; and University of Bristol. The services of the Bodleian Library in Oxford have been indispensable.

Among the published works listed in the Bibliography which follows, I am particularly indebted to William Temple's *Life of Bishop Percival* and the works of Clifton's two historians, Octavius Christie and Derek Winterbottom.

The Watts portrait of Percival is in the possession of Lance Percival, and the photograph of it is by Catherine Barne, who has also kindly supplied the illustration of the plaque in Hereford Cathedral, which is taken from an original photograph in the possession of Marion Lloyd. The photographs of the 1997 view of Clifton College, the Woolner bust and Percival's tomb are by Bromhead Photography of Clifton.

Finally, I wish to thank my publisher Ben Glazebrook, the Chairman of Constable, for his great kindness and my wife for her ever-ready advice and support.

Any errors are my own.

Bibliography

Printed Books

ABBOTT, EVELYN & CAMPBELL, LEWIS: *Life and Letters of Benjamin Jowett* 1897
ADAMS, PAULINE: *Somerville for Women* 1996
BAMFORD, T. W.: *Thomas Arnold* 1960
— *Rise of the Public Schools* 1967
BELL, CLIVE: *Old Friends* 1956
BELL, G. K. A.: *Randall Davidson* 1952 (3rd edition)
BENSON, A. C.: *The Life of Edward White Benson* 1899
BLAKISTON, HERBERT E.D.: *Trinity College* 1898
BRADBY, G. F.: *The Lanchester Tradition* 1914 (new edition 1954)
BRIGGS, ASA: *Victorian People* 1970 (revised edition)
BROWN, T. E.: *Collected Poems* 1900
Thomas Edward Brown, A Memorial Volume 1830–1930 1930
BROWNING, OSCAR: 'Arnold & Arnoldism' in *Education*, Dec. 1890
CARLETON, DON: *A University for Bristol* 1984
CHADWICK, OWEN: *The Victorian Church* Part 1 1971 (3rd edition)
— *The Victorian Church* Part 11 1972 (2nd edition)
CHANDOS, JOHN: *Boys Together* 1984
CHRISTIE, O. F.: *Clifton School Days (1879–1885)* 1930
— *A History of Clifton College* 1935
Clifton College Annals and Register 1862–1912 1912
Clifton College Annals and Register 1862–1925 1925
Clifton College Endowed Scholarships and Prizes 1914
Clifton College Register 1862 to 1887 1887
Clifton College: *125 Years of Clifton College* 1987
The Cliftonian
COHEN, MORTON N.: *Lewis Carroll* 1995
COLVIN, HOWARD: *Unbuilt Oxford* 1983
COTTLE, BASIL & SHERBORNE, J. W.: *The Life of a University* 1959 (revised edition)
DAVID, A.A.: *Life and the Public Schools* 1932
DICKINSON, G. LOWES: *J. McT. E. McTaggart* 1931

The Dictionary of National Biography 1975 (compact edition)

ELLMANN, RICHARD: *Oscar Wilde* 1987

ENSOR, R. C. K.: *England 1870–1914* 1936

FABER, GEOFFREY: *Jowett* 1957

FARRAR, F. W.: *Eric, or, Little by Little* 1858

— (Ed.) *Essays on a Liberal Education* 1867

FLETCHER, FRANK: *After Many a Day* 1937

FRASER, G. M. (intro.): *The World of the Public School* 1977

GATHORNE-HARDY, JONATHAN: *The Public School Phenomenon* 1977

GLENDAY, NONITA & PRICE, MARY: *Reluctant Revolutionaries* 1974

— *Clifton High School 1877–1977*

Great Public Schools (pub. Edward Arnold) c.1895

GREEN, ROGER LANCELYN: *A. E. W. Mason* 1952

GREEN, V. H. H.: *A History of Oxford University* 1974

GROSSKURTH, PHYLLIS: *John Addington Symonds* 1964

— (Ed.) *The Memoirs of John Addington Symonds* 1984

HAMMOND, N. G. L. (Ed.): *Centenary Essays on Clifton College* 1962

HENSON, HERBERT HENSLEY: *Retrospect of an Unimportant Life* (3 vols.) 1942, 1943, 1950

HIBBERT, CHRISTOPHER: *The Encyclopaedia of Oxford* 1988

HILL, C. P.: *The History of Bristol Grammar School* 1951

HINCHCLIFFE, EDGAR: *Appleby Grammar School* 1974

HODGKIN, R. H.: *Six Centuries of an Oxford College* 1949

HONEY, J. DE S.: *Tom Brown's Universe* 1977

HOPE SIMPSON, J. B.: *Rugby since Arnold* 1967

HOW, F. D.: *Six Great Schoolmasters* 1904

HOYLAND, GEOFFREY: *The Man Who Made a School* 1946

IREMONGER, F. A.: *William Temple* 1948

IRWIN, SIDNEY T.: *Clifton School Addresses* 1912

— (Ed.) *Letters of Thomas Edward Brown* 1900

The Jubilee Book of The Clifton High School 1877–1927 1927

KENT, JOHN: *William Temple* 1992

KITCHENER, F. E.: *Rugby Memoir of Archbishop Temple 1857–69* 1907

LATIMER, JOHN: *Annals of Bristol* 1887 (reprinted 1970)

MACK, EDWARD C.: *Public Schools & British Opinion since 1860* 1941

MACLAGAN, M.: *Trinity College 1555–1955* 1955

MAGNUS, LAURIE: *Herbert Warren of Magdalen* 1932

MALLETT, C. E.: *A History of the University of Oxford* (Vol. III) 1927

MARSHALL, MARY PALEY: *What I Remember* 1947

MCLEOD, HUGH: *Religion and Society in England 1850–1914* 1996

The Morality of Cumberland and Westmoreland 1865

MOZLEY, JOHN RICKARDS: *Clifton Memories* 1927

NEWBOLT, F. G.: *Clifton College Twenty-Five Years Ago: The Diary of a Fag* 1904

— *Clifton College Forty Years Ago: The Diary of a Praepostor* 1927

NEWBOLT, HENRY: *The Island Race* 1898
— *The Twymans: A Tale of Youth* 1911
— *Poems: New and Old* 1912
— *My World as in My Time: Memoirs of Sir Henry Newbolt* 1932
NEWBOLT, MARGARET (Ed.): *The Later Life and Letters of Sir Henry Newbolt* 1942
NEWMAN, JOHN HENRY: *Apologia pro Vita Sua* 1864
— *Tracts for the Times* from 1834
OAKELEY, EDWARD M.: *Bishop Percival, A Brief Sketch of a Great Career* 1919
PALMER, BERNARD: *Reverend Rebels* 1993
PARKIN, G. R.: *Life and Letters of Edward Thring* 1898
Parliamentary Debates 1900–1913
Parliamentary Papers 1906 (Royal Commission on Ecclesiastical Discipline)
PERCIVAL, ALICIA: *The Origins of the Headmasters' Conference* 1969
— *Very Superior Men* 1973
PERCIVAL, J.: *A Sermon Preached at the Opening of Clifton Chapel on Tuesday, September 30, 1862* in *Sermons* (Bodl.100.i.4(11))
— *Some Helps for School Life: Sermons Preached at Clifton College 1862–79* 1880 (Bodl.100 bb 75)
— *On the Relation of the Universities to School Education* c.1872 in *Educational Pamphlets* (Bodl.2624 e. 78(2))
— *But what can I do? A young man's duty to his neighbours, a sermon* 1883 (Bodl.100 e. 113 (19))
— *Sermons at Rugby* 1905 (Bodl.100 e. 1236)
— *Undergraduate Life at Oxford and Cambridge* 1909 (Bodl.2625 e. 42(6))
PRESTIGE, G. L.: *The Life of Charles Gore* 1935
PURVIS, JUNE: *A History of Women's Education in England* 1991
RAWNSLEY, W. F.: *Edward Thring* 1926
Redland High School 1882–1982
ROUSE, W. H. D.: *A History of Rugby School* 1898
SANDFORD, E. G. (Ed.): *Memoirs of Archbishop Temple* 1906
SCHUELLER, HERBERT M. & PETERS, ROBERT L. (Eds.): *The Letters of John Addington Symonds* (3 Vols.) Detroit, 1967
SELFE, SYDNEY: *Chapters from the History of Rugby School* 1910
SHERBORNE, J. W.: 'The College and the Community: University College, Bristol' in *University & Community: Essays to mark the Centenary of the Founding of University College, Bristol* 1976
SHROSBEE, COLIN: *Public Schools & Private Education* 1988
SIMON, BRIAN & BRADLEY, IAN (Eds.): *The Victorian Public School* 1975
SMILES, SAMUEL: *George Moore, Merchant & Philanthropist* 1878
Somerville College Oxford 1879–1979

STANLEY, ARTHUR PENRHYN: *The Life & Correspondence of Thomas Arnold D.D.* 1844

STEDMAN, ALGERNON M. M.: *Oxford, Its Social and Intellectual Life* 1878

STRACHEY, LYTTON: *Eminent Victorians* 1918

TARVER, JOHN CHARLES: *Some Observations of a Foster Parent* 1897

TEMPLE, WILLIAM: *Life of Bishop Percival* 1921

TERRAINE, JOHN: *Douglas Haig, the Educated Soldier* 1990

Twenty-Four Anglican Charges 1848–1901 (Bodl.1005 e. 43(23))

VICTORIA, QUEEN: *The Letters of Queen Victoria* (third series, Vol. II) 1931

VIDLER, ALEC R.: *The Pelican History of the Church of England* Vol. V 1961

WARD, MRS HUMPHRY: *Robert Elsmere* 1888

— *A Writer's Recollections* 1918

WARD, W. R.: *Victorian Oxford* 1965

WATSON, WILLIAM: *The Year of Shame* 1897

WESTON, FRANK: *The One Christ* 1907

WILSON, JAMES M.: 'A Lecture on Mathematical Teaching' in *Pamphlets Educational* (Bodl.2624 e 78)

— 'Morality in Public Schools, and its Relation to Religion' in *Journal of Education* No. 148, 1 Nov. 1881

— *Sermons Preached in Clifton College Chapel* 1883,1891

— *An Autobiography 1836–1931* 1932

WINTERBOTTOM, DEREK: *Clifton After Percival* 1990

— *John Percival, The Great Educator* 1993

— *T.E.Brown, His Life & Legacy* 1997

WOODWARD, E. L.: *The Age of Reform 1815–70* 1938

WOOLF, VIRGINIA: *Roger Fry, A Biography* 1940

YOUNG, G. M. (Ed.): *Early Victorian England 1830–65* 1934

— *Portrait of an Age – Victorian England* 1936

YOUNGHUSBAND, FRANCIS: *The Heart of a Continent* 1904 edition

Archives

Bodleian Library, Oxford; Clifton College; Cumbria Record Office, Kendal; Durham University; Eton College; Headmasters' Conference, Leicester; Hereford Cathedral Library; Hereford Record Office; Lambeth Palace Library; National Library of Scotland; The Queen's College, Oxford; Rugby School; St Andrews University; Somerville College, Oxford; Trinity College, Oxford; University of Bristol.

Manuscripts

Diary of Mabel Scott, the property of Martin Scott; Household Receipts, the property of Andrew Thornhill.

Source References

Chapter 1: Character and Upbringing

1. Clifton College archives: annotation in T. W. Dunn's copy of Temple.
2. Oakeley, 9.
3. Temple, 42.
4. Temple, 2.
5. William is mentioned as a 'full brother' in Percival's will, but his name does not appear in the parish register of baptisms. There was little time for him to have been born during his parents' brief marriage. Had he been, there would be no reason for his birth to go unrecorded by Temple when mentioning his sister, Anne.
6. Cumbria Record Office, Kendal: parish and census records.
7. Ibid. She was buried at Brough on 29 July 1838, aged 29.
8. Temple, 2, 3.
9. Cumbria Record Office, Kendal: Brough parish records. The half-sisters are mentioned in Percival's will.
10. Anne is recorded in the Brough parish register as living at Drybeck when she died. It seems probable that she and her brother were living together near his school.
11. Hodgkin, 10, 11.
12. Mallett, 287.
13. Sermon at Great St Mary's, Cambridge, 28 February 1909: Temple, 6, 7.

Chapter 2: The Influence of Arnold and Rugby

1. A. A. David, quoted in Hope Simpson, 191.
2. Hope Simpson, 24, 30.

3. Rouse, 124.
4. Hope Simpson, 188.
5. David, 140.
6. Letter dated May 9, 1836: Stanley, Vol.II 37.
7. Stanley, Vol.I 51.
8. Quoted in Chandos, 253.
9. Stanley, Vol. I 103.
10. Christie *School Days*, 113.
11. Selfe, 135–137.
12. David, 141.
13. Quoted in Kitchener, 32.
14. Bamford *Rise of Public Schools*, 248.
15. Sandford, Vol. I 222.
16. Kitchener, 72.
17. Stanley, Vol.I 127.
18. Simon & Bradley, 63.

Chapter 3: A New School for Bristol

1. Latimer, Vol. 3 46.
2. Christie *History*, 17.
3. Christie *History*, 19.
4. CC Register 1887, 10.
5. Christie *History*, 26.
6. CC Council minutes.
7. Temple, 12.
8. Ibid.
9. CC Council minutes.
10. Christie *History*, 26.
11. CC Council minutes.
12. *Cliftonian*, Vol . XXII 379, 380.
13. 1 Corinthians 3, 7.
14. Percival, *Sermons*.
15. Ibid.
16. Ibid.

Chapter 4: New Teachers, New Teaching

1. Temple, 18.
2. Ibid.
3. *Thomas Edward Brown*, 32.
4. Newbolt *Later Life*, 336.

5. *Thomas Edward Brown*, 31, 78, 79; Irwin *Letters*, 29, 30.
6. *Thomas Edward Brown*, 31.
7. Mozley, 21.
8. *Thomas Edward Brown*, 37.
9. *Cliftonian*, December 1897.
10. Christie *History*, 46; Mozley, 113, 114.
11. Herbert Warren in *Thomas Edward Brown*, 103.
12. Christie *History*, 68.
13. CC *125 Years*, 9.

Chapter 5: The Town House and Other Innovations

1. Newbolt *My World*, 47.
2. Bamford *Arnold*, 109.
3. Temple, 37.
4. Winterbottom *Clifton after Percival*, 12, 13.
5. CC Council minutes, 25 May 1875.
6. CC Council minutes, 22 June 1875.
7. CC Council minutes, 18 Jan. 1878.
8. Temple, 75.
9. Wordsworth, *Lines composed a few miles above Tintern Abbey*.
10. Bamford *Rise of Public Schools*, 248.
11. Temple, 39.
12. Christie *History*, 123.

Chapter 6: Wife and Family

1. Temple, 104.
2. Alice Winkworth, quoted in Temple, 15, 16.
3. Marshall, 36.
4. CC archives: annotation in T. W. Dunn's copy of Temple.
5. Mrs Watson, quoted in Temple, 16.
6. Household Receipts MS, property of Andrew Thornhill, f.145.
7. Ibid.
8. Household Receipts MS, f.98.
9. Temple, 139.
10. *Cliftonian*, Vol. XIV 259, 260.

Chapter 7: Growth and Achievement

1. Temple, 30.
2. Christie *School Days*, 16.

3. *CC Endowed S&P*: Dunn, 16–22.
4. CC AGM Report, 18 Sep. 1867.
5. Christie *School Days*, 9.
6. Christie *School Days*, 92.
7. CC Register 1887, 106.
8. Christie *School Days*, 113.
9. J. A. Neale in *Cliftonian*, June 1880.
10. Christie *School Days*, 13.
11. *CC Endowed S&P*: Dunn, 16–22.
12. Wilson, *Sermons*, 1883.
13. Christie *School Days*, 12.
14. Publication began in 1859.
15. *CC Endowed S&P*: Dunn, 16–22.
16. Issue dated December 1860, quoted in Chandos, 327.
17. Tarver, 141.
18. Tarver, 143.
19. Tarver, 157,158.
20. Issue dated 4 Dec. 1918.

Chapter 8: Ethos

1. Stanley, Vol. I 118.
2. Christie *School Days*, 101.
3. Headmasters' Conference Report 1873, 56.
4. Temple, 29.
5. Christie *School Days*, 24.
6. Hope Simpson, 113, 114.
7. *Cliftonian*, Vol. XV 299.
8. Percival *Some Helps*, 254.
9. *Thomas Edward Brown*, 32.
10. Percival *Some Helps*, quoted in *CC Endowed S&P*, notes 29.
11. *Thomas Edward Brown*, 32.
12. CC Annals & Register 1925, xiv.
13. 'The Best School of All'.
14. 'Clifton Chapel'.
15. *Diary of a Fag*, 91.
16. *Thomas Edward Brown*, 32.

Chapter 9: Games

1. Quoted in Briggs, 163.
2. Newbolt *My World*, 62, 63.

3. Hereford Record Office, R95/31.
4. In 'Vitaï Lampada'.
5. Newbolt *My World*, 52.
6. Christie *History*, 66, 67.
7. Headmasters' Conference Report 1873, 54.

Chapter 10: Clifton or Rugby?

1. CC Council minutes, 8 Nov. 1869.
2. Rugby School archives.
3. Hope Simpson, 90.
4. CC Council minutes, 8 Dec. 1869.
5. Ibid.
6. CC Council minutes, 5 Jan. 1874.
7. Rugby School archives.
8. Quoted in Temple, 50.
9. Quoted in Temple, 51.
10. *CC Endowed S&P*: Dunn, 16–22.
11. Newbolt *CC Forty Years Ago*, 163.
12. Quoted in Temple, 31.

Chapter 11: Constitutional Reform

1. Latimer, Vol. 3 450, 451.
2. Ibid.
3. Ibid.
4. CC Council minutes, 18 June 1870.
5. Ibid.
6. Hammond, 48.
7. CC Council minutes, 7 & 9 March 1871.
8. Hammond, 48.
9. St Andrews University archives.
10. CC Council minutes, 5 Oct. 1876.
11. Minutes of meeting, 18 Dec. 1876.
12. Christie *History*, 92.
13. Christie *History*, 29.

Chapter 12: Two Rebels

1. Christie, quoted in Newbolt *My World*, 64.
2. David, 5.

3. Quoted in Newbolt *My World*, 63, 64.
4. *The Twymans*, 90.
5. CC *125 Years*, 14.
6. *Old Friends*, 68.
7. Woolf, 37.
8. Woolf, 38.
9. Newbolt CC *Forty Years Ago*, 124, 125.
10. Dickinson, 9.
11. Dickinson, 10.
12. Dickinson, 18.
13. Dickinson, 13.
14. Newbolt *Later Life*, 15.

Chapter 13: Illegitimacy and Impurity

1. Issue dated 24 April 1865.
2. Ibid.
3. Cohen, 22.
4. Chandos, 290.
5. Christie *School Days*, 98.
6. Chandos 287, 289.
7. Schueller & Peters, Vol. II 264.
8. Grosskurth *Memoirs*, 94.
9. Grosskurth *Memoirs*, 98.
10. I am indebted to Richard Bland for drawing my attention to the relevance and implication of these dates.
11. Grosskurth *Memoirs*, 105.
12. Schueller & Peters, Vol. I 666, 667.
13. Ibid.
14. Schueller & Peters, Vol. I 612.
15. Grosskurth *Symonds*, 128.
16. Grosskurth *Memoirs*, 194.
17. Grosskurth *Memoirs*, 297.
18. Ellmann, 31.
19. Grosskurth *Memoirs*, 100.
20. Christie *History*, 48.
21. Magnus, 58, 59.
22. Christie, *History* 48.
23. Schueller & Peters, Vol. I 830.

Chapter 14: The End of a Reign

1. Oakeley, 4.
2. Temple, 34.
3. Oakeley, 4.
4. CC archives: file RS2/93.
5. CC Annual Report 1878.
6. *Cliftonian*, Feb. 1919, 6.
7. Hammond, 48, 49.
8. Smiles, 224; Temple, 41, 42.
9. 36 impressions during the author's lifetime.
10. Wilson *Autobiography*, 58, 59.
11. Wilson *Autobiography*, 89.
12. Newbolt *My World*, 67.
13. *Redland High School*.
14. Newbolt *My World*, 64.
15. CC archive: file RS2/93
16. Wilson *Autobiography*, 113.
17. *DNB*
18. Christie *History*, 100; Newbolt CC *Twenty-Five Years Ago*, 71.
19. Percival *Some Helps*, 265, 270.

Chapter 15: Ex-Headmaster

1. Wilson *Autobiography*, 112, 113.
2. Wilson *Autobiography*, 162.
3. Christie *School Days*, 24.
4. Wilson *Autobiography*, 104.
5. Wilson *Autobiography*, 111, 112.
6. Temple, 21, 22.
7. Schueller & Peters, Vol. III 501.
8. Christie *History*, 138.
9. In *Christianity and Social Order*, 91.
10. CC Council minutes, 1 Dec. 1909.
11. Iremonger, 149.
12. Iremonger, 132.
13. Kent, 1.
14. *Cliftonian*, Vol. XX 237.
15. Ibid.
16. CC archives: file K.44.
17. CC archives: file RS3/143.

Chapter 16: Percival's Men

1.   Percival *Sermons*, 273.
2.   Christie *School Days*, 66.
3.   Annotation in T. W. Dunn's copy of Temple.
4.   Hammond, 12.
5.   Temple, 28.
6.   Newbolt *Later Life*, 292, 293.
7.   'Clifton Chapel'.
8.   Newbolt *Later Life*, 7.
9.   Younghusband, 229.
10. Younghusband, 249.
11. Newbolt *Later Life*, 8, 9.
12. Ibid.
13. 'An Essay in Criticism' in *The Islanders*.
14. Temple, 206.
15. 'Clifton Chapel'.

Chapter 17: A University for Bristol

1.   Temple, 258.
2.   Carleton, 1.
3.   Cottle & Sherborne, 6.
4.   See Temple, 260–262.
5.   Temple, 263.
6.   Abbott & Campbell, Vol. II 60.
7.   *Reminiscences* of Marion Pease: typescript in University of Bristol archives, DM 219 (1).
8.   Issue dated 22 Jan. 1887.
9.   Cottle & Sherborne, 17.
10. Letter to J. W. Arrowsmith, 31 March 1906: University of Bristol archives, DM 219 (2).
11. Prof. G. H. Leonard, quoted in Temple, 264.
12. Temple, 263.

Chapter 18: Educational Reform

1.   Bodl.2624(e), 78(2).
2.   Chandos, 322; Mack, 28.
3.   Shrosbee, 219.
4.   *Education*, Dec. 1890.
5.   Parkin, Vol. I vii.

6. Parkin, Vol. I 103.
7. Ibid.
8. Parkin, Vol. I 104.
9. Headmasters' Conference Report 1875, 8.
10. Headmasters' Conference Report 1878, 49.
11. Headmasters' Conference Report 1873, 54.
12. Headmasters' Conference Report 1876, 72.
13. Bodl.2624 e 11.1 (6).
14. Temple, 276–278.
15. Durham University Library, MS 378.4281.
16. Bodl.2625 e 42(6).
17. See Woodward, 474–501.

Chapter 19: President of Trinity

1. Oakeley, 8.
2. Iremonger, 371.
3. Temple, 64,65.
4. Maclagan, 28.
5. Temple, 66; Magnus, 111–112.
6. Bodl. G. A. Oxon c.287, no. 158
7. Temple, 76.
8. Prestige, 23.
9. Mallett, Vol. III 412.
10. Trinity Record of College Meetings.
11. Quoted in Hibbert, 465.
12. Temple, 72.
13. Temple, 73.
14. Young *Early Victorian England*, Vol. 2 493.
15. Stedman, 54–69.
16. Christie *School Days*, 27.
17. Green R.L., 33.
18. Prestige, 23.
19. Temple, 69.
20. Colvin, 135.
21. Maclagan, 16.
22. Colvin, 151.
23. Temple, 74.
24. Temple, 132.

Chapter 20: Frustration at Oxford

1. Prof. E. A. Freeman, quoted in Mallett, Vol . III 464.
2. Canon Galpin, quoted in Temple, 89.
3. Temple, 75.
4. Temple, 84.
5. Browning, *A Grammarian's Funeral*, 1.129.
6. Prof. Ingram Bywater, quoted in Temple, 69.
7. *Robert Elsmere*, Chap. XLI.
8. *Robert Elsmere*, Chap. XLVI.
9. 1861: Abbott & Campbell, Vol. I 338.
10. Hereford Cathedral Library, Percival 6282.
11. Temple, 78.
12. Temple, 84, 85.
13. Issue dated 14 Nov. 1886.
14. Temple, 265.
15. Temple, 79.
16. *But what can I do?*, a sermon (1883).
17. Vaughan Nash, quoted in Temple, 81.
18. Temple, 82.
19. Ibid.
20. Temple, 96.

Chapter 21: Somerville and Education for Women

1. Temple, 259.
2. Hammond, 23: the epithets are John Betjeman's.
3. *Jubilee Book*, 20.
4. *Redland High School*.
5. Somerville Council minutes.
6. Ibid.
7. Adams, 15.
8. Temple, 76.
9. Somerville Council minutes, 5 Feb. 1900.
10. Somerville Council minutes, 14 Nov. 1885.
11. Adams, 114.
12. Issue dated 26 May 1897.
13. Temple, 274.
14. Temple, 276.

Chapter 22: A New Arnold at Rugby

1. Eton College archives.
2. Temple, 93, 94.
3. Ibid.
4. *The Times*, 18 Nov. 1886.
5. Temple, 94, 95: letter from H. Lee Warner.
6. Ibid.
7. Temple, 95, 96.
8. Temple, 97.
9. *The Times*, 18 Nov. 1886.
10. *The Lanchester Tradition*, 43.
11. *Journal of Education* No. 152, March 1882.
12. Temple, 101.
13. Temple, 102.
14. Iremonger, 34.
15. Rugby School archives: letter to Francis Dallin, dated 8 March 1922.
16. *Cliftonian*, Vol. XX 237, 238.
17. Iremonger, 310.
18. *DNB*.
19. Fletcher, 76.
20. Fletcher, 75, 76.
21. Temple, 116.
22. Temple, 112, 113.
23. Scott diary, 6 July 1890.
24. Temple, 113.
25. Temple, 104.
26. Rugby School archives: letter dated Jan. 1888.
27. Temple, 103.
28. Scott diary.
29. *Sybil* No. 13, 22 Nov. 1892, 91.
30. Temple, 110.
31. Scott diary, July 1895.
32. Ibid.
33. Fletcher, 79.

Chapter 23: Rugby's Two Reformers

1. *The Meteor* No. 295, 1891–95, 76.
2. *DNB*
3. Fletcher, 75, 76.
4. H. E. Butler (later Prof.): Temple, 109.
5. Percival *Sermons at Rugby*, 74, 32.

6. Percival *Sermons at Rugby*, 41, 42.
7. Christie *School Days*, 31.
8. Temple, 124.
9. *The Meteor* No. 339, 4 April 1895.
10. Temple, 108.
11. Hope Simpson, 80.
12. Interview in *The Sunday Strand* 1900, 406–410.
13. Bamford *Arnold*, 78.

Chapter 24: Welsh Disestablishment

1. Issue dated 4 May 1894.
2. Temple, 121.
3. Nat. Lib. of Scotland: letter dated 30 Aug. 1894.
4. Nat. Lib. of Scotland, Rosebery Papers, f.101.
5. *Letters of Q.V.* third series, Vol.II 468–471.
6. Ibid.
7. Ibid.
8. Nat. Lib. of Scotland: letter dated 19 Aug. 1898.
9. Bell G. K. A., 241.
10. *Letters of Q.V.* third series, Vol. II 498.
11. Nat. Lib. of Scotland, Rosebery Papers, f.16.
12. Benson, Vol. II 629.

Chapter 25: Bishop of Hereford

1. Temple, 166.
2. Temple, 154.
3. Issue dated 16 Dec. 1918.
4. Temple, 145.
5. Temple, 136.
6. Temple, 137.
7. Interview in *The Sunday Strand* 1900, 406–410.
8. Temple, 155, 148.
9. *Twenty-Four Anglican Charges*.
10. *Parliamentary Papers* 1906, Vol. xxxiv 287.
11. Temple, 164, 165.
12. Temple, 303.
13. Temple, 308.

Chapter 26: A Divided Church

1. Ensor, 137.
2. Woodward, 503.
3. *Parliamentary Papers* 1906, Vol. xxxiv 288.
4. Quoted in Temple, 150.
5. *Parliamentary Papers* 1906, Vol. xxxiv 288.
6. Chadwick Part I: Evangelicals.
7. *Twenty-Four Anglican Charges.*
8. Vidler, Vol. 5 129.
9. Ward *Recollections*, 133, 134.
10. Lambeth Palace Library: Letters & Papers of F. Temple, 31 ff 172–194.
11. McLeod, 11, 12.
12. *Parliamentary Papers* 1906, Vol. xxxiv 291.
13. Temple, 312.
14. Temple, 325.
15. Temple, 328.
16. Bell G.K.A., 635, 636.
17. Temple, 306.
18. Temple, 307.
19. Temple, 350.
20. Temple, 345.
21. Temple, 347, 348.
22. Temple, 348.
23. Oakeley 9, 10.

Chapter 27: Political Causes

1. Temple, 248: letter dated 26 Jan. 1900.
2. Nat. Lib. of Scotland, Rosebery Papers: letter dated 18 July 1895.
3. Ibid.: letter dated 12 Dec. 1901.
4. Ibid.: letter dated 18 July 1895.
5. Issue dated 20 Nov. 1895.
6. Issue dated 13 Sep. 1902.
7. Issue dated 19 Sep. 1902.
8. Issue dated 11 Dec. 1906.
9. Temple, 199.
10. *Parliamentary Debates*, Fourth Series, Vol. LXXXVI 818.
11. Hereford Record Office: Papers of John Percival, R95/51.
12. *Parliamentary Debates*, Vol. V 753.
13. *Parliamentary Debates*, Vol. 178 1543–47.
14. *Parliamentary Debates*, Vol. 178 1550.

15. *Parliamentary Debates*, Vol. XCI 664–667.
16. *Parliamentary Debates*, Vol. 139, 493.
17. *Parliamentary Debates*, Vol. I 813.
18. *Parliamentary Debates*, Vol. 134 869.
19. *Parliamentary Debates*, Vol. XII 408.
20. *Parliamentary Debates*, Vol. XII 408–419.
21. *Parliamentary Debates*, Vol. XIII 833.
22. Issue dated 4 April 1903.
23. *Parliamentary Debates*, Vol. I 813.
24. Hereford Record Office: Papers of John Percival, R95/33.
25. Temple, 237, 238.
26. Temple, 239.
27. Nat. Lib. of Scotland, Rosebery Papers: letter dated 15 July 1901.
28. Nat. Lib. of Scotland, Rosebery Papers: letter dated 12 Dec. 1901.
29. Temple, 254.
30. Nat. Lib. of Scotland, Rosebery Papers: letter dated 30 April 1896.
31. Temple, 255, 256.
32. *Parliamentary Debates*, Vol. CXVI 342.
33. *Parliamentary Debates*, Vol. CXVI 940–942.
34. *Parliamentary Debates*, Vol. 146 447–450.
35. Speech on 6 July 1906, quoted in Temple, 253.
36. *Parliamentary Debates*, Vol. III 94.
37. *Parliamentary Debates*, Vol. XIII 1109, 1110.

Chapter 28: War and Peace

1. Hereford Record Office: Papers of John Percival, R95/37.
2. Temple, 248: letter dated 26 Jan. 1900.
3. Temple, 251.
4. Nat. Lib. of Scotland, Rosebery Papers: letter dated 12 Dec. 1901.
5. Temple, 200.
6. Micah 4, 3.
7. Temple, 202.
8. Temple, 207.
9. Bell G.K.A., 452, 453.
10. Temple, 257.
11. Temple, 356.
12. Temple, 257.
13. Temple, 355.

Chapter 29: Letting Go

1. Nat. Lib. of Scotland, f.128: letter dated 30 Aug. 1894.
2. Letter to author from Mrs Margery Probyn.
3. At Stoke Bishop.
4. Letter to author from Mrs Margery Probyn.
5. Interview in *The Sunday Strand* 1900, 406–410.
6. Temple, 368.
7. Henson, Vol. I 225 & 253.
8. Henson, Vol. I 271–273.

Chapter 30: Conclusion

1. The Queen's College archives.
2. Issue dated 4 Dec. 1918.
3. Issue dated 4 Dec. 1918.
4. Issue dated 6 Dec. 1918.
5. Temple, 371.
6. Temple, 371, 372.
7. Reported in *Church Times*, 13 Dec. 1918.
8. Temple, 374, 375.
9. Rugby School archives: MS letter dated 8 March 1922.
10. Telegrams in CC archives.
11. Winterbottom *Clifton After Percival*, 9.
12. Tennyson, *Ode on the Death of the Duke of Wellington*.

Index

(Note: Percival is abbreviated to P. throughout Index)